English Rural Communities

CULTUS EX MENTIS CULTU

English Rural Communities:

The Impact of a Specialised Economy

EDITED BY

DENNIS R. MILLS

MACMILLAN

First published 1973 by

THE MACMILLAN PRESS LTD
London and Basingstoke
Associated companies in New York Dublin
Melbourne Johannesburg and Madras

SBN 333 14961 0 (hard cover)
SBN 333 14962 9 (paper cover)

Text set in 11/12 pt. Photon Times printed by photolithography,
and bound in Great Britain at The Pitman Press, Bath

Contents

Acknowledgements

'The effect of the depression of the mining industry on the cultural landscape of Cleator Moor, Cleator, Frizington, Moor Row, Bigrigg and Woodend, Cumberland', by Joyce Kneale, Ilkley College of Education dissertation, 1971, cited by permission of Joyce Kneale

'The Lord and the Landscape', by H. Thorpe, *Transactions of the Birmingham Archaeological Society,* LXXX (1965), by permission of H. Thorpe

'The Development of Rural Settlement around Lincoln' by D. R. Mills. *East Midland Geographer,* No. 11 (June 1959), by permission of *The East Midland Geographer*

'Dispersed and nucleated settlement in the Yorkshire Wolds, 1770–1850', by M. B. Gleave, *Transactions of the Institute of British Geographers,* No. 30 (1962), by permission of the Institute of British Geographers

'The Social Study of Family Farming', by W. M. Williams, *Geographical Journal,* CXXIX (1963), by permission of the Royal Geographical Society and W. M. Williams

'Population Changes over the West Cumberland Coalfield', by T. H. Bainbridge, *Economic Geography,* XXVI (1949), by permission of *Economic Geography*

'The Model Village at Bromborough Pool', by J. N. Tarn, *Town Planning Review,* XXXV (1964–5), by permission of J. N. Tarn

'The Economic Geography of Craven in the early Nineteenth Century', by R. Lawton, *Transactions of the Institute of British Geographers,* No. 20 (1954), by permission of the Institute of British Geographers

'The Geographical Effects of the Laws of Settlement in Nottinghamshire', by D. R. Mills, *East Midland Geographer,* V (1970), by permission of *The East Midland Geographer.*
'Rural Depopulation in 19th Century Britain', by R. Lawton, in *Liverpool Essays in Geography: a Jubilee Collection,* edited by R. W. Steel and R. Lawton, Longman (1967), by permission of Messrs Longman Green

'Rural Population Changes since 1851: Three Sample Studies', by June A. Sheppard, *Sociological Review,* X (1962), by permission of *Sociological Review*

'The Metropolitan Village', by F. I. Masser and D. C. Stroud, *Town Planning Review,* XXXVI (1965–6), by permission of *Town Planning Review*

The maps and diagrams have been prepared for the press by Mr A. Hodgkiss of the University of Liverpool and Mr H. Dobson and Mr J. Hunt of the Open University

Introduction

THE student may already turn to a significant number of books dealing with the establishment of the basic settlement patterns of England in the Anglo-Saxon, Scandinavian and medieval periods (for example, Thorpe in Watson and Sissons (1964), Mitchell (1954), Chapters III and IV; Darby (1936); Hoskins (1955), Chapters II and III; and the Domesday Geographies edited by Darby's team). More recently he has been provided with texts exploring rural location patterns with a strong emphasis on the role of distance factors (for example, Chisholm (1962) and Everson and Fitzgerald (1969)), while Clout (1972) has written an extremely useful introductory survey of rural geography, mainly from the standpoint of the present day.

It is more difficult for the student to investigate the impact of a specialised economy upon the geography of rural communities over the last four or five centuries. Considerable contributions have been made by historians, such as Beresford and Hurst (1971), Hoskins (1957), Laslett (1965) and Saville (1957). Geographers have paid attention to many landscape features associated with this impact, such as the survival of ridge-and-furrow and the building of canals and railways. Nevertheless, the student of geography who is interested more specifically in the relationship between economy and community must hunt up articles scattered through a wide range of journals, some of them of limited circulation.

In bringing together a selection of such articles, I hope I shall at one and the same time shorten the student's search and stimulate him to extend it wider afield in the bibliography provided. A further hope is that those many students who write dissertations on small localities will find between these covers some of the guidance they may need, in the form of methodology by example.

The book is divided into three parts, the first of which is concerned with some of the effects of specialised forms of agriculture on rural communities, landscapes and spatial patterns since the fifteenth century. For reasons that are made clear below, the middle part of the

For references to this Introduction, see page 26.

book is made up of readings on industrial aspects of the subject, while the final part is devoted to mobility. Increased mobility of goods and people was a pre-condition of increased specialisation, but its greatest effects have been felt in the century and a quarter since the railway network was established. In order then to provide a very broad chronological sequence, the three readings illustrating mobility have been placed at the end of the book.

METHODOLOGY

Early geographical studies of rural settlements placed a heavy emphasis on environmental determinism. Characteristic of this phase were investigations into the relationships between geology, soils, water supply, drainage and vegetation on the one hand and settlement patterns on the other. Not surprisingly, these investigations concentrated on the earlier periods of our history, before the advance of technology apparently liberated Man from close reliance on Nature.

The doctrine of possibilism admitted that Man was a free agent, having the wit to make a choice between one location and another, with the result that he did not always finish up with settlement patterns logical in terms of the physical environment. Thus since 1945 historical geography and related disciplines have explored many aspects of cultural systems that render more intelligible the locational decisions of the past, within the English countryside and elsewhere. In some way or other most of the readings in this book belong to this school of thought, among others. For instance, the estate system is prominent in Thorpe's paper; the technological system of agriculture in Gleave's; family farming as a social system in Williams; the social structure of a factory village in Tarn's and the poor law system in my own paper on Nottinghamshire.

Now it is fair to say that probably none of the authors concerned consciously wrote their papers to exemplify the technique of study known as systems analysis, with its highly conscious structuring of information and its striving for generalisations. The geographical study of rural communities is a highly complex field, since such a wide range of physical and cultural factors make their influence felt on settlement patterns. Moreover, in the case of *rural* settlements geographical inertia has been so strong that it is quite impossible to arrive at a satisfactory geographical explanation for any given date without referring back to the earlier history of an area. This is one of the principal reasons why the whole of Thorpe's article has been printed. The early pages of his article summarise, mainly with respect to one community, many of the important developments in English lowland settlement before the fifteenth century.

To return, however, to the remainder of the book, the empirical writing here provides one platform from which more highly systematised accounts of the historical geography of rural communities will emerge. The readings represent an interim stock-taking at an important point in the development of the subject. In this development Baker (1972) has distinguished between 'real', perceived and theoretical approaches to the subject material. We are not particularly concerned here with the theoretical strand, if by that is meant an emphasis on maximising behaviour, spatial analysis and theories of locational competition.

On the other hand these studies, although firmly planted in the 'real' geographies of particular areas, also make a contribution towards an understanding of the perceived environments of particular places and periods. They demonstrate, albeit for the most part unconsciously, that locational decisions are taken in the context not of real environments, but of environments as perceived by their inhabitants. Such perceptions would be influenced by social status, technological considerations, a sense of philanthropy, limitations of knowledge relating to opportunities for financial gain, obligations to kin, neighbours, church and so forth.

To take a case in point, the act of *founding* a village at Bromborough Pool could possibly be interpreted in terms of maximising the efficiency of the labour force at this new industrial location, but the *character* of the village must be interpreted in the light of the social values of the time, the status of the early factory owners and their sense of philanthropy. This example shows an entrepreneur not as a maximiser, but as a satisficer, i.e., one who aims to obtain levels of profit satisfactory to the achievement of goals, some of which are financial, some social, some religious and so on. (Simon (1959) very clearly described the distinction between satisficing and maximising behaviour.)

Thus one important criterion in the selection of articles was the need to bring to the fore the geographical implications of the existence of a variety of institutions which guided the locational decisions of people in times past. The institution of landownership was one of the most potent forces acting upon rural communities. For instance, the redistribution of farmsteads within the fields might have come about in different ways in England had individual owners been less powerful, had there been the periodic reallocation of land as in some European countries, and so forth.

Finally, under methodology, it is always important in historical geography to guard against the tendency to judge situations from the standpoint of a present day outlook. An interesting illustration of this point arises out of a comparison between present day commuting and its implications, as described in Masser and Stroud's article 'The Metropolitan Village' and commuting movements in nineteenth century Nottinghamshire, as mentioned in my paper of 1970. Strange to our way of thinking, the direction of flow then was outwards from the market towns and large villages to farms in parishes with insufficient cottage accommodation, and the reasons for this pattern of movement were largely associated with the institutions of the time.

HOW DO WE DEFINE RURAL COMMUNITIES?

No matter which methodological approach is made to a given field, the field itself must be defined as adequately as possible. With rural settlement this objective is not particularly easy to attain. Perhaps 'settlement' can be disposed of with reasonable accuracy, in post-colonisation studies, by enlarging the phrase to 'settlement patterns' and by defining these as 'the distribution of houses and other residential units, with their associated landscape features, such as farmsteads, workshops and street patterns'. For the modern geographer, however, we must add various non-landscape distributions, such as the functions of settlements, the spatial aspects of religion or socioeconomic variables. Thus the term 'communities' is to be preferred in the context of this book, using community in the sense of a primary group, a group of people between whom face-to-face relationships were made possible by residential proximity. But what do we say about 'rural'?

Broadly speaking geographers have spent much more time and energy in studying English rural settlement at the time of the original colonisation, or at any rate in its early stages, than during the post-medieval period to which this book is devoted. Thus an implicit consensus of opinion has grown up that rural was synonymous with agricultural and that the hamlet or village can be regarded as a settlement inhabited only or very largely by farmers. While this definition of rural settlement is acceptable enough in, say, the context of

Domesday studiés, from the later part of the Middle Ages onwards it becomes increasing untenable, until we arrive at the very complex present day position in which workplace and residence are so often quite separate, bringing many thousands of urban workers to 'rural' residences. (On the rural–urban continuum see the important references of Pahl (1966) and Frankenberg (1966).)

In the traditional economy, industry was a widespread activity in the countryside; it amounted not only to craftsmen who worked for a purely local market, but also included the development of regional specialisation in particular products from the late medieval period onwards. One of the earliest and best known examples was the woollen industry of villages in the Cotswolds, Norfolk and Suffolk and the Pennines, which goes back to the thirteenth century as a countryside activity.

Rural industries were related spatially to a number of different factors. In the extractive industries, the state of technology often limited workings to a small scale of activity. For example, the depth of coal pits was limited by ignorance of modern methods of shaft driving, drainage and haulage. Thus the coalfields, although destined in most cases to become highly industrialised and urbanised, for long retained a rustic appearance. The mining population was relatively small and its integration with the farming population was further assured by many individuals and families combining the two activities in one dual economy.

In the manufacturing sector, the range of factors obviously varied with industry and area. Raw materials, power, fuel, water, labour, food, skill and capital might be important, either singly or in varying combinations. Many examples may be found in the *Industrial Archaeology* series published by David and Charles. In Hertfordshire, for instance, paper making was (and is) an important industry in the Chess and Gade valleys, where both water and water-power were important locational factors (Branch Johnson, 1970, 37). In the woodland areas, timber was extensively used as a raw material and a fuel for such activities as iron making, glass blowing, potting, lime burning, charcoal burning and the manufacture of bows and arrows, tools, vehicles and other objects made of wood (Birrell, 1969).

It has been widely recognised that an urban concentration of industry was sometimes limited by the relative lack of food supplies, as for instance in the woollen and worsted industry of East Anglia. This is almost the same as saying that industries were attracted to rural labour supplies, as in the case of the Midland industries of lace making, framework knitting, boot and shoe making and straw plait and hat manufacture (Smith, 1963; Mounfield, 1964–6; Law, 1968 and Hooson, 1968). Certainly, none of these industrial locations can be satisfactorily explained in terms of raw material and fuel supplies.

In this phase of industrialisation, often referred to as the domestic economy, the major distinguishing feature of the town was a specialisation in commerce. While the term 'town' was used of any nucleated settlement, the description 'market town' was reserved for those central places in which the vast bulk of the country's commerce was carried on (provided, of course, we extend the term up the hierarchy to include the county towns, the provincial capitals and London itself).

As the industrial revolution progressed, the scale of industrial units increased and under the influence of steam power industry began to concentrate at points where coal was easily obtainable, on the coalfields themselves, at seaports and at inland locations well served by river or canal transport. Out of this there gradually developed an increasingly sharp dichotomy between rural-agricultural areas and urban-industrial areas, but not as quickly as has sometimes been supposed. Reference to figures 31, 32 and 33 of Watson and Sissons (1966) shows that only five English counties, even as late as 1851, were completely devoid of industry. These were Herefordshire, Rutland, Cambridgeshire, Sussex and, surprisingly, Middlesex.

Now what was the significance of industry in villages? Firstly it enabled population to reach higher levels than would have been possible by relying on agriculture alone. Secondly, it had important socioeconomic implications within the village community. In places where a craft or industry was well-developed, another significant social group was added to those one would ordinarily expect to find, such as landless labourers, farmers, landowners and tradesmen. Moreover the industrial group was closely integrated with the rest of the community through the existence of dual occupations. Where this occurred the social, economic, political and judicial hegemony of the landed classes was open to challenge.

A good example has been investigated by Hey (1969) in the south Yorkshire parish of Ecclesfield, about four miles north of Sheffield. In the northern part of the parish nail making was important, while on the Sheffield side cutlery was manufactured. Both of these occupations dualled with farming and about one household in seven or eight contained a smithy in the 1670s. There is evidence to show that the dual economy brought prosperity to the area and to individuals. Contrary to modern notions of wealth based on intensive specialisation, many of the nailers and cutlers were better off than those who got a living from farming only and some were able to rank with the yeomen. Many rural industries were still expanding in 1800, but by 1851 the tide had turned. This is the date at which, for the first time, the census indicated that over 50 per cent of the population lived in settlements generally accepted as 'urban'. This coincided broadly with the point at which several important industrial processes succumbed to the use of coal and/or steam power: for example, brick making, framework knitting and handloom weaving. At the same time the railways became an effective system whereby the country craftsman gradually found himself put out of work by mass manufactured products.

So far we have recognised the traditional economy, in which industry was widespread in the countryside. This was followed by a second phase, from about 1850 to about 1920, in which the urban–rural dichotomy was at its sharpest owing to the concentration of industry into relatively small areas of the country. With a declining share of the country's industry and commerce, the rural areas became increasingly dependent on agriculture. Significant use of labour saving machinery from the mid-century and the agricultural depression from the late 1870s were among the factors contributing to rural depopulation, as described in Lawton's paper in part three of the book.

By the end of the century many rural areas bore the hallmarks of depressed areas: falling population, low incomes, unemployment and under-employment, and a lack of new investment whether in old or new activities. It is not surprising, therefore, that the provision of amenities, such as water supplies, sanitation, decent housing regulations, transport, street lighting, public open spaces, education and medical services should lag so far behind what was deemed desirable in the urban areas in the same period. Only a dour stoicism, a superabundance of fresh air, low population densities and a slight, but significant rise in the labourer's real wages around the end of the century prevented a public outcry until the 1914–18 War revealed the poor physique of working class recruits from urban and rural areas alike (Burnett, 1968, 283).

The First World War was a watershed in this matter as in so many others. It was followed by an official willingness to help bring the amenities of depressed areas, rural and urban, up to the standards of the more fortunate parts of the country. Lack of funds slowed down progress throughout most of the inter-war period, but during the same years the motor bus and the car were to achieve a great deal more in blurring the social and economic boundaries between town and country. For the first time in our history, or that of any other Western country, it was possible for a significant number of people to live in villages and work in towns. An adventitious population had emerged.

With this in mind it is interesting to turn to Mrs Robertson's work (1961) on the occupational structure of the population in the Rural Districts of England and Wales based on the 1951 Census. Using some simple statistical devices, she distinguished three types of occupational structure. In the first a minimum of 52 per cent of the occupied population was employed on the land and this was known as the 'agricultural-rural' type. The intermediate type, referred to as 'rural' had an agricultural population ranging from 33–52 per cent, while all areas with less than 33 per cent were classed as 'rural-urban'.

The 'agricultural-rural' structure was found in Devon and Cornwall, the Norfolk–Suffolk border, large areas in the Fens, part of Cumberland and East Yorkshire, and extensive areas of Wales, spilling over the border into England. Intermediate areas were often adjacent to these most highly specialised areas, but others were found in the Cheviots and Pennines, the limestone belt north east and south west of Bristol and even in Kent and Essex. No less than three out of every four Rural Districts fell into the third category, the 'rural-urban', with adventitious populations ranging from around 25 per cent right up to 70 per cent.

Rural Districts with populations so heavily engaged in urban forms of employment were often an indication not only of the need to redraw local government boundaries, but also of an increasing interdependence between town and country, which rendered a complete restructuring of local government very necessary. This interdependence has been growing ever since 1920 and now in the 1970s, with only three per cent of our employed population engaged in agriculture, it is possible to speak of an entirely urbanised nation so far as many aspects of life are concerned. This fact has been recognised in the new local government structure, within which, over the whole of the country outside the metropolitan districts, the distinction between urban and rural has been almost entirely removed. The concentration of employment and commerce in urban areas which began in earnest in the middle of the nineteenth century has continued, but for the last half century there has been a significant and growing residential movement in the opposite direction. It remains to be seen how long will have to pass before industry and commerce also begin a really noticeable movement towards rural locations, separated by greenbelt from the existing large built-up areas. The plans for hyper-markets are, however, one pointer in that direction.

Looking back over the three phases, before 1850, 1850–1920 and since 1920, it is possible to isolate two relatively constant characteristics of rural communities. First, they contain a large agricultural population relative to towns; and secondly, they provide relatively little employment in the commercial and other service occupations. While this is not a precise definition of rural communities, if read with the qualifications discussed above, it will serve as a working approximation, and better an approximation than a definition of misleading simplicity!

THE READINGS

I. *Specialisation in agriculture*

Whether farmsteads were dispersed or grouped together in nucleated villages, their original function was to pursue unspecialised, or subsistence agriculture. While the arable/pasture balance varied from one part of the country to another and there were also spatial variations in crop and animal types and combinations, agriculture was of a subsistence nature throughout the period of primary settlement (or colonisation) of the country. In the later Middle Ages, however, the degree of specialisation by end-product reached a significant level and began to have an impact upon the local economies of individual parishes and the settlement patterns within them.

The most marked effects were experienced in places where the common field rotation of arable crops was replaced by enclosed fields in which the manorial lords or their large tenant farmers specialised in cattle or sheep farming and the subsistence economy disappeared. It is important to recognise that enclosure in itself did not necessarily lead to desertion or depopulation of a village, for in some areas small scale peasant farming carried on long after enclosure for pasture had been carried out. Whereas the big landlord took product-specialisation to its limits, the peasant farmer still used some of his land as a means of subsistence and this prevented the population from shrinking to a fraction of its former self. At a given state of the economy, therefore, institutional factors may prove to be as important to farming as soil types and climate.

Thorpe's article, which opens the book, traces the evolution of the settlement pattern in a Warwickshire parish. First he describes the period of subsistence agriculture, then the transition to the specialised economy when it suffered depopulation, passes on to the re-establishment of the village, and finally describes its cultural landscape in the 1960s. In fact, Wormleighton, as it was both a deserted medieval village and a planned estate village, is a classic instance of the influence of a powerful landowning family, the Spencers, upon an English village community. In this case, the importance of the behavioural environment in explaining changes in the phenomenal environment needs little advocacy. The phenomenal environment consists of both natural and man-made phenomena, while the behavioural environment is comprised of knowledge, values, ideas, socioeconomic processes, etc. (Kirk, 1963, 364 ff).

In the poor law literature of the first half of the nineteenth century the terms 'open' and 'close' (closed) were used to point the contrast between villages or freeholders and those controlled solely by large landowners. This theme is brought out in full in an article (Mills, 1970) in the second part of the book. For the moment, the earlier onset of specialisation in closed villages like Wormleighton needs to be registered. These were closed systems in which the social and economic processes were guided by one dominant personality or family.

Following Thorpe's article is a paper on settlement changes around Lincoln in the eighteenth and nineteenth centuries. In this I have mentioned the differences betweeen open and closed villages, but the main theme is the secondary dispersal of farms which was associated with the agricultural revolution of that period. This is continued by Gleave in his detailed study of two East Riding parishes.

While the disappearance of subsistence farming was exceptional in the fifteenth century, when Wormleighton was depopulated, by the eighteenth century its last remains were rapidly disappearing from the whole of England. The secondary dispersal of settlement, which affected large parts of the country, was common to both open and closed villages. Even where relatively small farms persisted, profit maximisation had become a much more important objective and the relocation of farmsteads should be seen as a means to that end.

The development of specialised, larger scale units was particularly rapid in the eastern, arable areas of the country, such as the East Riding and Lincolnshire. Williams' paper, which comes at the end of this part of the book, being devoted to a Devon community helps to redress the balance. Moreover, his focus is more directly on the *social* study of farming than the earlier studies. Although the Bishop family owned a considerable part of the parish during a portion of the study period, 'Ashworthy' may be regarded as an open village. Its openness is strikingly demonstrated by Williams' account of the movement of families into and around the landowning and landholding system of the village. Thus although the system itself was stable, it was openly accessible to a large number of participants.

II. *Specialisation in industry*

While specialisation in agriculture affected the whole of rural England in varying degrees, the direct impact of industrial specialisation was confined to particular parts of the country. The significance of this point, in the context of the industrial revolution, was emphasised by E. L. Jones (1968): 'Concentrations of rural domestic industry appeared in areas of densely-populated pastoralism which were not well placed for cereal growing. . . . The division of the country into cereal surplus areas and areas of pastoralism with rural domestic industry was in accordance with the principle of comparative advantage'. (p. 61.)

While there are possible exceptions to this rule, such as straw plaiting in south Bedfordshire, Jones' list of rurally based industries bear it out on the whole and the two examples mentioned in this part of the book, the textile industry in Craven and framework knitting in west Nottinghamshire, both illustrate this general principle.

The broad industrial division of the country between pastoral and arable areas was later emphasised by the fact that all the main coalfields of England are situated in the pastoral areas. In the extractive industries local specialisation was reinforced, if not initiated, by the limited availability of workable deposits of such minerals as coal, iron, lead, copper and tin. In many mining areas this same factor led to a punctiform pattern of settlement in which, although the bulk of the population was non-agricultural, the agglomerations never reached sufficient size and/or diversity of economy to qualify outright for urban status, in the commercial sense defined above. This contrast between extractive and manufacturing industries is brought out by a reading of Bainbridge's article on the West Cumberland coalfield and Lawton's on the Craven district of the West Riding.

Unfortunately, most geographical studies of mining areas have concentrated on their economic development and broad population changes, although the very recent work of P. N. Jones (1969) on colliery settlement in south Wales and Jackson's wider west European survey (1970) have done much to strengthen the social geography of coalfields, while a particular case study of the Durham mining villages is available in Blowers (1972). As Bainbridge's essay on Cumberland was written without much reference to the geography of communities, it is appropriate to supplement it here with a few extracts from a student dissertation on the neighbouring haematite ore field (Kneale, 1971). This is also an example of the kind of observational study that can be undertaken in a small area during a limited time-span. The area studied is about twelve square miles in extent and includes the villages of Cleator Moor, Cleator, Frizington, Moor Row, Bigrigg and Woodend (see figure I.1 and figure 5.1).

Although the working of haematite was recorded as early as 1682, large scale mining only began in the middle of the eighteenth century and the boom period did not occur until about 1830–80. Immigration from Ireland, Cornwall and Wales, as well as local agricultural areas supplied the necessary increase in the skilled and unskilled labour forces respectively. Cleator Moor, Moor Row and Woodend were entirely new settlements, while the other three changed out of all recognition. As mining activities moved around the ore field, there arose a need for miners' accommodation in different locations, until the coming of the railway about 1857 brought a degree of stability through extending the range of daily commuting.

After the peak years at the end of the nineteenth century, employment fell drastically, but as can be seen from figure 1, these villages have not disappeared. On the contrary, rehousing and the building of additional houses have caused the built-up area to expand. On balance, the population reached a maximum in 1891, fell substantially to 1901 and has fluctuated around this level since then (table I). It would be difficult to find a better example of geographical momentum asserted through the medium of settlement in an area where the original economic base has almost completely disappeared.

Population has been maintained by workers commuting to Distington and Workington (see figure 5.1) and by the establishment of light industry in the 1940s onwards. For example, the Cross Paper Works at Cleator had a payroll of over a thousand in 1970. The last mine closed in 1946, leaving the Bigrigg stone quarry as the only form of mineral extraction.

The recent settlement history of this district, therefore, falls into

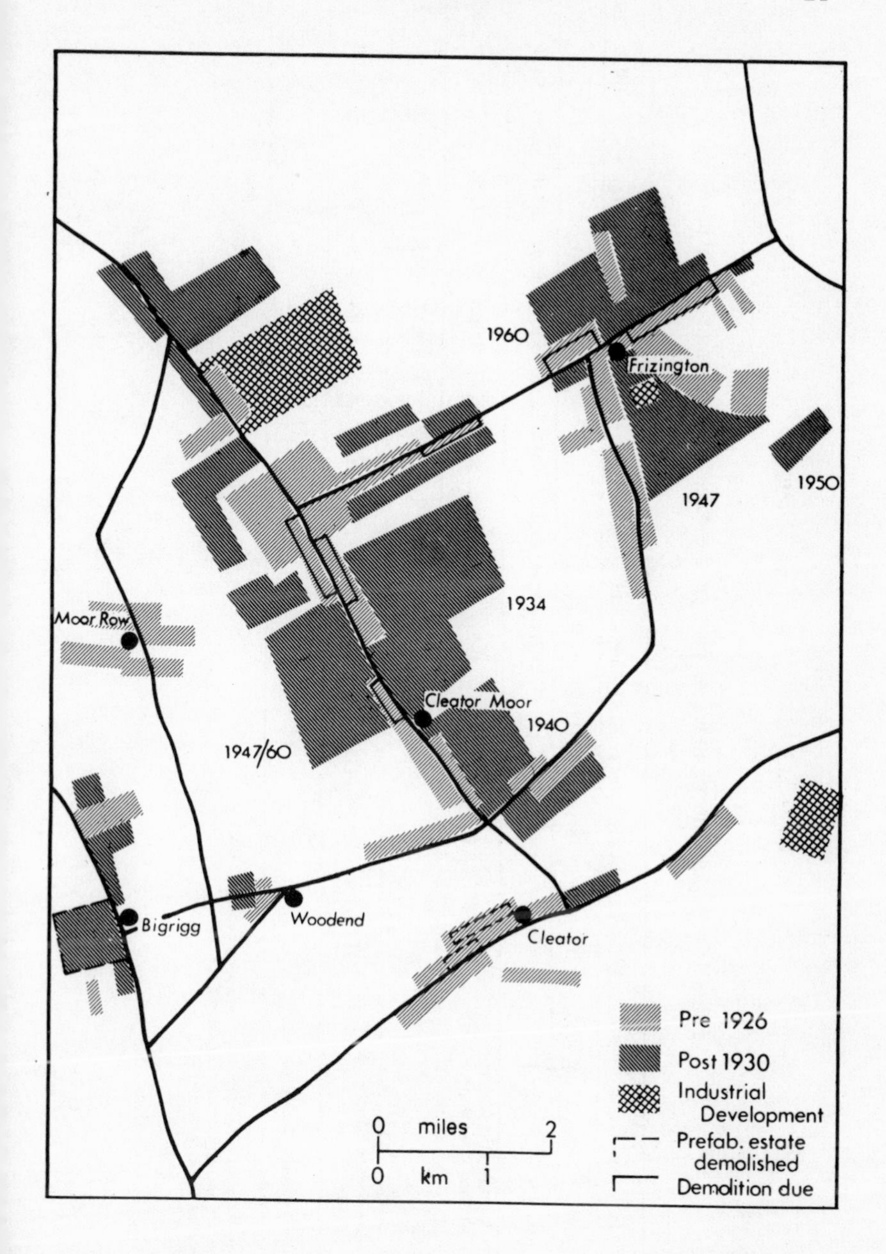

Fig. I.1 Settlement and the relics of iron mining, Cleator Moor, Cumberland

Table I: Population changes in part of the West Cumberland ore field

	1801	1811	1821	1831	1841	1851	1861	1871	1881	1891	1901	1911	1921	1931	—	1951	1961
Cleator	362	571	818	487	763	1779											
Cleator Moor							3995	7061	10,420	9464	8120	8301*	8291	6581		6411	7123
Arlecdon, including Frizington and Willimore Townships	354	438	478	475	558	643	1550	3426	6651	5697	5341	5183†	5151	4328		4247	4094
Frizington only					211							3612	3656				
Egremont, including Moor Row and Bigrigg	1515	1556	1741	1741	1750	2049	3481	4529	5976	6105	5761	6305‡	6582	6017		6213	6943
Moor Row and Bigrigg only												2323	2180				

* Cleator Moor U.D. from 1911 census onwards.
† Arlecdon and Frizington U.D. from 1911.
‡ Egremont U.D. from 1911.

three phases: rapid establishment in boom conditions of mining, stability and stagnation as the boom tails off and collapses, and a new phase of optimistic stability brought about by industrial relocation. What do these villages look like now? The answer to this question can be phrased in Joyce Kneale's own words:

> Today these houses stand out because of their uniformity and monotonous symmetry. Of all the settlements, Moor Row is the most spectacular, insomuch as it was purpose-built for the miners. There is no trace of any pre-existing settlement. What is even more remarkable about this compact community is that, originally, it was Cornish; this can be seen from the place names: Penzance Street and Dalyell Road.
>
> At Woodend, a row of houses was built for the railway workers; this was an important junction in relation to the engine shed and shunting yard at Moor Row. Woodend never grew any larger, until 1965 when new bungalows were built and to date only seven new buildings have been erected.
>
> On the other hand, Cleator had a nucleus of a community on which to build; it also had the added advantage of a flax mill, built by Ainsworth around 1811. This man was responsible for much of the housing, for not only did he provide houses for his mill workers, he built houses for the miners when his business interest changed.
>
> As with most property owners, he built himself a mansion, The Flask at Cleator and John Lindaw, another noteworthy in mining, built his mansion, Ehen Hall, only half a mile away . . .
>
> These houses were ornate, but a regularity of style was used for the miners' cottages. No gardens were provided, although allotments were, and still are, tended near by. Washing was hung on a common green out of sight of the main road. They still have outside toilets and are basically known as 'two up and two down houses'. This style was nationally adopted, particularly in industrial centres. More are to be found at Wath Brow: Trumpet Terrace which stretches for at least a quarter of a mile. These were built by another eminent mineowner, Stirling, who was responsible for many other public buildings.
>
> It is surprising how many business owners built houses for their workers even though their concern was small. For example, Joseph Spedding, who took over a flour mill near the Forge, built the only existing houses near the river. The total is only four, but at least it shows that the owners were beginning to consider the welfare of their workers, a far cry from the attitude that existed at the beginning of the Industrial Revolution. This can be partially explained by

the attitude of the workers, for if there were no houses the workers often refused to leave the home they had.

Houses were built at both Cleator and Cleator Moor for the furnace workers. The Old Hall was built in a different style for the foremen or overseers. It is of a more grandiose style, possessing a garden, enclosed with a wall. Titus Salt at Saltaire followed this pattern of making the foreman's house different from the rest. As the rank of a worker increased, so too did the size and standing of the house.

Frizington had not grown greatly in comparison to Cleator and Cleator Moor. It was a well established hamlet dating from 1160, which grew to an elongated street village with the advent of mining. This row pattern is a prevalent design in the study area. Moor Row is the only exception, as despite its name it is more accurately described as a clustered or heap settlement. (p. 17–20.)

While these villages were unique in some ways, they shared with Lowca, Aspatria, Broughton Moor and Pica in the west Cumberland coalfield, the characteristic row of many mining settlements. One of them almost acquired urban status, or perhaps more accurately, acquired it and lost it again, for we learn that 'Most housewives relied on the twice weekly market at Cleator Moor, which drew people from all the outlying areas. There was, therefore, little need for visits into the larger towns of Workington and Whitehaven, for which public transport did not cater (until 1938)' (Kneale, 1971, 24–5). Thus for a time it would have been possible to define a small urban hinterland around Cleator Moor. This half urban, half rural character is to be found in many of the industrial regions that filled up with population during the nineteenth century, for example, the footwear villages of Northamptonshire, the stockingers' villages in Derbyshire, Leicestershire and Nottinghamshire, the textile areas of the West Riding and Lancashire. At one extreme the built-up area of Pennine valleys has been made more continuous, or apparently continuous, by the constraints of steep valley sides. At the other extreme, the limitations of mineral deposits sometimes restricted the growth of population to scattered moorland hamlets.

We should also notice in West Cumberland a paternalism that was common to many of the new industrial locations of the nineteenth century, where it was necessary for the entrepreneur to provide accommodation in order to obtain a labour supply (Pollard, 1964). This is also exemplified in Tarn's essay on Bromborough Pool, which follows that by Bainbridge. A model village was built there by Price's Patent

Candle Company on a then rather isolated site by the Wirral bank of the Mersey. In these industrial contexts there is a parallel to the agricultural estate villages described in earlier parts of the book by Thorpe and Mills. Perhaps it is not forcing the analogy too far to say that in the present century this paternalism has been continued on local authority housing estates (Thomas, 1966, 93) and in the New Towns dominated by development corporations. On the other hand, where industrial development started earlier, say in the sixteenth and seventeenth centuries, where the industrial unit remained small until relatively late and where overall expansion was modest, there were better chances for the the survival of pre-existing open communities.

My own article, which completes this part of the book, to some extent cuts across the methodological approach of some of the earlier passages in that I have concentrated on one aspect of the behavioural environment, namely the operation of the laws of settlement, for its own sake. This institutional factor does, however, help to explain the distribution of both industrial and agricultural population in rural Nottinghamshire in the mid-nineteenth century and in that sense the relationship between the behavioural and phenomenal environments is made clear.

III. *Mobility*

Between the wars, it was not uncommon for historical geographers to cling to a series of 'static pictures' representing the geography of a region at particular points in history. Discussion of change over time seemed to be difficult without using the narrative form of the historian (Mills, 1972, 49–52). In more recent decades, however, with the confidence born of experience, geographers have begun more consciously to study geographical change, of which migration in its different forms is an important aspect.

There is little need of further introduction, because Lawton's paper (1967) takes a broad, national standpoint, therefore complementing the two localised studies that follow. These are also complementary to each other in the sense that Sheppard described a rural area in which depopulation was still occurring, whereas Masser and Stroud discussed the movement of population outward from a metropolitan city into the surrounding countryside.

However we define rural England today, these two opposites of depopulation (or at the most stagnation) and suburbanisation stand out as the most prominent problems, both academic and practical. The study of the city in the country is a theme that will see much development in the next decade. There are already several substantial pieces of work, by Clout, Coppock, Giggs, Lewis and Pahl (1965), to which the student may refer. Many county planning authorities, including Hampshire, Kent, Cambridgeshire, Nottinghamshire, Lindsey, East Sussex and Norfolk have undertaken studies to guide the development of dormitory villages.

Although rural planning authorities are naturally anxious to cushion the economic and social effects of depopulation and stagnation, where these occur, the nature of our planning system is such that they have difficulty in reversing established trends (Green, 1971, chapters 6 and 9). No such inhibitions, however, need apply to academic studies in this field. June Sheppard's article of over ten years ago still remains an isolated endeavour. Perhaps this set of readings will give some of their readers the perspective and interest which will project them into their own studies of present day 'truly rural England'.

REFERENCES

Baker, A. R. H. (ed) (1972) *Progress in historical geography.*

Beresford, M. W., and Hurst, J. G. (1971) *Deserted medieval village studies.*

Birrell, J. (1969) 'Peasant craftsmen in the medieval forest', *Agric. Hist. Rev.,* XVII.

Blowers, A. (1972) 'The declining villages of County Durham', in Open University, *New Trends in Geography, III: Social Geography.*

Branch Johnson, W. (1970) *The industrial archaeology of Hertfordshire.*

Burnett, J. (1968). *Plenty and want: a social history of diet in England from 1815 to the present day.*

Chisholm, M. (1962) *Rural settlement and land use.*

Clout, H. D. (1972) *Rural geography: an introductory survey.*

Coppock, J. T., and Prince, H. C. (1964) *Greater London,* Chapter 11, 'Dormitory settlements around London'.

Darby, H. C. (ed) (1936) *An historical geography of England before 1800.*

Domesday Geographies of England are published by Cambridge University Press.

Everson, J. A., and Fitzgerald, B. (1969) *Settlement patterns.*

Frankenberg, R. (1966) *Communities in Britain: social life in town and country.*

Giggs, J. A. (1970) 'Fringe expansion and suburbanization around Nottingham: a metropolitan area approach', *East Mid. Geogr.,* V.

Green, R. J. (1971) *Country planning: the future of the rural regions.*

Hey, D. G. (1969) 'A dual economy in south Yorkshire', *Agric. Hist. Rev.,* XVII.

Hooson, D. J. M. (1968) 'The straw industry of the Chilterns in the nineteenth century', *East Mid. Geogr.,* IV.

Hoskins, W. G. (1957) *The making of the English landscape.*

Jackson, R. T. (1970) 'Mining settlements in Western Europe: the landscape and the community', in Beckinsale, R. P. and Houston, J. M. (eds) *Urbanization and its problems.*

Jones, E. L. (1968) 'Agricultural origins of industry', *Past and Present,* XL.

Jones, P. N. (1969) *Colliery settlement in the South Wales coalfield, 1850–1926,* University of Hull Occasional Papers in Geography, XIV.

Kirk, W. (1963) 'Problems of geography', *Geography,* XLVIII.

Kneale, J. (1971) *The effect of the depression of the mining industry on the cultural landscape of Cleator Moor, Cleator, Frizington, Moor Row, Bigrigg and Woodend,* unpublished dissertation, Ilkley College of Education.

Laslett, P. (1965) *The world we have lost.*

Law, C. M. 'Luton and the hat industry', *East Mid. Geogr.,* IV.

Lewis, G. J. (1967) 'Commuting and the village in mid-Wales', *Geography,* LII.

Mills, D. R. (1972) 'Has historical geography changed?' in Open University, *New Trends in Geography, IV: Regional, Historical and Political Geography.*

Mitchell, J. B. (1954) *Teach yourself Historical Geography.*

Mounfield, P. R. (1964–6) 'The footwear industry of the East Midlands', *East Mid. Geogr.,* III, 293–306, 394–413, 434–44 and IV, 8–23.

Pahl, R. E. (1965) *Urbs in rure,* London School of Economics, Geographical Paper No. 2.

Pahl, R. E. (1966) 'The rural-urban continuum', *Sociologia Ruralis,* VI, reprinted in Pahl, R. E. (1968), *Readings in urban sociology.*

Pahl, R. E. (1970) *Patterns of urban life.*

Saville, J. (1957) *Rural depopulation in England and Wales, 1851–1951.*

Simon, H. A. (1959) 'Theories of decision-making in economics and behavioural science', *Amer. Econ. Rev.,* XLIX; reprinted in Castles, F. G. (*et al.,* eds) (1972) *Decisions, organizations and society.*

Smith, D. M. (1963) 'The British hosiery industry at the middle of the nineteenth century: an historical study in economic geography', *Trans. Inst. Brit. Geogrs.,* XXXII.

Thomas, C. J. (1966) 'Some geographical aspects of council housing in Nottingham', *East Mid. Geogr.,* IV.

Watson, J. W., and Sissons, J. B. (eds) (1964) *The British Isles: a systematic geography.*

Part One
Specialisation in Agriculture

1 The Lord and the Landscape

illustrated through the changing fortunes of a Warwickshire parish, Wormleighton

H. THORPE

EVERY settlement is unique, not simply in terms of its location on the earth's surface but more particularly because it represents the end product, as we see it today, of the intensive occupation by successive generations of a relatively small tract of land for varying periods of time. In its general adaptation to the broad physical, social, and economic patterns of the local region a settlement may have much in common with its neighbours, but within its own territorial unit appraisals of micro-physical conditions on the one hand and the influences of individual men, women, and their institutions on the other have often conspired to produce a distinctive personality, etched deeply on the landscape, for each town, village, hamlet, parish, or township. Whereas the lowly peasant had often little choice but to conform with local custom and practice, a lord of the manor had scope to influence the activities of a whole community and so might change the very look of the landscape itself. Wealthy, wise, and powerful lords with a long established interest in, and sense of obligation towards, their lands and folk could encourage good farming and soften the blows of famine and disease. Dissolute lords, and particularly those whose manors changed hands frequently, might neglect or abuse their peasantry to the point where the hardy fled to growing towns while the weak were hard pressed to scrape even a bare living from the soil. In this study the growth and prosperity of an English village, Wormleighton in Warwickshire, is traced from Anglo-Saxon times to the Norman Conquest and beyond, until suddenly at the end of the fifteenth century the settlement was destroyed in order that its arable lands could be used as pastures for sheep and cattle. The depopulated manor was then purchased in 1506 by an energetic and ambitious Warwickshire sheep farmer, called John Spencer, who not only re-established the village but quickly amassed great wealth in livestock and land in the surrounding area. After John Spencer was knighted soon after 1518, the family became one of the leading titled families in England. The manor of Wormleighton has remained in the possession of the Spencers until the present day, and I am greatly in-

For references to this chapter, see p. 76.

debted to the 7th Earl Spencer of Althorp for kindly allowing me to consult the fine collection of maps and documents relating to Wormleighton in the muniment room at Althorp. With the aid of these documents it has been possible to study in some detail the historical geography of Wormleighton from the late fifteenth century onward. The influence of the great family is still strongly discernible in the village today, though several of their farms have been sold since 1924 to cover death duties.

REGIONAL SETTING

The parish of Wormleighton, with an area of 2451 acres and a present population around 150 of whom about 110 live in the nucleated village itself, lies on the borders of south-east Warwickshire, its boundaries abutting both Oxfordshire and Northamptonshire to the east (figure 1.1). From the heavily dissected scarp slope of the Cotswolds embracing the eastern half of the parish, the land drops gently from a height of about 515 ft around the village itself to 315 ft on its western boundary. The sharp break of slope between the Cotswold Fringe and the broad plain of the Feldon of south Warwickshire coincides with a geological contrast between the resistant, dark-brown Middle Lias Marlstone above 500 ft and the heavy, impervious greyish-brown Lower Lias Clay below (figure 1.2). Numerous springs, fed by seepage through the porous Marlstone and the glacial sands and gravels that occasionally overlie it, appear along the scarpfoot and contribute to the headstreams of the river Itchen draining northward to the Leam and Avon. A long narrow spur slightly exceeding 400 ft curves westward from the village of Wormleighton and divides the lower land into a northern and a southern block. From the latter, movement south-eastward across the Cotswold scarp was rendered easy by the Fenny Compton gap, due partly to headward erosion of dip-slope streams like the Clayholme Brook draining to the Cherwell (figure 1.2) and partly to downcutting associated with an overflow of glacial Lake Harrison.[1] This gap was to be used successively by road, canal, and railway leading south towards London.

WORMLEIGHTON BEFORE THE DEPOPULATION OF 1499

Dense forest, with a high proportion of oak, covered most of Warwickshire in Neolithic times and this was true of the Wormleighton area, particularly on the heavy clays. By Early Iron

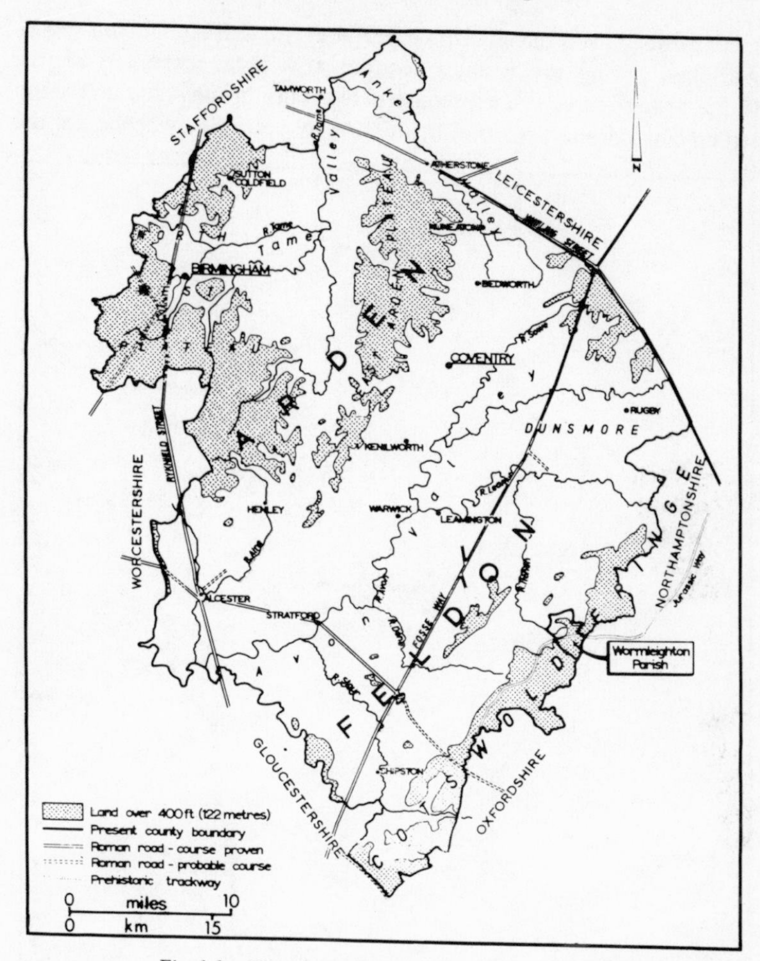

Fig. 1.1 Wormleighton: location in Warwickshire

Age times a good deal of clearing and settlement had taken place both along the river terrace sands and gravels of the Avon valley, and around a line of Celtic hill forts following the scarp-top of the Cotswolds. The prehistoric trackway, known to archaeologists as the Jurassic Way,[2] that ran diagonally across England linking these hill forts appears to have crossed the Fenny Compton gap near Wormleighton, perhaps following in part the course of the Anglo-Saxon 'Ridge Way' shown in figure 1.2. But although some clearing may have occurred along the trackway, there is no evidence for settlement around Wormleighton before the Anglo-Saxon colonisation. Although during the Roman occupation a great arterial road, the Fosse Way (figure 1.1), was constructed south of the Avon and many settlements sprang up along it, there is as yet little evidence for the

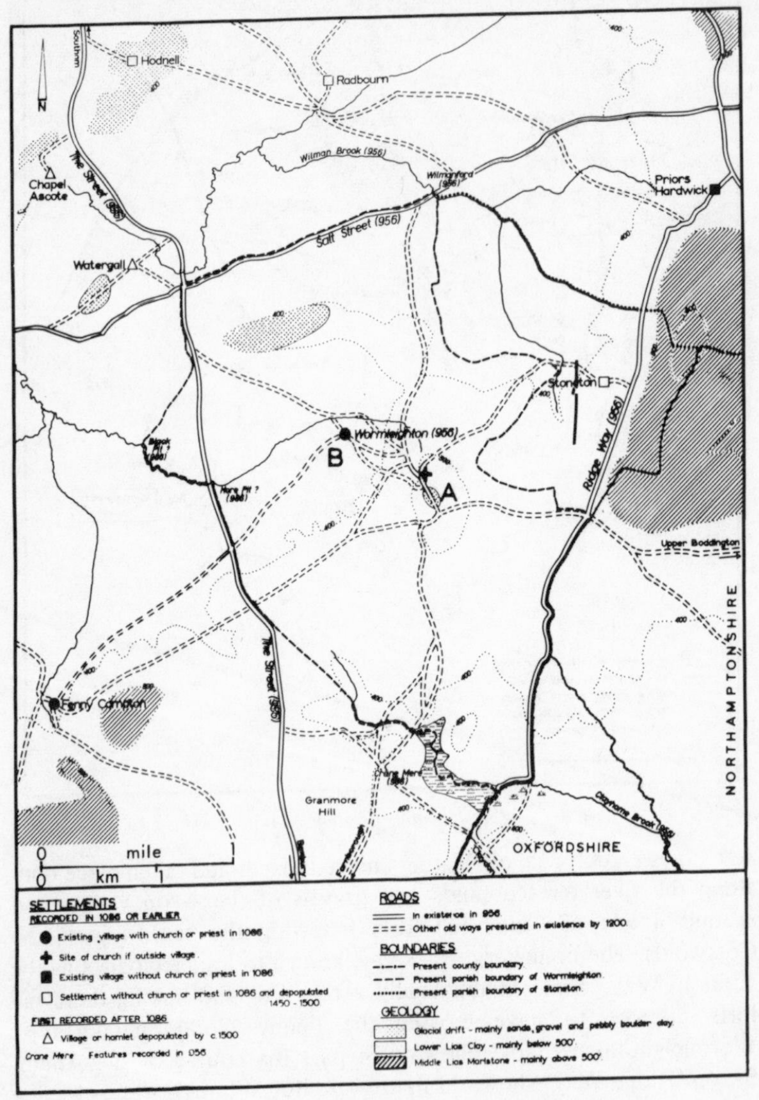

Fig. 1.2 Wormleighton and environs circa 1200

spread of Romano-British population across the densely wooded Lower Lias Clays into the Cotswold Fringe. Scattered finds, such as pottery and coins, along the valleys of the rivers Itchen and Dene may encourage one to look more closely for evidence of Roman settlement around Wormleighton, but, apart from a wooden coffin associated with Roman coins[3] found between Wormleighton and Stoneton, nothing has so far come to light.

When the Anglo-Saxon settlers entered Warwickshire about A.D. 500 they were quick to take advantage of land already cleared in Romano-British times, particularly along the Avon Terrace Belt but also along the line of a great road like the Fosse. Their expansion southward from the Avon valley, with its numerous Anglo-Saxon cemeteries, towards the Cotswold scarp was both early and vigorous, and was associated with the establishment of strongly nucleated villages with distinctive Anglo-Saxon place names, many having characteristic endings in *-ton* and *-ham.* Regional differentiation within Warwickshire was now becoming marked, for whereas the Avon Terrace Belt and the Feldon to the south were to be closely settled, the Forest of Arden to the north contained relatively few major settlements and the scattered hamlets, with distinctive clearing names ending in *-ley, -worth,* and *-field,* so typical of the region today, were to come into being only later as small groups of venturesome settlers spread north into the dense oak wood making individual hedged clearings.[4] This distinction was deemed worthy of comment by topographers such as Leland and Dugdale centuries later and still remains strong today.[5]

Anglo-Saxon settlement at Wormleighton appears to have been associated with a small group of colonists, one of whom, called *Wilma* or *Wilmund,* gave his name not only to the present village but, as we shall see, also to other topographic features in the vicinity. The earliest form of the name *Wilman lehttune* (Wilma's kitchen garden) appears in a charter[6] of King Eadwy dated 956, granting an estate to Earl Ælfhere. The ancient boundaries of the land-holding, which are very carefully recorded in this and other charters,[7] can still be identified within reasonable limits on the ground today and have been plotted on figure 1.2. The perambulation begins at *Cranmere* (presumably Crane Mere), which almost certainly occupied a small depression in the clays of the Fenny Compton gap since utilised as a reservoir to provide water for the Oxford Canal. The mere was actually larger than the reservoir, as the extent of alluvium plotted from field work and also shown on the unpublished Six Inch sheets of the Geological Survey[8] confirms. Further support for its location is provided by the current place name Granmore Hill for the rising ground south of the depression, while the stream issuing from the mere in 956 was called *Cranmeres broc* or *Claeihæma broc* (Clayhome Brook) which today flows by the village of Claydon![9] From the mere the boundary ran along 'the street', which appears to be the road from Southam to Banbury, to a 'hore pit' (mud hole) and a 'black pit' which presumably were pools on or adjoining the little stream flowing west. Thereafter the boundary followed the *sealt straet* (Salt Street)[10] eastward to *Wilmanford,* where it crossed *Wylman broce* (Wilman Brook), and so to join the *hricweg* (Ridge Way) running from north to south along the scarp-foot to cross the Cranmere Brook just east of the mere. It will be clear from figure 1.2 that these boundaries agree remarkably closely with those of the later parish established in the post-Norman period, indicating that here, as elsewhere, many of our local administrative units are territorially of great antiquity. The extent of the land unit of Wormleighton in 956 was somewhat larger than the present parish, as it appears then to have included Stoneton, now a separate parish of significantly 'immature' shape (figure 1.2). Both places remained closely linked for many centuries and were still considered as one land-holding when the first large-scale map was made in 1634 for Lord Spencer (figure 1.8).

Wormleighton was just one of a great cluster of Anglo-Saxon villages and hamlets in the Feldon, the majority lying only one or two miles apart. Of its neighbours shown on figure 1.2, Fenny Compton[11] records in its name both the location of the settlement in a valley (combe) at the scarp-foot and the water-holding character of the Lower Lias Clays that receive copious spring-line water from the base of the Marlstone. Stoneton to the east may have derived its name, 'stone farm', from rock exposures or from actual quarrying along the scarp, while Radbourn (*Hreodburna* = 'reed stream' in 998) described the reed-fringed brook near by. Further reference to the damp conditions of the clay land is contained in the name, Watergall, signifying soggy, infertile ground. By contrast, Hodnell ('Hoda's hill') appears to have taken its name from the wise choice made by a colonist called Hoda of a dry sand and gravel capped hill rising above 400 ft as the site of his dwelling. Ascote probably means simply 'Eadstan's cottage(s)', the association with a chapel coming much later. The grant of land at Wormleighton in 956 tells us nothing about the precise location of the village or hamlet. An attractive site for settlement was provided by the small flat-topped hill marked *A* on figure 1.2. Here the site was dry and wells could be sunk into the small expanse of glacial sands and gravels capping the hill which slightly exceeded 500 ft. It is not unlikely that some early occupation did take place here, but, from evidence to be given later, it would seem that the main settlement actually occupied site *B* (figure 1.2) in a shallow valley in the Lower Lias Clays just to the north-west of *A*. Field work has shown that *B* was not a particularly damp site, despite its position on the clays, and it had the advantage of good spring water issuing from the base of the sands and gravels below *A* and feeding northward into a small stream.

In common with other settlements in the vicinity the inhabitants of Wormleighton probably practised mixed farming, having large open arable fields on the cleared clay lands of the valley with extensive grazings for cattle, sheep, and swine on the higher ground adjoining to the east. At first plentiful timber was available for fuel and for construction purposes, but as population grew, clearing in the Feldon generally and in Wormleighton in particular appears to have proceeded so vigorously that by Domesday times the landscape had already become markedly 'open', and in succeeding centuries wood was very scarce. The road south through the Fenny Compton gap, and the Ridge Way which it intersected, ensured that Wormleighton did not suffer from isolation, while the Salt Street from Droitwich brought in not only salt, so important for preserving meat and fish, but other commodities too. During the period of Scandinavian invasions Warwickshire eventually lay on the border between resistant Anglo-Saxon England to the west and the Danelaw to the east, the frontier between the two closely following the line of the great Roman road, the Watling Street, which later formed the north-eastern boundary of the county (figure 1.1). Whereas Danish influence on settlement along the eastern fringe of Warwickshire was slight and sporadic, in the adjoining counties of Northamptonshire and Leicestershire to the east it was very strong as the place names indicate. There is no evidence to show whether Wormleighton was attacked at this time, but together with other places it was probably called upon to contribute in men, money, and goods to the defence of the shire and particularly of the Hundred of *Honesberie* to which it apparently belonged.

The charter of 956 is preserved in the cartulary of Abingdon, and it appears from a later charter[12] that the estate belonged to the Abbey for a period in the eleventh century, though they had lost it by 1066.

From that remarkable national survey, Domesday Book, prepared for William of Normandy in 1086, one can obtain a good general picture of the social and economic geography of the vill of Wormleighton twenty years after the Norman Conquest. Unfortunately we know virtually nothing about the fate and changing fortunes of the local Anglo-Saxon lords and their peasantry during the early years of the Norman occupation. For example, we do not know whether those who had supported King Harold at the Battle of Hastings continued to organise local resistance for a time and whether their villages suffered in consequence. From the Domesday evidence it would seem that Norman control was quickly asserted in Wormleighton and neighbouring vills, and judging by the general paucity of Norman defensive works[13] of motte and bailey type in the area peaceful conditions quickly obtained. At the time of the Domesday Survey Wormleighton was divided into three estates, the largest of which was still in the hands of an English lord by the name of Turchil of Warwick who had granted it to a tenant called Warin who may or may not have lived in the village.[14] The size of Turchil's holding was 3 hides, a hide[15] being a conventional assessment unit comprising, in Warwickshire, 4 virgates. The remaining two estates were in Norman hands; that of the Count of Meulan, which comprised 1½ hides, was leased to a tenant called Gilbert; that of Geoffrey de Mandeville, amounting to only ¾ hide, was held by someone known as William.

Consolidating the information for the three estates in order to obtain an overall picture for the entire vill, one finds that there were no less than 14½ ploughlands in Wormleighton worked by 23 ploughteams, of which 7 belonged to the three demesnes and 16 to the ordinary folk. The intensive nature of arable land-use not only in Wormleighton but in the Feldon of Warwickshire as a whole in Domesday times has already been clearly demonstrated by Professor R. H. Kinvig in a fine series of distribution maps which merit careful study.[16] It is interesting to find that the number of recorded ploughteams was considerably in excess of the number of recorded ploughlands, and one wonders whether this indicates that the arable land was being very intensively worked at this time. If this were so, one would like to know whether the fertility of the soil was standing up to such intensive farming, but the Survey is unfortunately silent on such matters. Whereas plentiful woodland is recorded for vills in the Forest of Arden, north of the Avon, it is significant that none is recorded for Wormleighton and neighbouring vills, which again suggests that much clearing for arable and pasture had indeed taken place. The value of the vill had also increased considerably since just before the Conquest, when the three parts were worth 130 *s.*, to 305 *s.* in 1086, though whether this considerable increase was entirely due to more intensive land-use or to harsh reassessment is unfortunately not known. In view of the apparent prosperity of Wormleighton in 1086 it is rather surprising to find that no mill is recorded there, whereas they were common in comparable vills in other parts of the Feldon.

Some measure of the importance of livestock in Wormleighton may be gained from the reference to 45 acres of meadow, providing the valuable hay crop on which cattle and sheep depended for supplementary feed in the harsh winter months following Martinmas. The principal meadows no doubt occupied the wetter clay land bordering the stream flowing just to the north of the village, with a second source around Crane Mere (figure 1.2). If one includes the three tenants of the separate estates, who may not necessarily have lived in Wormleighton, the total recorded population amounted to fifty, made up of 30 villeins, 8 bordars, 6 serfs, 1 priest, and 2 Frenchmen besides the three tenants. Assuming that the majority of these were heads of families, the total population of Wormleighton in 1086 must have been between 200 and 250, which is greater than that of today. The reference to two Frenchmen within Turchil's estate suggests that a small number of Norman folk had already entered the settlement, perhaps in the capacity of overseers. From the mention of a priest in both Wormleighton and Fenny Compton it would seem probable that a church had been established in each village, that at Wormleighton presumably occupying its present site on the hill overlooking the old village (*B* in figure 1.2). The sharp separation of church and village may appear unusual, but in Warwickshire there is nothing exceptional in this, for the churches at Warmington, Avon Dassett and Burton Dassett, all close to Wormleighton, stand aloof on the hill above the old village. The present Church of St Peter at Wormleighton contains remnants of an early twelfth century structure in the surviving angles of the original nave, but no Anglo-Saxon material has come to light.[17] Presumably the early church, perhaps merely a wooden building, was rebuilt soon after the Norman Conquest to conform more closely with the architectural standards of the foreign lord.

In the century following the Domesday Survey the three separate manors in Wormleighton continued in being, but nothing more is heard of the Mandeville holding after 1221. The two remaining holdings appear to have been consolidated and their overlordship passed entirely into Norman hands, first to Henry de Newburgh, Earl of Warwick, and then to the Crown. Henry I seems to have granted the manor to his Chamberlain, Geoffrey de Clinton, whose son later gave the church of Wormleighton to Kenilworth Priory.[18] The high degree of organisation that the Normans brought to their new land holdings, especially in the early years following the Conquest when the aim in the first flush of victory was to make their manors as profitable as possible, no doubt gave rise as we have seen to some increase in farming efficiency and intensity in Wormleighton and elsewhere. With the coming of peace and prosperity population numbers in many villages increased, being accompanied in some cases by the establishment of dependent hamlets. From the twelfth century onward the opportunities for expansion and further colonisation were particularly good north of the Avon where large tracts of Arden woodland still remained to be cleared and settled.[19] In the Feldon, however, one suspects that not only was *Lebensraum* already considerably reduced, but also that the carrying capacity of many soils, particularly those of the heavy Lower Lias Clays intensively used by strong village communities for five centuries or more was rapidly reaching a limit. This limit was related to soil and climatic conditions on the one hand, and to complex social and economic factors, as well as to technological skill, on the other. Confirmation that saturation point had already been reached in many Feldon vills is contained in the Warwickshire Hundred Rolls of 1279 which have been very thoroughly analysed for the Hundreds of Stoneleigh and Kineton by Dr J. B. Harley.[20] Comparison of the recorded populations for Feldon vills between 1086 and 1279 shows that in general only slight increases of population had occurred in these two centuries, several vills had remained almost stationary, while in the Hundred of Kineton (which then included Wormleighton) seven parishes out of the forty examined showed slight decreases. Apart from John Peche, who held 2 carucates in demesne, and John Passelewe, who held a further 2 carucates of him, the landholding population in Wormleighton in 1279 amounted to 36 villeins holding $23\frac{1}{4}$ virgates, 6 freemen with $2\frac{1}{4}$ virgates, and 3 cottagers with 1 virgate, making a total of 47 recorded persons with 4 carucates and $26\frac{1}{2}$ virgates. The recorded population was therefore very slightly below that of 1086, though the amount of ploughland would appear to have been greater, perhaps about one-third of the parish area then being arable.

It is tempting to conclude from this evidence, supported by data for other vills, that long before the Black Death had catastrophically upset the life of many villages in the middle of the fourteenth century, stagnation in the growth of both population and farming resources had already been reached in parts of the Feldon. Lords of the manor must have struggled to increase or even maintain their profits, while village folk must have experienced increasing difficulty in getting an adequate livelihood from the land. Under such conditions of increasingly delicate equilibrium the influence of any disrupting forces – social and economic change, inclement weather, political unrest, famine and disease – was acutely felt, and magnified, leaving its impress deeply on both man and land. It is interesting to consider to what extent the vulnerability of a parish to social and economic change was partly reflected in taxation returns. Thus, in the Lay Subsidy[21] of 1327 Wormleighton and Fenny Compton were assessed at 62*s.* and 61*s.* 4*d.* respectively, Ladbroke at 54*s.*, Priors Hardwick at 35*s.*, Hodnell at 22*s.* and Radbourn at 9*s.* 6*d.* The two latter places were depopulated by 1486, whereas the remainder still exist as villages today although, as we shall see later, Wormleighton must be treated as a special case. It may well be that the Lay Subsidy of 1327 had already foreshadowed the decline of Hodnell and Radbourn, whereas Wormleighton was still fairly prosperous, as the assessment suggests, though it, too, was to suffer later. The decline in Hodnell[22] must have been particularly pronounced, for the parish appears then to have included also Chapel Ascote and Watergall, both subsequently depopulated (figure 1.2). The number of taxpayers listed in the Subsidy and the magnitude of the total amount of tax paid for each vill also give some indication of the relative prosperity, and possibly population size, of the settlements. Thus, whereas in Radbourn 6 taxpayers subscribed a total of only 9*s.* 6*d.* and the 14 taxpayers of Hodnell only 22*s.*, the corresponding figures for Wormleighton were 22 taxpayers (62*s.*), Fenny Compton 16 (61*s.* 4*d.*), Ladbroke 23 (54*s.*) and Priors Hardwick, owned by the Priory of Coventry, 18 (35*s.*). Among the taxpayers listed for Wormleighton in 1332[23] and 1337 were Sir John Peche, who held the main manor, and Nicholas Passelewe, holding a sub-manor, while the remainder included a hayward, a smith and a reeve. Although from the Lay Subsidies quoted above Wormleighton (parish area 2425 acres in 1894) yielded slightly less than its neighbour Fenny Compton (2157 acres in 1894), other evidence suggests that it was more prosperous. In Domesday times the value of the manor of Fenny Compton was only £6 compared with £15. 5*s*. 0*d*. for Wormleighton, while the recorded value of the Spiritualities in the Pope Nicholas *Valor*[24] of 1291 were £7. 6*s*. 8*d*. and £10 respectively. Similarly, the recorded value of sheaves, fleeces and lambs in the *Nonarum Inquisitiones*[25] of 1342 amounted to £33. 6*s*. 8*d*. for Fenny Compton, but no less than £50 for Wormleighton.[26]

Figure 1.2, which attempts to show Wormleighton in its local setting during perhaps the peak of its post-Conquest prosperity, provides a good example of the density of nucleated rural settlement in this part of the Feldon and indicates some of the principal roads and fieldways that appear to have existed at this time. In plotting these lines of communication use was made of the evidence of aerial photographs giving complete cover for the district, and I am greatly indebted to Mr D. J. Pannett[27] for checking the information against his maps of the distribution of ridge-and-furrow patterns, old open-field boundaries and headlands for Wormleighton and neighbouring parishes. Wormleighton appears to have been well served by routeways at this time, many of them continuing in use today. The little stone church on the hill appears to have benefited from the short period of prosperity after the Conquest, having acquired a thick-walled tower and two narrow aisles by the end of the twelfth century. The rapid succession of priests in Wormleighton, Fenny Compton, Ladbroke, Burton Dassett, Avon Dassett and Warmington between 1348 and 1350 is probably an index of the severity of the great plague, the Black Death, in the area and similar evidence could no doubt be produced for many other parishes within and outside Warwickshire.[28] Conditions at the end of the Black Death must have been chaotic in many parishes where a severely depleted, half-starved and under-stocked labour force had to cope with portions of neglected fields. Little wonder that many parishes never had a chance to regain their old equilibrium before they were beset with other physical and human problems. Little wonder, too, that lords of large manors now lacking an adequate labour force should be ready to consider other forms of land-use than arable farming, or be willing to sell land to the first bidder. And who could blame the dispirited peasants, short of plough teams and seed corn, if they tried to sneak away to the growing towns where employment might be found in tanning, metal working or the woollen industry?

Professor R. H. Hilton[29] has clearly demonstrated the unprofitable nature of peasant farming in such Feldon villages as Compton Verney and Kingston around 1400, when many peasants were voluntarily surrendering their arable strips to their lord who in turn often had great difficulty in finding new tenants for his surplus land. Moreover, in many vills the peasants had already commuted their customary services and renders into annual money rents and were now hard pressed to pay these fixed sums, particularly when the demand for their wage labour both by the lord and by prosperous freemen had declined sharply. The outcome appears to have been a general reduction in the intensity of arable farming under the old open-field system and a corresponding increase in the acreage under grass. The demands of the growing cloth industry for ever increasing quantities of wool now encouraged many peasants and tenant farmers, as well as the lord of the manor himself, to graze sheep on unwanted arable land, with the result that blocks of enclosed pasture sprang up on the old ridge-and-furrow landscape of the open fields. For example, in 1354–5 a flock of nearly 800 sheep was kept on the demesne at Great Chesterton.[30] At the end of the same century some 400 sheep were folded on the lord's demesne at Radbourn[31] (figure 1.2), while a bailiff's account roll for Kingston shows that over half the manorial receipts in 1393–4 were derived from the pasturing of tenant beasts.[32] It is not surprising, therefore, that by the late 1430s many lords of the manor had recognised the advantages to be gained by converting all their arable land to great sheep walks. This was especially easy in villages where there were few or no freemen and ruthless lords could drive the peasants from the land and even destroy the village itself. One or two herdsmen could then tend the stock, their wages were only a small item, and the profits to be gained from commercial stock raising were considerable. In consequence by 1460 rural depopulation had become a serious national problem affecting many counties besides Warwickshire. The severity of depopulation in Warwickshire alone may be judged by the fact that at least 100 settlements were to be affected, although many of these did not disappear entirely.

Professor M. W. Beresford has already provided most interesting and fully documented accounts of the medieval depopulations for England in general, and for Warwickshire in particular, and it is unnecessary to enlarge on these here.[33] Instead the writer proposes to make one or two observations on the reasons[34] generally advanced for the depopulations before discussing in detail the fate of Wormleighton itself. In the first place, one would emphasise that too much weight has probably been attached to wool alone by those seeking to explain the reasons for the widespread conversion of open arable to enclosed pasture during the fifteenth and early sixteenth centuries. While it is not denied that wool commanded a very high price both at home and abroad, one would stress, too, that growing towns of the period, such as Birmingham and Coventry, required meat as well as bread. Nor was mutton the only flesh, for large herds of cattle were kept in many parts of Warwickshire, providing not only beef, butter and cheese for the townsfolk, but also hides for the flourishing leather industry in local centres like Birmingham, Coventry and Lichfield. In the second place, one would emphasise that the maintenance of good arable farming on the heavy Lower Lias Clay of many parts of south Warwickshire depended as much on weather conditions as on general soil fertility and favourable social and economic conditions. That these sticky soils, so prone to water-logging, can yield good crops of corn in favourable years was seen during the ploughing-up campaign of the Second World War, but once the emergency was over many farmers lost no time in allowing this intractable land to tumble down to grass again as feed for cattle and sheep. Indeed, during wet years there can be little doubt that the best crop for much of this land is grass.

Several authorities[35] would agree that Europe in general experienced a humid peak in the fourteenth century, followed by a preponderance of unfavourable climatic conditions in the first half of the succeeding century. One might inquire whether this was the reason for the disappearance of vine growing in England towards the end of the fourteenth century. Even today the farmers of southern Warwickshire require a good dry spell before they can tractor-plough their heavy clays. If they are able to do so in a dry autumn then the action of winter frost breaks down the heavy clods and sowing in a dry spring is easy. But if a wet autumn is succeeded by a wet spring the land may never be ploughed in time to crop that year. Medieval peasant farmers were clearly much more vulnerable to the harsh effects of inclement weather than the modern farmer whose bread corn may come from as far afield as Australia or Canada. Thus, if they missed a crop or saw a large proportion of their seed rot in sodden fields, they would be near to starvation the following year. A succession of only two wet autumns and springs would thus bring famine to peasants farming the heavy clays, unless they had a compensating pastoral land-use. At the very least, then, one must consider weather conditions as one of the factors, together with changing social and economic conditions, that might here upset the delicate balance between man and land at this time. A deterioration in each, operating simultaneously, could quickly change both the fortune and the appearance, of a Feldon parish. Some settlements succumbed early, particularly if their lord took the line of least resistance and sold his manor; others struggled for a while and then gave in; yet a third group, worthy of more detailed study than has yet been accorded them, survived as open-field mixed farming units with land still in strips until as late as last century. It is to the second of these groups that Wormleighton belonged.

DEPOPULATION A.D. 1499

Manors held by absentee lords, including especially those estates that changed hands frequently in the fluid land-market conditions of the late fourteenth century onward, were likely targets for depopulation. Professor H. J. Habbakuk[36] has also emphasised the important part that 'good and bad demographic luck' might play in the fortunes of great families and so in that of their estates. Thus failure of male issue, as well as changes of fortune, might lead to the transfer of a manor from the hands of a family that had been associated with the place for generations to an 'outside' family that cared little for either the land or the folk. Such change may have occurred in Wormleighton on the death in May 1386 of Sir John Peche, who then held the principal manor there. Sir John left a widow and two daughters, and the manor passed successively to his widow for life and then to his daughter, Margaret, who married Sir William Mountfort of Coleshill in Warwickshire.[37] So the manor came in due course into the hands of their grandson, Sir Simon Mountfort, who had the misfortune to be attainted for treason in 1495, all his lands being seized by the king. Although there is no direct evidence that the manor in Wormleighton had suffered considerable neglect following the death of Sir John Peche in 1386, it is very probable that this was so. As will be seen later, the manor house is thought to have been in a very dilapidated condition towards the end of the fifteenth century, presumably because it no longer served as a major residence for an important family; indeed, it may well have sheltered only a bailiff or an ambitious tenant farmer at this time. Similarly, if one compares the recorded population of Wormleighton in Domesday times with that at the end of the fifteenth century, the settlement must have declined by over half even before the final depopulation occurred in 1499.

After Wormleighton came into the hands of the king in 1495, part of the manor, comprising 10 messuages, 200 acres of arable land, 40 acres of meadow and 200 acres of pasture,[38] appears to have been granted for a time to a John Spicer. A prominent grazier of Hodnell (figure 1.2) by the name of John Spencer held 1 messuage and 3½ virgates from John Spicer in 1497, and it is not unlikely that most of this land was in pastoral use then.[39] In the account that is to follow of Wormleighton's historical geography during and after the depopulation we shall be closely concerned with the Spencer family over a period of more than four centuries extending to the present day. At this time they were prosperous freemen farmers[40] who appear to have taken full advantage of the opportunities that depopulation had offered elsewhere of first renting and later purchasing abandoned arable, pasture and meadow land in the Feldon. As their fortunes grew through the accumulation of land and stock, so their social standing rose through marriage ties with the local nobility and gentry. In 1498 William Cope,[41] who had married the daughter of John Spencer of Hodnell and who was Cofferer to the Household of Henry VII, was granted the manor of Wormleighton by the king at an annual rent of 20 marks (£13. 6*s*. 8*d*.), having previously rented the manor from John Spicer.[42] He promptly set about purchasing all the lands and tenements of minor lords in Wormleighton, including those of Sir Edward Raleigh.[43] Having gained control of the entire parish he proceeded in 1499 to destroy 12 messuages and 3 cottages, converting 240 acres of arable land to enclosed pasture for animals and driving 60 persons from the land.[44] If one includes a further 6 messuages that had been destroyed by Sir Edward Raleigh,[45] the total destruction in Wormleighton around 1499 amounted to no less than 18 messuages and three cottages with an estimated population of about 85. That an enclosed, depopulated manor was now more valuable than one in which village folk still derived a livelihood from mixed farming may be judged by the fact that the annual rent due to the Crown from Wormleighton, which before depopulation had been £8, increased after enclosure to £13. 6*s*. 8*d*.[46] Similarly the value of the land to Cope rose from £40 to £60 per annum.[47]

Using aerial photographs, documentary evidence and field investigations, an attempt has been made in figure 1.3 to reconstruct the fifteenth century settlement pattern and rural landscape of the immediate neighbourhood of Wormleighton before the final depopulation. The major settlement, of village status, nestled on fairly well-drained land close to a stream about one-third of a mile from the church. In common with many Warwickshire villages, both past and present, the settlement seems to have consisted of two parallel rows of rectilinear homesteads and crofts separated by a long narrow green[48] that extended from the ford, close by the road to Southam, south-east towards a suite of fishponds.[49] Investigation with the aid of soil augers of the small mounds and long narrow banks forming the rectilinear mesh of former cottages, gardens and closes, with their associated lanes, has revealed little stone walling, and one supposes that the homesteads on these heavy clays were simple thatched structures of

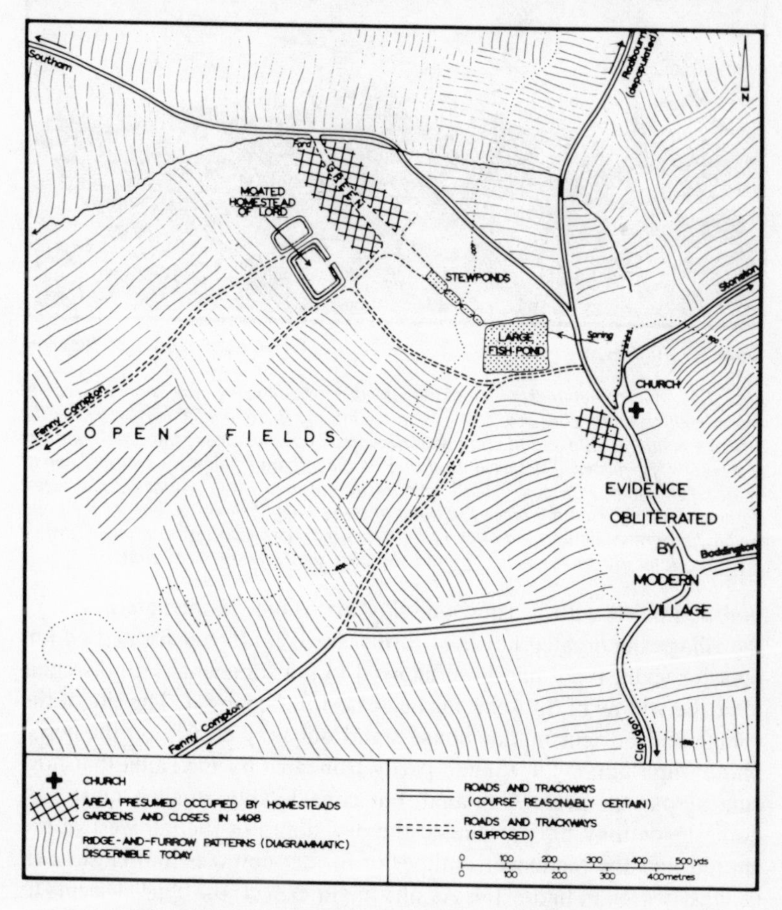

Fig. 1.3 Wormleighton circa 1498 (pre-depopulation)

Dr J. K. St. Joseph *Crown Copyright Reserved*

Fig. 1.4 Aerial photograph looking north-west showing the old church of Wormleighton and a cluster of cottages on the hill-top (bottom left); earthworks of the deserted medieval village and rectangular moated homestead near the canal; outlines of a secondary cluster of deserted dwellings on the hill flank below the church; a great square fish pond with four small fish-breeding tanks (now drained); old water channels leading from the large fish pond into the valley below; remains of the great double hedgerows set up soon after 1499; ridge-and-furrow patterns of former arable land-use in the fields around the past and present settlements.

timber, infilled with brushwood, clay and daub. Immediately west of the village the moated house of former lords no longer formed an impressive sight, for it had been allowed to fall somewhat into disrepair after the widow of Sir John Peche ceased to occupy it. The site of the village and ancient manor house stand out very clearly on the aerial photograph figure 1.4, though partly truncated by the canal that now cuts across the area. A second, but considerably smaller, cluster of homesteads may have occupied the dry slopes of the hill west of the church and the rectilinear outlines of former cottages and closes can be clearly seen in figure 1.4. As one might expect, the church seems to have received few major additions during the fifteenth century, though

Dr J. K. St. Joseph *Crown Copyright Reserved*

Fig. 1.5 Aerial photograph of the modern estate village of Wormleighton looking north-east and showing the T-pattern of roads flanked by the remnants of the village green; the orderly rows of cottages with their large gardens; farmsteads with their out-buildings; the old gatehouse with the remains of the manor house beyond; the church with its square tower on the extreme left of the photograph; old ridge-and-furrow patterns of former arable land-use beyond the great hedges that sharply define the rectangular limits of the village

the south porch (which could be either early fifteenth century or late fourteenth), the clerestory above the nave, and the rood-screen and loft were added then.

Prominent on figure 1.3 and figure 1.4 are the fishponds (now dry), the largest of which was fed by the spring issuing half way down the drift-capped hill. The controlled effluent from this large embanked pond seems to have led off from the north-east corner following a small runnel along its northern edge to enter the smallest of the four fish-breeding tanks. Surplus water could be directed from the large pond down a small channel into the main stream in the bottom of the valley below, by-passing the village (figure 1.4). The size of the great square pond reminds one of the importance of fish-breeding in medieval times, a fact well borne out for Warwickshire by recent research by Dr B. K. Roberts.[50] Before Wormleighton was enclosed in 1499 great open arable fields crossed by ridge and furrow lay around the village, and to give a general impression of this orderly patterned landscape the incidence of ridge and furrow, discernible both on the ground today and on aerial photographs such as figure 1.4, has been plotted on figure 1.3. It is certainly not claimed that the ridge-and-furrow patterns seen today are all a direct relic from medieval times. One has only to look at the corrugations that cross the bed of the large drained fishpond to realise that many of these patterns have been etched on the landscape, or parts thereof, since the depopulation. Yet one must also bear in mind that many aspects of open-field patterns, particularly those contained within headlands and field ways, were semi-permanent features of the medieval landscape, and in Wormleighton, with such a strong pastoral tradition after enclosure, the surviving ridge-and-furrow grid may still give a reasonable picture of the topographic framework of strip cultivation during the fifteenth century. Recent research work on ridge and furrow has also led one to think that the actual pattern of ridges and furrows may have changed very little during several centuries of cultivation. Co-aration in medieval times on the Lower Lias Clay of Wormleighton would have found ridging a great convenience, not only in identifying strips of land but more particularly for ensuring good drainage in times of excessive rainfall. Unfortunately little is known about the nature of the field system that was operated at Wormleighton itself in medieval times, though four compact fields survive as names on the estate plan of 1634. On the Bishop of Worcester's vills in the neighbourhood a two-field system was favoured, and this may well have been customary over extensive areas of the southern Feldon.[51] By contrast further north three-field and four-field farming was often practised.

The aerial photograph figure 1.4 reveals a remarkable variety of ground patterns, some of which are residual elements from the pre-depopulation landscape, whereas others, particularly the hedgerows and buildings other than the church, are more recent. In describing aerial photographs of 'lost village' sites many research workers have tended at times to see the present landscape merely as a doubly exposed photographic plate, one horizon revealing skeletal features of the old village organism, the other containing 'modern' features that are still viable topographic elements, though such features as roads may yet be very old beneath the surface. As will be seen later, the years immediately following the abandonment of a settlement were often associated not only with the destruction of all or part of the old village or hamlet, but also with further alteration of the landscape to meet the needs of the changed economy. Thus many closes and folds, as well as great pastures strongly hedged, banked and ditched, were fashioned from former open fields and village remnants. Surviving homesteads may have been quickly converted to provide shelter for stock, particularly for use in lambing or calving time, while new shelters may have been provided for herdsmen or animals elsewhere. The problem of feeding larger numbers of livestock during the winter months gave a boost to hay production and storage, while any opportunities for irrigating pastures and meadows were quickly seized upon. All these activities left their impress on the landscape, and there is no doubt that many earthworks once thought to have been associated with villages before their abandonment actually came into being in the period immediately following the depopulation. Figure 1.4 must therefore be viewed as a three-stage or four-stage landscape at least.

Before following the story of Wormleighton after the depopulation, it would be useful at this point to examine briefly the fate of some of the neighbouring settlements in the difficult days of the fifteenth century. As we have already seen, Hodnell, Chapel Ascote, Watergall and Radbourn (figures 1.1, 1.2 and 1.6) seem to have been relatively small settlements that had suffered gradual decline since the fourteenth century.[52] John Rous, a chantry priest of Warwick, who died in 1491, was so incensed by the ruthless depopulations both in the county and elsewhere that he presented a petition to Parliament in 1459 asking for legislation against it. Later in his *Historia Regum Angliae*[53] Rous gives a long list of villages in south Warwickshire that had been destroyed, adding; 'If such destruction took place in other parts of the kingdom as in Warwickshire it would be a danger to the whole country'. In his list, which was probably prepared about 1486, Rous mentions Hodnell, Chapel Ascote and Radbourn as already depopulated, and it would seem that those responsible were either the monks of Combe Abbey or the Catesby family.[54] From circumstantial evidence Stoneton would also appear to have suffered some depopulation, but the precise details are not known. By contrast Fenny Compton and Priors Hardwick seem to have suffered little, despite the fact that part of the former, like Wormleighton, had passed to the Mountforts after the death of Sir John Peche in 1386 and so came into the hands of the

Crown in 1495. When William Cope, Cofferer to the king, obtained the manor of Wormleighton in 1498 he was also granted a manor in Fenny Compton to hold in socage,[55] but whereas Wormleighton had been declining throughout the century and was ripe for final depopulation, Fenny Compton seems to have been a thriving settlement of several manors that stoutly resisted interference.

REHABILITATION AND THE RISE OF THE SPENCERS

The Spencers first come prominently to our notice in the latter part of the fifteenth century, when, as prosperous Warwickshire farmers, they began to concentrate on the raising of stock on land that they had purchased or leased, particularly within parishes that had already suffered depopulation. For example, in 1485 we find John Spencer, who lived in Hodnell, leasing for a period of one hundred years all William Catesby's lands in Hodnell and Chapel Ascote, with some additional land in Radbourn.[56] As a result of depopulation, great blocks of abandoned arable land had been put down to pasture in the area, and even today one can recognise these in distinctive local names of late origin such as Wills Pastures[57] (the name of a small extra-parochial district of 149 acres, between Wormleighton and Hodnell). The families, Catesby and Spencer, were clearly on very friendly terms, entered into many transactions[58] together, and were later to be related by marriage. For example, it is interesting to find in an undated letter,[59] thought to be pre-1486, that John Catesby of Althorp in Northamptonshire, requests 'Master Spenser of Hodynhill' to sell him 300 wether hoggerels to help stock his farm. (A wether was a castrated ram; a hoggerel was a sheep between one and two years old.) At the time of his death in 1497 John Spencer had extensive leases[60] of land in Napton, Lower Shuckburgh, Burton Dassett, Ascote and Wormleighton, all close to Hodnell, as well as more distant holdings in Stretton-under-Fosse east of Coventry (figure 1.6). Apart from Napton all these parishes appear to have been affected by depopulation in some degree before 1497 or very soon after, though John Spencer does not seem to have been responsible. Instead he was probably very quick to take advantage of any leases being offered on enclosed tracts of former open field now put down to grass. From the list of his holdings given in the *Inquisition Post Mortem*[61] it is clear that he usually held messuages as well as land in the respective parishes, though many of the homesteads had probably already been abandoned. In Burton Dassett he held a virgate of land from Sir Edward Belknap in 1497, but we know that Belknap proceeded to enclose 360 acres of arable land here in 1499 and destroyed 12 messuages, later putting down a further 240 acres to grass.[62] The entry for Chapel Ascote refers simply to 20 virgates of land without reference to messuages, which had probably already been removed. Mention has already been made of the holding in Wormleighton of a messuage and 3½ virgates in socage.

John Spencer of Hodnell had a brother, William, who lived in Radbourn and probably farmed in a similar way to his brother. William's son, who was also called John (henceforth to be called John Spencer I to distinguish him from his uncle), was destined to set in motion a great advance in the fortunes and social standing of the family. Before his uncle's death in 1497 John Spencer I was farming the manor of Snitterfield on the edge of the Avon valley west of Warwick (figure 1.6), and about this time he married Isabel, daughter and coheiress of Walter Graunt of Snitterfield,[63] which no doubt brought important additions to his estate. On the death of his uncle he moved to Hodnell to look after the extensive grazing business until his cousin, Thomas, came of age. His female cousin, Joan, had married William Cope, Cofferer to the king, who was granted the manors of Wormleighton and Fenny Compton in 1498, so John Spencer I quickly acquired powerful friends and relatives, and was in a good position to obtain grazing lands of his own in the vicinity, first by lease and later by purchase. Thus in the early years of the sixteenth century we find him renting land in Hodnell from the Priory of Nuneaton, the manors and pastures of Wormleighton and Fenny Compton from William Cope, the manors of Ladbroke and Radbourn from Sir John Rysley, a pasture in Stoneton from Sir Edward Raleigh and other persons, and the rectory of Radbourn from the Priory of Henwood [64] (figure 1.6).

With the quick profits derived from intensive grazing on these rented pastures John Spencer I soon acquired sufficient capital to enable him to purchase estates outright, commencing with the manor of Wormleighton and another in Fenny Compton bought from William Cope for no less than £1900 in 1506.[65] In the latter part of the fifteenth century depopulation had also been proceeding vigorously in the county of Northampton that adjoined Warwickshire to the east, and opportunities for John Spencer I to acquire lands there soon arose. Moreover, after his death in 1522, there were two sons not only

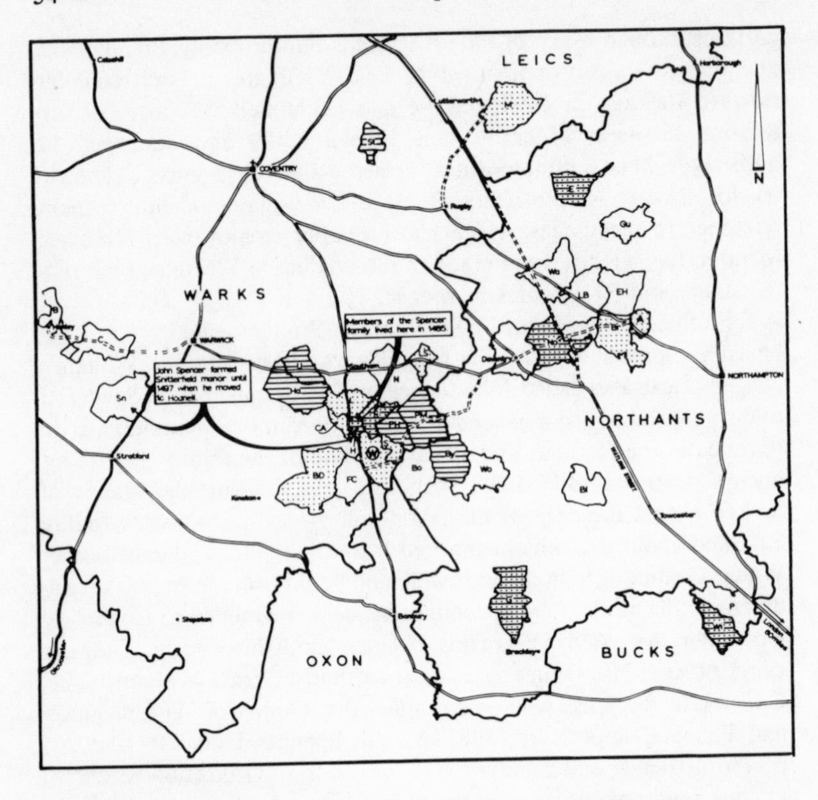

PRESENT COUNTY L	N	W	PARISH WITHIN WHICH A MANOR OR LAND WAS HELD	DATE OF FIRST RECORDED ACQUISITION BY SPENCERS	LEASE TO SPENCERS
	A		Althorp	1508+	
		B	Beaudesert	1568	
	Bl		Blakesley	1573	
	Bo		Boddington	1590+	
	Br		Brington	1511+	1577+
	By		Byfield	1557	
		BD	Burton Dassett		pre-1497
		C	Claverdon	1577	
		CA	Chapel Ascot		1485
			Daventry	pre-1559	
	E		Elkington	1589+	
	EH		East Haddon	pre-1559	
		FC	Fenny Compton	1506	c1500
	G		Greatworth	1628	
	Gu		Guilsborough	pre-1577	
		Ha	Harbury	pre-1559	
		H	Hodnell		c1485+
		L	Ladbroke		c1500
	LB		Long Buckby	1563+	
		LS	Lower Shuckburgh	pre-1559	pre-1497
M			Misterton		1576
		N	Napton		pre-1497
	No		Norton	1575	
	P		Passenham	1585	
		PH	Priors Hardwick	1585+	
		PM	Priors Marton	1602	
		R	Radbourn	1632	1485+
		S	Stoneton	1518	c1500
		Sn	Snitterfield	pre-1497	
		Str	Stretton-under-Fosse		pre-1497
		U	Ufton	1559	
		W	Wormleighton	1506	pre-1497
	Wa		Watford	1563+	
	Wi		Wicken	1502+	
	Wo		Woodford	1580+	

L - Leics N - Northants W - Warks
+ Denotes subsequent additions

Parish known to have suffered some depopulation c.1450-1500.
Parish containing important monastic lands disposed of after Dissolution.
Parish associated with both depopulation and disposal of monastic land.
N.B. The actual extent of the Spencer land holding in each parish is not shown.
Cathedral City.
County Town.
Market Town.
Major Road of the period.
Important link roads carrying Spencer livestock.
Present county boundary.
Present parish boundary.

0 miles 10
0 km 15

Fig. 1.6 Growth of principal Spencer land holdings along the Warwickshire–Northamptonshire Border circa 1485–1633

to establish a strong male line, but also to carry on the process of acquiring more land. The gradual acquisition of local holdings by purchase or lease up to 1633 is summarised in figure 1.6.[66] From this it will be seen that a great block of land suitable for pasture and hay was acquired by the Spencers along the borders of Warwickshire, Northamptonshire, and, to a less extent, Leicestershire. Geologically the area included large expanses of impervious clays of the Lower and Upper Lias, producing long succulent grass, with shorter, drier pasture on the uplands of the Middle Lias Marlstone, Northampton Sands and Oolitic Limestone. Clearly the opportunities for transhumance between parishes of contrasting physical and economic character were great. In 1508 John Spencer I purchased the manor of Althorp for £800 from the Catesbys.[67] This estate had been depopulated some time previously, and it would seem that although the Spencers never had either the brutality or the opportunity[68] to engage in wholesale depopulation themselves, they did not hesitate to turn to profitable use the fat pastures and former arable lands of abandoned settlements. Althorp was eventually to become not only a centre from which surrounding estates were administered, but also the great seat of the family. Wormleighton, too, was now to become the nodal point for vast pastures spanning the Warwickshire–Northamptonshire border, and a second family seat. As figure 1.6 shows, communications between Wormleighton and Althorp were good, and both places were near important roads leading to London. Stoneton, which was once part of the parish of Wormleighton though it is separate today, was also purchased in 1518; despite the fact that it was in Northamptonshire until 1896, it was from now on considered as a joint manor with Wormleighton, and the two are still administered partly as a joint estate today.

The severe depopulations to which we have referred above could not continue for over half a century without public outcry both in Warwickshire and elsewhere. The complaints of John Rous in 1459 probably had little immediate effect, but by the end of the century the State was compelled to take notice of the evils of depopulating enclosure and introduce legislation against it. Thus the general Statute of 1489 aimed at limiting depopulation, while the Act of 1515 forbade the conversion of tilled land to pasture.[69] A Bill connected with the latter complained that 'many merchant adventurers, clothmakers, goldsmiths, butchers, tanners and other artificers and unreasonable and covetous persons do encroach many more farms than they are able to occupy'.[70] The reference to butcher-graziers and tanners is particularly significant. Despite these moves to restrain depopulators little seems to have been achieved, with the result that in 1517 Cardinal Wolsey set up his famous Commissions of Inquiry. The greater part of the findings of the Commissions was printed in 1897 by Leadam,[71] under the title of *The Domesday of Inclosures,* and one can learn a great deal from these about the sequence of events in Wormleighton following the depopulation by William Cope in 1499. When Wolsey's Commissioners inquired into the facts of the depopulation at Wormleighton, William Cope[72] had been dead for four years so John Spencer I appears to have had some difficulty in convincing the Exchequer that he was not directly responsible. In proclaiming his innocence he disclosed many interesting details about changes that had been wrought on the landscape of Wormleighton since he purchased the manor in 1506, and these we will now examine.

John Spencer I, who by now had held the office of High Sheriff of Northamptonshire in 1511 and was to be knighted by Henry VIII soon after 1518, not only denied responsibility for the depopulation but in a letter of 1519[73] claimed to have partly rebuilt the settlement and to have made many improvements. The new settlement had been established on the hill-top adjoining the church, the site being much drier than the earlier one on the clays in the valley. Yet there was no difficulty in obtaining water, for wells could easily be sunk into the sand and gravel capping. By 1519 he claimed to have built himself a new manor house on the hill, as well as four houses for his servants, and the total population in 1519 was stated to be only twenty less than had occupied the settlement before its depopulation in 1499. Later the number of houses appears to have been further increased to six,[74] and finally to twelve[75] by 1522 when Sir John I died, the total population then being only a little less than sixty. There is abundant evidence on the ground, in manuscripts, and on estate maps (e.g. that of 1634, figure 1.8) to show that Sir John Spencer I had indeed built a new settlement of some size, perhaps almost an early 'model village', on the hill.[76] The very range of his grazing activities required that he had shepherds, cowherds, drovers and general labourers around him, as well as great barns for the storage of wool and fodder. Until about 1516 John Spencer I continued to live in his uncle's house at Hodnell until his cousin came of age.[77] After that he may have continued to live there for a while, or else moved temporarily into what he describes as the 'sory thached hows' which is presumably a reference to the dilapidated moated manor house in the valley.[78] In the meantime he was engaged in building a fine redbrick house on the hill that was probably begun in 1516 and completed by 1519.[79] It is interesting to find that John Spencer I had been given licence to castellate his manors of Althorp and Wormleighton in November 1512, though this does not appear to have been carried out until later.[80] The northern portion of this fine house still stands today and some idea of its original appearance may be gained from figure 1.7 which shows

Fig. 1.7 Wormleighton House from the magnificent Sheldon tapestry map bearing the date 1588. The fine Tudor building and strong gatehouse are depicted from the south with the square tower of the church rising behind. The tapestry map is on display in the County of Warwick Museum, Market Place, Warwick

Wormleighton manor house, looking from the south, with the square-towered church behind, from the famous Sheldon tapestry map[81] of Warwickshire dated *circa* 1588. From this it will be seen that the house was a large Tudor building with a strong stone gatehouse and probably with embattled parapets.[82] The considerably modified gatehouse can be identified easily in the top left portion of the modern aerial photograph (figure 1.5). John Spencer I also pleaded that he had spent a large sum of money in repairing the church 'whiche he found greatly in decay'. From the present architectural features of the church this does not appear to have involved any rebuilding, but rather a general renovation. He had also bought a 'Crosse, Bookes, Coope, Vestementes, Chalisis and Sensers', and had organised regular choral services, whereas even before the depopulation the congregation 'were so poore and lyvd so poorely that they had no bookes to syng servis on in the Churche'. Finally, he emphasised that whereas the community had been served in the past by only a single priest, he now intended to have two or three, though whether he really did so is doubtful.

Away from the newly established settlement on the flat hill-top the former landscape of open field had given place to great enclosures, bounded by hedges and ditches, within which large flocks of sheep, smaller herds of cattle, and occasional groups of horses[83] grazed on the grassy corrugations of ancient ridge and furrow. The presence of new banks and ditches on depopulated sites was frequently mentioned by contemporary writers, and it is clear that not only were abandoned buildings, gardens and closes pressed into use for the penning of stock but a rectilinear grid of new closes grew up around or alongside them. Before 1491 Rous[84] complained that the depopulators 'enclose the area of the village with mounds and surround them with ditches', the like of which can clearly be seen on the lost village site at Wormleighton today. Thus the rectilinear ground patterns seen on the left of the four small fishponds in the aerial photograph (figure 1.4) appear from field work to belong to this group, the ponds themselves then being convenient watering places for cattle and horses. The long branching pattern of what appear at first glance to be sunken roads or old water courses that once led from the right of the ponds on figure 1.4 down to the stream (now to the canal) in the valley bottom also appears to be a post-depopulation feature. Although the courses, like the ponds, are dry today they were clearly not roads, for their branching heads lead straight to the ponds. Field work, including the running of levels along each course, suggests that there were indeed old water channels related to an irrigation scheme for watering meadows. Water from the spring, and also from the overflow in the north-east corner of the large square pool, appears to have been collected in a channel running along the northern edge of the large pool. From this channel, the flow into which was controlled by a small sluice, water could be released into the smaller ponds if required or could be directed into the network of small runnels. By blocking these runnels at convenient points a good flow of water across the fairly impervious surface was made possible. The small stream, emerging from a spring that fed this system of pools and channels, is today called the Washbrook and takes its name from a small stone-lined pit[85] that was once used for washing sheep.

Part of the higher ground around the newly established settlement on the hill-top still remained in arable use to provide grain for the community, but apart from this most of the parish was given over to pasture. Different kinds of stock were carefully segregated in great closes, while frequent movement of animals from one part of the parish to another, or even from one parish to another, ensured that no pastures were overgrazed. Such control had a strong landscape expression in the great hedges and ditches that separated the shrunken arable from the expanded pasture, one pasture from another, and grazing areas from the valuable meadowland. In his replies to Wolsey's Commissioners John Spencer I has much to say about the fine hedges and ditches some now twenty years old, that he, and William Cope before him, had constructed. He also stresses that when he came to Wormleighton there was 'noo wood nor tymber growing within xij or xiiij myle' and poor folk had to 'bren the strawe that theire cattell shuld lyve by'. To remedy this shortage of timber, which certainly presented a serious problem in many parts of the Feldon at this time, he had set acorns 'bothe in the heggerowes, and also betwixt the hegges adioynyng to the old hegges that William Coope made before'. It is interesting to notice that on two occasions he refers to his great field divisions as 'doble dyched and doble hegged' with trees set between. This was no exaggeration, for these great double field boundaries form a characteristic feature of the parish today and have been mapped in figure 1.8. Several good examples can be seen in the aerial photograph (figure 1.4), for instance the field boundary immediately to the left of the large fishpond.

Various remarks by John Spencer I confirm the impression already gained that Wormleighton's land area had been very intensively used for arable and pasture in the four centuries preceding depopulation. Not only had almost complete deforestation made timber 'a gretter commodyte then eyther corne or grasse', but he complains that there was no intercommon remaining in the parish to provide free grazing for his tenants, a fact confirmed by the estate map of 1634. In view of our contention earlier that the clays of the Lower Lias are suitable for arable farming in favourable weather but in the long term are certainly better under grass, it is interesting to find that the same conclusion had been reached over four centuries ago by John Spencer who stressed that his manor 'was nevir good for corne as the cuntrey will testefye'. Perhaps the most illuminating part of Spencer's statement is the description of his occupation. He pleads to be allowed to retain his hedges and enclosed pasture 'for his lyvyng ys and hathe byn by the brede of cattell[86] in his pastures, for he ys neythir buyer nor seller in common markettes as other grasyers byn, but lyvyth by his owne brede of the same pastures, and sold yt when it was fatt to the Citie of London and other places yerely'. Further reference to the breeding of livestock is made in a letter to the Commissioners written in the winter of *circa* 1521–2 when Spencer pleads that if he had to sell his stock in mid-winter he would lose heavily 'for he hathe no maner of fatt cattell now lefte hym at this tyme but his brede'.[87] This might be taken as referring only to ordinary breeding ewes and heifers, but, as will be seen later, the Spencers were also engaged in selective breeding and in the sale of breeding stock. The importance of good road connections between Wormleighton, Althorp and London has already been mentioned, and in the succeeding years large numbers of fat stock were to be sold in the London market by the Spencers. Discreetly perhaps, there is no mention of the sales of wool which must also have been very great at this time, as will be demonstrated later. The pleas of John Spencer I were successful, he was allowed to keep his great pastures, the family fortunes continued to increase and he was knighted not long before his death on April 15, 1522.[88]

THE PERIOD OF INTENSIVE STOCK RAISING AND THE ACQUISITION OF MORE ESTATES

The rise of the Spencer family has been described in considerable detail by Dr M. E. Finch[89] for the period from 1540 to 1640, and I am grateful to her for allowing me to make use of her material in this paper. After the death of Sir John Spencer I the family's acquisition of grazing land in Warwickshire and Northamptonshire continued, aided in some degree by the Dissolution of the Monasteries in 1536–9, though in few if any cases did the Spencers purchase an ecclesiastical estate direct from the Crown. Thus, selecting examples from figure 1.6, which records the growth of holdings, the manor of Byfield (purchased in 1557) had belonged to Sheen Priory, the manor of Wicken (1588) to Snelshall, and those of Priors Marston (1602) and

Priors Hardwick (1633) to Coventry. The wealth of the Spencers also enabled them to make good marriages among important families, and in due course the estate was wisely entailed so that successive father and eldest son of the main line had only a life tenancy. In consequence the estate remained a remarkably stable entity for long periods of time. Although a great deal of the wealth of the early Spencers was vested in land, a very large proportion was also held as stock on their pastures. Indeed, the holdings shown on figure 1.6 constituted an enormous, closely integrated stock farm organised around two main centres, Wormleighton and Althorp. Wormleighton, with its great enclosed pastures and many small pens and folds, was the main centre for livestock, whereas Althorp, with a great park soon to be added, became the principal residence, though still functioning as a secondary stock centre. Apart from a large white stone monument to John, son and heir of Sir Robert Spencer, who died in 1610, the lack of Spencer tombs in the old church at Wormleighton is an eloquent reminder that the main domestic life of the family was centred elsewhere, namely at Althorp with a mortuary chapel in the church at Brington. Local hearsay still maintains that up to 20,000 sheep were grazed on the Spencer estates during the sixteenth century, and it is interesting to find that Dr Finch's analysis of the shepherds' accounts shows a total flock of about 14,000 sheep in May–June 1568 and again in October 1576. Of this total about 10,500 sheep and lambs appear to have been kept on the pastures peripheral to Wormleighton and between 3000 and 3500 on those around Althorp.[90]

We are fortunate in having an account of the manor of Wormleighton in 1554 which shows that it comprised '21 messuages, 21 tofts, a dovecot, 21 gardens, 1100 acres land (arable land), 560 acres meadow, 2500 acres pasture, 240 acres wood, 20 acres land covered with water and 540 acres heath'.[91] Compared with the present parish acreage (2451) this amounted to no less then 4960 acres in 1554. Even allowing for variations in the size of an acre between then and now it is clear that the manor of Wormleighton so described was a larger unit than the present parish, no doubt including the whole of Stoneton, part of Fenny Compton, as well as Watergall and Wills Pastures. The large amount of pasture does not surprise us, nor the 540 acres of heath which probably lay partly on the dry hills of the Middle Lias Marlstone and partly on the damp tracts of Watergall, but the reference to as much as 1100 acres of arable land is unexpected. A large proportion of this arable area was probably in Fenny Compton, which, as will be seen later, was not enclosed until as late as 1778–9; the growth of population in Wormleighton, too, had no doubt required an extension in its arable acreage. The coincidence in the numbers of messuages, tofts and gardens suggests that the grant referred simply to 21 homesteads with their adjoining plots of land. The large amount of meadow is to be expected, and the 20 acres of water would be approximately covered by the fishponds, other pools and the shrunken remnants of Crane Mere. Although the amount of woodland would certainly suggest that Sir John Spencer I's policy of planting trees had been sound, it is again likely that some of this lay along the steep scarp in adjoining parishes, though the map of 1634, to be discussed in detail later, shows several square copses or coverts set amid the large enclosed pastures (figure 1.8).

Unfortunately no reference is made in the above account to the great house at Wormleighton which was often used as the home of a married son or other close relative now that the main seat of the family was at Althorp. A large shearing yard (shown on the estate map of 1634) and a great wool barn[92] are known to have adjoined Wormleighton house, and in the summer of 1577 a great deal of the wool from close on 10,000 sheep known to have been shorn that year on all the Spencer estates probably passed through this great barn. The purchasers of Spencer wool during the sixteenth century are not known, and one wonders what quantity of wool, if any, went to local cloth centres such as Coventry. Early in the seventeenth century a single buyer or a partnership took the entire clip, most of which went outside the local area to places like Norwich or London.[93] How great the clip might be is shown by a valuation of no less than £1500 for that in the woolhouse at Wormleighton in February 1628.[94] That this was not exceptional may be judged by Dr Finch's calculation that Robert, first Baron Spencer of Wormleighton, received £1067. 7*s*. 0*d*. for wool and £1539 for stock in his London accounts for the winter of 1610–11.[95]

In 1519 John Spencer I had stressed the importance of his 'brede of cattell' which referred to both sheep and cattle, and one cannot doubt that breeding stock formed the backbone of the great grazing enterprise. For example, in October 1576 the breeding flock to be carried forward to the next year amounted to 5286 female sheep and 251 rams requiring extensive grazing and supplementary winter feed.[96] Unfortunately, the figures for cattle are not available, but from various references it is clear that they were an important subsidiary at both

Wormleighton and Althorp.[97] The local landscape at this time must have presented a most colourful picture with closely segregated flocks of lambs, hoggerels, breeding ewes, rams and wethers grazing the great hedged and ditched pastures with smaller pens holding stock selected for sale or slaughter. In smaller closes, near to water, cattle and horses were to be seen, while along the trampled green roads flocks and herds were being driven to new pastures or to markets. Aloof from this constant movement were the strongly hedged corn fields on the hill, and the narrower meadows glistening with water in the valley bottom. An entry in the Shepherds' Charges gives a list of the sheep counted in several closes of Wormleighton on 14 October 1580 and most of the closes named can be identified on the estate map of 1634. Thus in the great pasture of 'Sherton hill' there were 860 store ewes, in the 'great meadow' 79, and in 'Burmesleys Close' 60. Carefully separated were 135 store rams in 'the one part of the Town Hill', and 54 more in 'the nether part'.[98] Local sales of fat stock, surplus lambs and calves to local butchers, such as those of Lutterworth, appear to have been on a small scale only and the pattern established by Sir John Spencer I of selling the bulk in the profitable London market seems to have persisted through to the first quarter of the seventeenth century.[99] One would like to know more about the arrangements by which stock were driven south for delivery to London butchers. For example, were the animals handed over to butcher-graziers on the outskirts of London to spend a period in fattening pastures before slaughter, or did they go direct to the butcher after a journey of 100 miles by easy stages? As we have seen already, the Spencers were also willing to sell sheep to stock the estates of other great landowners, and in due course they acquired a reputation for the quality of their animals. We do not know the type or types of sheep that the Spencers favoured, but by careful selection and good feeding it is clear that they had built up breeding stock better than most. Sales of breeding ewes and rams were made not only to their relatives and to important local families, but also to Robert Dudley, Earl of Leicester, in 1576 and to Thomas, Lord Burghley, in 1602.[100] Thus the influence of the Spencers on the establishment and improvement of some early breeds may have been considerable. Finally, in view of what has been described above, one might reasonably claim that many of the distinctive patterns etched on the lost-village site of Wormleighton (figure 1.4) are the result of vigorous and long-continued post-depopulation pastoral activity.

THE PERIOD OF LEASING OF SPENCER LAND

In the previous two sections we have seen how the Spencers used wealth gained from the leasing of great blocks of land to purchase large estates which were not dissipated like those of many other great families. The early profits that they derived from wool and meat were devoted to wise investment in land, which in turn supported further increases in their flocks and herds. Increase in wealth was matched by that in social status, for by 1603 Sir Robert Spencer had become Baron Spencer of Wormleighton, and in 1643 Henry Spencer, the third Baron Spencer, was created Earl of Sunderland. Commenting on the meteoric rise of the Spencers from humble graziers to a leading titled family within the short space of a century, J. H. Round has rightly emphasised that they owed their success 'neither to the favour of a court, nor to the spoils of monasteries, nor to a fortune made in trade, but to successful farming'.[101] The backbone of this farming had been grass, livestock and wool, but a change was to come during the second quarter of the seventeenth century associated particularly with a decline in wool prices relative to those of other agricultural products.[102] The cloth trade was now undergoing a period of stagnation and wool was less in demand than formerly. Faced with the threat of a heavy decline in their revenues derived from wool, the prices obtained for mutton alone did not appear sufficiently rewarding for the Spencers to maintain their great sheep flocks for much longer, and other uses for their land had to be considered. Dr Finch has shown that the numbers of sheep on their pastures remained high until 1628, after which a slow reduction may have set in while the Spencers debated whether or not to seek alternative forms of revenue.[103] In the previous half-century an increasingly important supplementary source of income had been derived from the leasing of land on those Spencer estates, distant from Wormleighton and Althorp, which do not appear to have been closely concerned with their grazing interests at that time. The rents derived from such leaseholds had been slowly increasing, and these sums may have insulated the family from the main shock of falling wool prices. The opportunities for leasing more enclosed land to upstart farmers, anxious to set up on their own as general producers of grain and livestock produce on compact holdings of a few hundred acres, were good, and the Spencers lost no time in taking advantage of this. Furthermore, small speculators could easily be found who, having seen the great profits that had been made in wool and meat, were now eager to try their hand at the grazing business hoping that the fall in wool prices was only temporary. Once again the changeover from stock ranching on great enclosed pastures to mixed farming by small leaseholders left its mark on the landscape.

By 1634 William, Lord Spencer, now a Knight of the Bath, appears to have made the decision to sub-divide even his lands in Wormleighton into compact blocks for leasing to tenants. It was even rumoured in February that year that some of the Wormleighton pastures might be leased for ploughing,[104] though in practice this probably did not come about for several years. It is most significant, however, that a large-scale estate plan of Wormleighton and Stoneton should have been made from a survey by Richard Norwood that year, and I am greatly indebted to the present earl for kindly allowing me to trace and photograph this.[105] Figure 1.8, which incorporates data from the Wormleighton portion of the map, shows not only the well-enclosed character of the parish in 1634 but also the distribution of the recorded arable and meadow land. One should stress that the enclosed fields were still very large by modern standards, as a comparison of figures 1.8 and 1.9 will indicate. A large block of arable land lay south-east of the settlement, and many of the pastures, which were equally large, carried a rectangular spinney or covert in the centre. Two of the large pastures north of 'The Old Town' (the 'lost' village site) show signs of recent subdivision, for in each a spinney now adjoins two minor field divisions of apparently later date. The tracts of meadow were generally smaller, though that adjoining Fenny Compton Meadow may also show signs of recent subdivision. The site of the depopulated village had by now taken on the character of a great park for the large redbrick manor house on the hill. Trees adorned the land around the fishponds which, though still holding water, had relinquished their old function and had become ornamental pools. So Wormleighton conformed in a modest way to the custom of the time, so well expressed in Christopher Saxton's map of Warwickshire and Leicestershire for 1576, that the fine house of a great lord should have its park.[106] Gone were the small stock pens, while the sluices that once controlled the entry of water into the small runnels that formerly drenched the meadows had silted up or rotted away. The village, aligned along the street axis, had three major components: the core of the settlement comprised the impressive manor house with its fine gateway, walls and great barns; south of this was a cluster of homesteads grouped along the street and bordering a small green with a 'stockbank' or pinfold for stray cattle (a stone 'bus shelter was built on the site of the old pound or pinfold in 1955); finally, to the north, a smaller group of homesteads nestled near the church, with an outlying windmill a quarter of a mile to the east. Apart from a single homestead near the sand-pits, everyone lived in the village. This particular homestead was probably the first farmstead to spring up outside the village, having perhaps developed from the

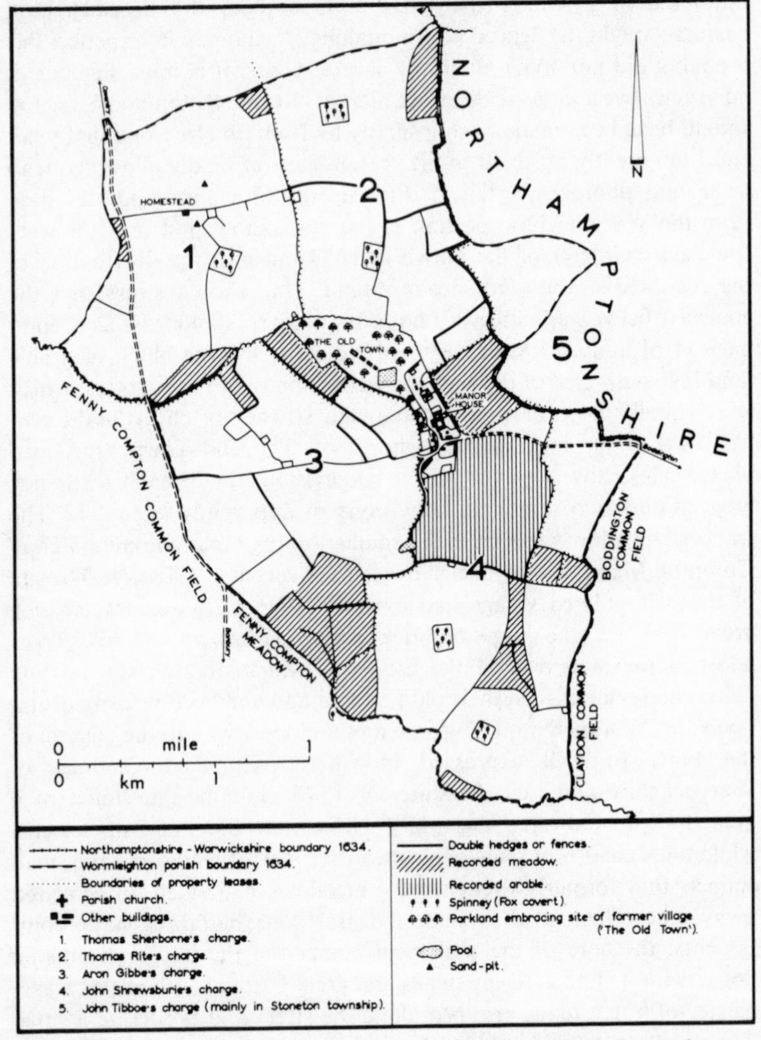

Fig. 1.8 Wormleighton 1634 from a survey by Richard Norwood

former cottage of a master shepherd now occupying a convenient central position within Lease No. 1. The double hedges shown on figure 1.8, although only remnants of the former pattern, preserve enough order and alinement to show that an important part of their function was to prevent the trespass of stock on both arable and meadow within Wormleighton parish, on the adjoining open fields of Claydon and Boddington, and within the village itself. Of particular interest on the estate map of 1634 is the subdivision of land in the parish of Wormleighton into four great 'charges', apparently meaning leases, with a further two charges in Stoneton, each charge being a well-balanced grazing unit with grass, meadow and water. (The blocks of land and their stock may once have been the responsibility of separate master shepherds employed by the Spencers.) On the original map each 'charge' bears the name of the individual either renting or responsible for the land, and it would seem most likely that the map had been expressly made to record the areas covered by each lease.[107] Those in Wormleighton, which were apparently held in 1634 by Thomas Sherborne, Thomas Rite, Aron Gibbe and John Shrewsburie, were more or less of the same size, averaging *circa* 500 acres (figure 1.8). The field names, which unfortunately could not be inserted legibly on figure 1.8, also suggest that at some time prior to 1634 each 'charge' had formed the nucleus of a single block of land. Thus 'Thomas Sherborne's Charge' (No. 1) embraced 'My Lady's Field' and 'Lady's Meadow', while that of Thomas Rite (No. 2) covered a former 'Windmill Field' now subdivided into three. Similarly the nucleus of No. 3 had once been called 'Shirton Hill' and No. 4 accorded closely with a former 'Banbury Field'. It is possible that these record an earlier four-field structure of pre-depopulation times. Leases Nos. 1, 2 and 3 on figure 1.8 apparently contained no arable land in 1634, and it might appear from this that at first the Spencers thought it advisable to maintain their land under grass and may well have sold part of their local stock to the first leaseholders. At least one of these leases must have changed hands very quickly, for Dr Finch records that in 1636 Lord Spencer leased a holding of 442 acres to a Matthew Clarke for twelve years at an annual rent of £489. 8*s*. 0*d*. which amounts to no less than 22*s*. an acre.[108] The size of this holding would seem to agree very closely with one of the 'charges' mentioned above. Within two years Matthew Clarke, having found that stock raising had lost its profitability, refused to pay his rent saying that it was too dear; he also removed his stock, some of which he had bought from Lord Spencer in 1636. The Spencers were now faced not only with the problem of declining revenues from sheep farming, but also with the difficulty of persuading others to lease land from them. During this period of flux a large proportion of the land around both Wormleighton and Althorp probably lay under-stocked, for by now the Spencer sheep flock appears to have declined to only one-third of its former size if one can make adequate calculation from the wool weighed at Wormleighton in September 1639.[109] The answer lay, firstly, in a change to more mixed farming on the great home farms of the Spencers, producing grain and meat for urban markets, and, secondly, in a gradual allocation of land under lease to a new class of tenant farmer that arose later on the estates.

The leases proposed on the 1634 map do not appear to have become permanent, for when opportunity arose and policy dictated, Wormleighton and Stoneton – still treated as one manor, though forming separate parishes – were leased *en bloc* to suitable tenants who in turn may have sub-let. As the Spencers had their main residence at Althorp, with 42 men and 11 women on the domestic staff[110] there in 1637, the fine house at Wormleighton formed an attractive residence for wealthy tenants, both relatives and outsiders. Tenants taking on a block lease of this kind may well have sub-let land to individual farmers within the village, but it is interesting to find that no farmsteads were established outside the village apart from that near the sand-pits (figure 1.8). Thus, a century later, when a new map[111] of the manor of Wormleighton was prepared by John Reynolds in 1734, the settlement pattern had apparently not undergone any major change, but the subdivision of former great fields had proceeded vigorously within each of the old 'charges' of 1634 which were not shown on the new map. This suggests that more intensive use was being made of the land by leasehold farmers living in the village and in the single outlying farmstead, and it is probable that several of these small enclosures had again felt the bite of the plough. Even so, most of the larger closes were no doubt still under grass.

The changes shown on the map of 1734 were not considered sufficiently great to warrant the inclusion of a separate illustration in this account. Changes within the village itself had included the addition of a small square pool on the hill slope immediately below the spring that still fed the old fishponds. As we have seen earlier, a sheep dip (later called the Washbrook) was located on this spring near the foot of the hill and the Spencers ensured that it was kept in good repair for the use of their tenants' stock.[112] Around the old fishponds the trees had now disappeared from the former parkland of 'The Old Town' (figure 1.8) and the land appears to have been used as a large pasture, which is its function today. The disappearance of the park should be considered in relation to a great decline in the appearance of the manor house between 1634 and 1734. By the latter date the house was only a shadow of its former self, for during the Civil Wars it had served as the headquarters for Prince Rupert and his cavalry before the Battle of Edgehill, fought in the autumn of 1642 when the crops had been harvested from the old open fields that still extended below the Cotswold scarp some five miles south-west of Wormleighton. As one would expect, the Spencers sided with the Royalists, and the manor house at Wormleighton, with its stout embattled walls and gatehouse, formed an important local stronghold controlling the gap through the Cotswold scarp. Indeed, when at a later date the Royalists had to retreat south before the Parliamentarian forces it was felt that the manor house should not be left to fall into enemy hands. A brief entry in the diary of Sir William Dugdale, the famous Warwickshire antiquary, records its fate on 7 January 1646: 'Wormleighton house, in Warwickshire, burnt by his Maties forces of Banbury, to prevent the Rebells making it a Garrison.'[113] The destruction was certainly severe, and the present house, which is only a remnant of the original, incorporates mainly the north wing of the old Tudor building and the two-storied gatehouse (bearing a date 1613) with many associated repairs and alterations, often crudely effected (figure 1.5). After 1646 the house degenerated into a large rambling farmstead, and still serves as such today, for there was no compelling need for the Spencers with their fine house at Althorp to rebuild it. The population had certainly remained fairly static at Wormleighton between 1634 and 1734 if one considers the pattern of buildings on both maps, a conclusion borne out by Dr William Thomas who recorded 12 houses and 15 families there in 1730,[114] figures not far removed from those of two centuries ago.

The Spencer fortunes seem to have revived through the renting of land, and as there was as yet no necessity to contemplate actual sales of land in Wormleighton or Stoneton the estate here continued intact. A sharp contrast in the rural landscape was still discernible between Wormleighton with its enclosed fields, and such adjacent parishes as Priors Hardwick, Priors Marston and Fenny Compton, which had never experienced drastic depopulation and still retained much open field. But this was to change in 1758, when some 770 acres in Priors Hardwick were enclosed by private Act and no less than 3800 acres in Priors Marston.[115] This was a period of feverish activity in such recently enclosed parishes, as a new pattern of fields and farms was established. Improvements in long-distance transport were also being discussed, and in April 1769 an Act was passed to build a canal from Coventry to Banbury and Oxford.[116] It was understandable that this should use the Fenny Compton gap, that had for so long carried a road through the Cotswold scarp, and that part of its course should run through the parish of Wormleighton. The course of the canal, which was opened between Coventry and Banbury by March 1778 and to Oxford by January 1790, is shown on figure 1.9. Local tradition stoutly maintains that the sinuous course was determined by Earl Spencer who would only consent to the canal crossing his land on condition that it passed through the land of each of his tenant farms! Although there would clearly be advantages in bringing in lime and other commodities, it appears more probable that the course of the canal merely conformed to the dictates of physical geography by closely following the 400 ft contour! From canal maps[117] dated 1777 and from a plan[118] of the manor of Wormleighton by John Corris, prepared in 1779, it is clear that only two farmsteads then lay outside the village, namely those called Grange Farm and New House Farm on the map of 1963 (figure 1.9), both located on the long spur within the great canal loop. The homestead of New House Farm had apparently been built between 1734 and 1777, and marks a belated second stage in the spread of tenant farmsteads outside the main village. A wharf had been established at the point where the road from Southam south to Banbury crossed the canal, and an inn soon sprang up on the Fenny Compton side of the road. Fenny Compton parish, with its strong village community, had now acquired a 'new look', not because of the canal, but as a result of the enclosure of no less than 2200 acres of former open field in 1778–9.[119] In the very south of Wormleighton parish, the shrunken remnant of Crane Mere (figure 1.2) that had been steadily silting up since Anglo-Saxon times was now dug out, embanked, and pressed into service again as a reservoir for the canal (figure 1.9). So man continually reappraises the latent opportunities of the landscape. Similarly, the old fishponds in the valley had been drained, and an enterprising tenant farmer had cropped the silty bed of the largest, leaving the ridge-and-furrow patterns still discernible in figure 1.4.[120]

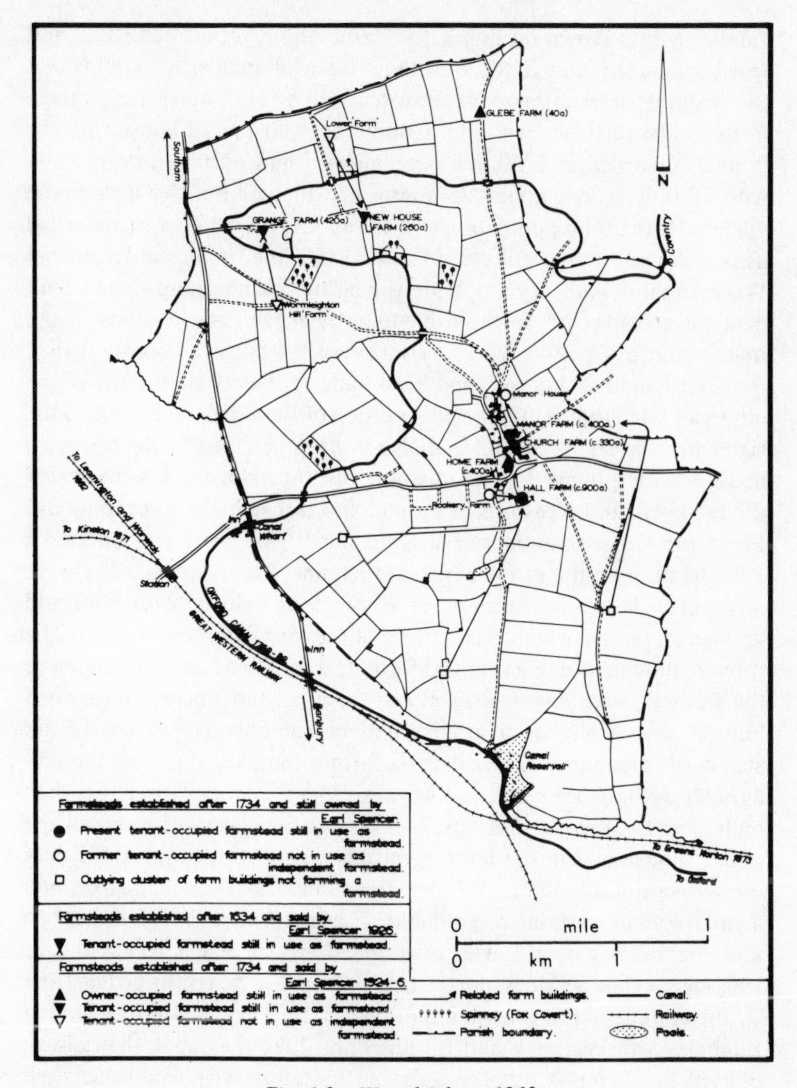

Fig. 1.9 Wormleighton 1963

When the formal programme of Ordnance Survey mapping at a scale of 2 in. to 1 mile crept northward across the Feldon in the years immediately following 1810, the pattern of fields in Wormleighton parish, surveyed around 1812, was not substantially different from that of 1734.[121] The great change to the present day landscape of smaller fields, shown on figure 1.9, came about soon after 1812, and was particularly associated with the growth of smaller leaseholds and the granting of permission for farmsteads to be built outside the village in the midst of their own land. Compared with the 12 houses and 15 families recorded in 1730, the population[122] had risen to 149 by 1801 with 28 families occupying 28 houses of which all but two were in the village. Of the total population of 149, no less than 127 were recorded as employed in agriculture. About 1850 the main settlement in Wormleighton had very much the appearance of an estate village, with neat farmsteads and cottages blending well with the remains of the manor house. In 1848 the orderly row of ten cottages, locally called the 'Ten Commandments', had been built, reputedly on the site of the old wool barn that had handled so much of the Spencer income in the sixteenth century. A school had also been established by the Spencers in 1839 with a house for the mistress, but the village folk were denied the comforts and pleasures of an inn, and this remains so even today! From the Census Enumeration Schedules[123] for 1851 one obtains a very detailed picture of the parish at this time. For example, there were now seven leasehold farmers, of whom four held between 460 and 480 acres, figures which recall those of the four 'charges' of 1634. The three remaining holdings ranged from 150 to 320 acres. All but one of the farmers were engaged in mixed farming, but one still described himself specifically as a grazier and presumably employed the six shepherds mentioned. The other six farmers employed no less than 53 agricultural labourers and two boys, so that the labour force was then high. The number of domestic servants (21) suggests that life in the manor house and in the large farmsteads was very comfortable, and the services of a jobbing gardener, three laundresses, a seamstress and a charwoman were also available. Contact between Wormleighton and the outside world was maintained by three carriers and two wagoners, while services along the canal were to be reinforced in 1852 by the completion of the section of the Great Western Railway linking Banbury with Warwick and Birmingham. Like the canal, the railway utilised the Fenny Compton gap and a station was established well outside the parish on the road running west from Wormleighton (figure 1.9). Unfortunately there is no tithe map[124] for Wormleighton, so one cannot describe the detailed land use of the parish in the second quarter of the nineteenth century. Instead, reference will be made to the Board of Trade Returns[125] for 1867, which confirm that although Wormleighton raised wheat, oats, beans and small acreages of peas, turnips, swedes and clover on 23 per cent of its area, the remainder of the large parish was still under grass. Certainly one's mind is carried back to Sir John Spencer I's assertion in 1519 that his manor 'was nevir good for corne as the cuntrey will testefye'. The livestock figures for 1867 – 617 cattle, 3480 sheep and 37 pigs – may not together equal those of the sixteenth century but they were still considerable. Farmers today continue to take pride in the strong pastoral tradition that has been established in the parish over the past four centuries. The emphasis on the rearing and fattening of cattle and sheep remains very great, and both cereal production and dairying have been of only slight importance until recently.[126]

THE TWENTIETH CENTURY: SALES OF SPENCER LAND

Within the parish today there are still seven separate farm units, four of which are worked from farmsteads within the village. Until early in 1924 all were tenant farms, and the maintenance of buildings and general supervision of the estate were carried out by agents of Earl Spencer living in the village. But a great change was to come about later that year when the present earl, who had succeeded to the title in 1922, was faced with the payment of heavy death duties on his father's estate. The decision was now taken to sell land within Wormleighton parish which had been in Spencer hands for over four centuries. Part of the sum was raised by the sale of two farms to their tenant occupiers in October 1924 – Home Farm (then 253 acres) within the village and New House Farm (then 262 acres) outside (figure 1.9).[127] In April 1926 Wormleighton Hill Farm[128] (424 acres), which had been established outside the village soon after 1834, was also sold, together with a very small farm (Glebe Farm *circa* 40 acres) on the northern extremity of the parish. Glebe Farm appears to have come into being as a small tenant holding soon after 1834. Since 1926 no further sales have been necessary, but some of the farms already sold have changed hands. Certain re-groupings of both buildings and land have also occurred, as well as confusing changes of farmstead names. Thus, of the farms no longer owned by the Spencers, Grange Farm and Wormleighton Hill Farm are now worked together as one holding, the buildings of the latter no longer serving as an independent farmstead. Similarly, New House Farm and Lower Farm (established soon after 1834) are 'paired', the latter's buildings no longer constituting a separate farmstead. Of the three remaining tenant farms, Manor Farm (*circa* 400 acres) has its farmstead in the village and an outlying cluster of barns that came into being about a century ago; Hall Farm (*circa* 900 acres) has a similar disposition with two outlying building-clusters of similar age, and part of a former farmstead, Rookery Farm, lying on the outskirts of the village. Finally the buildings of Church Farm (*circa* 330 acres) within the village include both the remains of the former Tudor manor house and a separate group near the old gatehouse (figure 1.9). (The present detached farmhouse known as Church Farm is thought by some to have been part of the bakehouse and kitchens of the manor house.) A close rectangular grid of fields, many dating from the period after 1734, is now associated with the farms, but the ghostly outlines of former larger fields can still be clearly traced on the ground today in ancient fieldways and in double ditches and hedges.

Visitors to the village today cannot fail to be impressed by its neat appearance and wise planning. The neat rows of cottages provide very good housing, and the spaciousness of the settlement owes much to the large gardens that surround them. In strong contrast to the estate cottages, all but six of which still belong to the Spencers, are the large rambling farmsteads, well-constructed in brick and stone, with fine outbuildings, yards and lawns. As one walks along the street, whose green – before the cottage gardens enclosed parts of it – was once much wider, one's attention is focused on the manor gatehouse adorned with a Spencer shield and through its archway to the square-towered church beyond. But an inn is lacking, and one must search diligently among the small cottages beyond the church for the tiny cottage shop and post office. The prominence of pumps in the gardens of the homesteads is an eloquent reminder that the village only acquired a piped water-supply as recently as 1963! This was long overdue, for until recently the village had no piped sewerage system and was dependent on the services of a 'night-soil man' who called periodically; in consequence the danger of water pollution in wells and pumps had been great. Similarly, it was not until as late as 1938 that a supply of electricity reached the village and made possible improvements in lighting, cooking and heating. The 'old world' character of village life changed dramatically during the Second World War, when evacuee families from Coventry were billeted there, raising the population perhaps to an all-time peak and bringing in a temporary flood of children to a village that had previously shown an ageing population structure. Since the war there has been a tendency for the dormitory element in the village population to increase. This is understandable when one recalls that less than twenty labourers are now employed on the farms, and only a handful on the estate, so that good cottage homes are available for renting to people who live in the village but work elsewhere. In particular men travel to Banbury and Coventry or work in a small factory near Fenny Compton station producing sectional concrete.

The tendency for younger people in Wormleighton to look beyond their own village for many services as well as for employment has been further encouraged by drastic changes in local administration. Thus, the village school, which had 42 scholars on the register in 1907, could only muster 12 in 1949. As a result the school was closed, and Wormleighton children now travel by 'bus to attend the primary school in more populous Fenny Compton and the secondary modern school in the former market town of Kineton, the latter over seven miles away. But the closure of the school brought one small benefit, for Earl Spencer kindly gave the building to the village for use as a much needed village hall for meetings and social functions. The services of teachers resident in the village had meant much to the social life of the community, and the reliance of the latter on their resident vicar now became even greater. But in 1954 a further blow was to fall, for in that year for reasons of economy the ecclesiastical parishes of Fenny Compton and Wormleighton were joined in a united benefice with a joint vicar resident in Fenny Compton. Wormleighton vicarage, which was now sold, became a private residence, and the community lost yet another key figure. A decade later there was some slight redress, for two teachers from Fenny Compton came to live in Wormleighton. Contact between Wormleighton and the 'outside world' is maintained by motor car and a skeleton 'bus service, and it is only in the last few years that the attractive character of the village and its interesting story have caught the attention of a small number of visitors. At the weekend an increasing number of motorists penetrates the seclusion of the village street, while with the coming of pleasure craft to the Oxford Canal summer visitors tie up for the night near the wharf where barges once offloaded.

Even today, with some 120 folk in the parish, of whom about 100 live in the estate village on the hill, Wormleighton probably has fewer people than lived in the earlier village down in the valley in Domesday times. The acreage of arable land is also probably considerably less today than it was then, while the corrugations of ridge and furrow on the present fat pastures remind one of great changes in land-use through time. It is not surprising that the severe disturbances associated with the depopulation of 1499, the sweeping changes from arable to pasture, the quick regeneration of the village on a new site with a different way of life, and the close dependence of the new community for so long on a distant lord have left structural weaknesses in the social and economic life of Wormleighton today. By contrast the neighbouring parish of Fenny Compton, physically similar but for long held by several rival lords, managed to escape depopulation, maintained its open-field husbandry until very late and, apart from minor setbacks (notably the general exodus from the land in the latter half of the nineteenth century), continued strongly in being to return a parish population of about 550 today. Innate strength and stability over many centuries have therefore secured for Fenny Compton a size and status somewhat above that of Wormleighton today. That this should be so between two contiguous parishes of similar extent cannot be satisfactorily explained in physical terms alone. Emphasis must be placed on their contrasting historical geography, so many aspects of which are tangibly incorporated into present landscape features, notably into field patterns and village morphology, but which at the same time still have a more subtle expression in the character and outlook of the very folk themselves.

SOURCE: *Transactions of the Birmingham Archaeological Society,* Vol. 80, 1965.

REFERENCES

1. G. H. Dury, 'A 400 feet bench in south-east Warwickshire', *Proceedings Geologists' Association,* lxii (1951), 167; 'A note on the Upper Cherwell', *Journal Northamptonshire Natural History Society,* xxxii (1953), 193. See also W. W. Bishop, 'The Pleistocene geology and geomorphology of three gaps in the Midland Jurassic Escarpment', *Philosophical Transactions of the Royal Society of London,* ccxli, no. 682 (1958), 255–306.
2. O. G. S. Crawford, *Archaeology in the field* (1953), ch. 7.
3. *The Victoria History of the Counties of England,* Warwickshire, i (1904, p. 249.
4. For a detailed account of the colonisation of Arden and Feldon *vide* H. Thorpe, 'The Growth of Settlement before the Norman Conquest', *Birmingham and its Regional Setting: A Scientific Survey* (British Association Handbook, 1950), pp. 87–112.
5. *Vide* Lucy Toulmin Smith (ed.), *The Itinerary of John Leland* (1906–10), ii. 47–51 and v. 155–6 for an account of Arden and Feldon, *circa* 1540; also William Dugdale, *The Antiquities of Warwickshire* (1656), Preface b3.

6. W. de G. Birch, *Cartularium Saxonicum* (1885–93), nos. 946–7. See also A. Mawer and F. M. Stenton, *The Place-Names of Warwickshire* (English Place-Name Society, xiii, 1936), p. 275 and *Victoria County History of Warwickshire*, v (1949), p. 218. E. Ekwall, *The Concise Oxford Dictionary of English Place-Names*, 4th edn. (1960), considers that the first element may be a river name *Wilme* or *Wielme* from O.E. *wielm* meaning 'flowing', and that the second element is O.E. *lēactūn* signifying '*tūn* where leeks grow'.
7. A. S. Napier and W. H. Stevenson, *The Crawford Collection of Early Charters* (1895), pp. 19–20, give details of grants of land at Ladbroke and Radbourn, adjoining Wormleighton, by King Æthelred to Ealdorman Leofwine around 998.
8. Photostat copies of 6-inch sheets SP.45.SW and SP.45.SE. can be obtained from the Geological Survey, London.
9. M. Gelling, *The Place-Names of Oxfordshire* (English Place-Name Society, vols. 23, 24, 1953–4), p. 418; E. Ekwall, *The Concise Oxford Dictionary of English Place-Names*, 4th edn. (1960), p. 110.
10. This 'salt street' ran from Priors Marston through Stratford-upon-Avon to the brine springs at Droitwich in Worcestershire. See F. T. S. Houghton, 'Salt-Ways', *Transactions Birmingham Archaeological Society*, liv (1932), 1–17 and map, plate 4.
11. For the meaning of these and other Warwickshire place-names see *The Place-Names of Warwickshire*, op. cit.
12. D. Whitelock (ed), *English Historical Documents*, i (1955), pp. 537–9.
13. See *Victoria County History of Warwickshire*, i. 345–406.
14. The complete Domesday entries for Wormleighton are given in *Victoria County History of Warwickshire*, i. 316, 324, 335.
15. Although a nominal figure of 120 acres is often stated as the approximate size of a hide, one should emphasise that the unit varied considerably from region to region. As the assessment was imposed from above, it would be rash to rely on the hidage as an index of the relative prosperity of different areas. See *Victoria County History of Warwickshire*, i. 298.
16. R. H. Kinvig, 'The Birmingham District in Domesday Times', *Birmingham and its Regional Setting* (1950), 113–34; see also his chapter on Warwickshire in H. C. Darby and I. B. Terrett (eds), *The Domesday Geography of Midland England*, 2nd edn, 1971, pp. 273–312.
17. *Victoria County History of Warwickshire*, v (1949), 221–4.
18. W. Dugdale, *The Antiquities of Warwickshire* (1656), pp. 404–5.
19. P. N. Nicklin, 'The Early Historical Geography of the Forest of Arden', *Transactions of the Birmingham Archaeological Society*, lvi (1932), 71–6 'Moated Sites in Midland England'; B. K. Roberts, 'Moated Sites', *The Amateur Historian* (Winter 1962), 34–8 and maps facing p. 40; *ibid.*, lxxx (1965), 26–37.
20. J. B. Harley, 'Population Trends and Agricultural Developments from the Warwickshire Hundred Rolls of 1279', *Economic History Review*, xi, no. 1 (August 1958), 8–18; also 'The Hundred Rolls of 1279', *The Amateur Historian*, Autumn 1961, 9–16.
21. W. F. Carter and E. A. Fry, 'Lay Subsidy Roll of 1327 for Warwickshire', Supplement to *Transactions Midland Record Soc.*, iii (1899), 1–12.
22. The derogatory name *Schytenhodenhull*, applied to part of the manor from 1232 to 1401, may have reflected this decline. See *The Place-Names of Warwickshire*, pp. 132–3.
23. W. F. Carter, 'Lay Subsidy Roll for Warwickshire, 1332', *Dugdale Society Publications*, vi (1926), 27.

24. S. Ayscough and J. Caley (eds), *Taxatio Ecclesiastica Angliae et Walliae Auctoritate Papae Nicholas IV circa 1291*. Record Commission (1809), 216–57. From the nature of the entries these two manors were better compared as regards Spiritualities than as regards Temporalities, though the latter may be generally more useful.
25. G. Vanderzee (ed), *Nonarum Inquisitiones in Curia Scaccarii*. Record Commission (1807), 438–48.
26. In the 1342 figures quoted above for Fenny Compton and Wormleighton the recorded values of the ninth of sheaves, fleeces and lambs have been multiplied by ten, to include the tithe and so give an overall index of wealth derived from agricultural production in these parishes.
27. Mr D. J. Pannett was a postgraduate research student of the Department of Geography, University of Birmingham. The results of his research are shortly to be presented in a dissertation entitled 'The Significance of Ridge and Furrow in the Agrarian Landscape of Warwickshire'.
28. Lists of incumbents are given in W. Dugdale, *The Antiquities of Warwickshire* (1656). See also *Victoria County History of Warwickshire*, i. 145–6, for further details of the severity of the Black Death in Warwickshire.
29. R. H. Hilton, 'A Study in the Pre-History of English Enclosure in the Fifteenth Century', *Studi in Onore di Armando Sapori*, i (1957), 675–85.
30. Willoughby de Broke MS. 393b (bailiff's account roll of Great Chesterton 1354–5) at Shakespeare's Birthplace Library, Stratford-on-Avon.
31. Public Record Office, *Ministers' Accounts* 1041/10 and 13. Even earlier, pasture for 600 sheep had been included in a grant of land in Radbourn to the monks of Combe. See W. Dugdale, 2nd edn., p. 329.
32. Willoughby de Broke MSS. 438 and 439.
33. M. W. Beresford, 'The Deserted Villages of Warwickshire', *Transactions Birmingham Archaeological Society*, lxvi (1945–6), 49–106; also *The Lost Villages of England* (London, 1954).
34. See H. Thorpe, 'The Lost Villages of Warwickshire', *Warwickshire and Worcestershire Magazine* (Feb. 1959).
35. G. Utterström, 'Climatic Variations and Population Problems in Early Modern History', *Scandinavian Economic History Review*, iii (1955), 3–47; H. Flohn, 'Klimaschwankungen im Mittelalter und ihre Historisch-geographische Bedeutung', *Berichte zur Deutschen Landeskunde*, vii (1949–50); C. E. Britton, *A Meteorological Chronology to A.D. 1450*, Meteorological Office Geophysical Memoir No. 70 (H.M.S.O. M.O. 409a), 1937; D. J. Schove, 'Climatic Fluctuations in Europe in the Late Historical Period (especially A.D. 800–1700)', University of London M.Sc. thesis, 1953.
36. See the Preface to M. E. Finch, 'The Wealth of Five Northamptonshire Families, 1540–1640', *Northamptonshire Record Society*, vol. xix (1956), pp. xii–xiii.
37. W. Dugdale, *The Antiquities of Warwickshire*, 2nd edn., revised by William Thomas (1730), i. 515.
38. Warwickshire Feet of Fines, 1345–1509, iii, no. 2767 (1498–9). *Dugdale Society Publications*, xviii, pp. 212–13.
39. *Calendar of Inquisitions Post Mortem, Henry VII*, ii. 245.
40. J. H. Round, *Studies in Peerage and Family History* (1901), pp. 285–9.
41. William Cope seems to have held land both from the Crown and from various individuals in several parts of southern England. In 1499 he was appointed steward of the lordships of Henley-in-Arden and Tanworth in Warwickshire (see *Calendar of Patent Rolls, Henry VII, 1494–1509*, p. 168). In 1503 he took possession of great parks in Guildford and Henley, Surrey (ibid., p. 339).

42. I. S. Leadam, *The Domesday of Inclosures 1517–1518 (1897),* ii. *485* (Earl Spencer's MS. of *circa* 1519). See also Spencer MSS. 1670, 1677 and 1685.
43. Ibid. ii. 656.
44. Ibid. ii. 403–4; see also Public Record Office, *Miscellanea of the Exchequer* 164/10/7. William Cope was associated with other depopulations, for example, at Irchester and Knuston in Northamptonshire (*vide* Leadam, i. 287).
45. W. Dugdale (1656), p. 405.
46. I. S. Leadam, ii. 485.
47. Ibid. 404. See also Spencer MSS. 1698 and 1699.
48. Villages and hamlets with their homesteads arranged around a central open space, or green, seem to have been common in many parts of England from Anglo-Saxon times at least. An examination of many lost village sites in England suggests that the green was often an important morphological feature.
49. See M. W. Beresford, *The Lost Villages of England,* pp. 32–8, 54; also 'The Deserted Villages of Warwickshire', *Transactions Birmingham Archaeological Society,* lxvi (1945–6), 78; H. Thorpe, 'The Green Village as a Distinctive Form of Settlement on the North European Plain', *Bulletin de la Société Belge d'Études Géographiques,* xxx, no. 1 (1961), 93–134; also the section and maps on Rural Settlement in *The British Isles: A Systematic Geography* published for the International Geographical Congress (1964).
50. B. K. Roberts, 'Moated Sites in Midland England', *loc. cit.,* p. 30. Dr Roberts was formerly engaged in post-graduate research in the Department of Geography, University of Birmingham; his Ph.D. thesis, 'Settlement, Population and Land Use in the Western Portion of the Forest of Arden, 1086–1350' (Thesis No. 619) was presented in 1965. I am indebted to him for help in locating various unpublished manuscripts relating to Wormleighton.
51. See H. L. Gray, *English Field Systems* (1915), pp. 499–500; R. H. Hilton, 'Social Structure of Rural Warwickshire in the Middle Ages', *Dugdale Society* (1950), pp. 22–5.
52. See M. W. Beresford, 'The Deserted Villages of Warwickshire', pp. 61, 65–7, 78, 86, 92–3, 94 and 98.
53. T. Hearne (ed.), 2nd edition (1745), pp. 122–3.
54. W. Dugdale (1656), p. 219a.
55. *Calendar of Patent Rolls, 1494–1509;* grants to William Cope, dated May 7, 1498 and Nov. 12, 1503, pp. 133 and 340.
56. Early Spencer Papers, Box 8, in the muniment room at Althorp, Northamptonshire.
57. *The Place-Names of Warwickshire,* p. 149. Wills Pastures may have been identical with Hodnell Pastures first mentioned in 1603. A family by the name of Willes lived in the area during the early seventeenth century.
58. For example, the will of William Catesby, Esquire, drawn up 25 August 1485, showed that John Spencer was then owed sixty pounds and possibly more. See W. Dugdale (1656), p. 586.
59. Early Spencer Papers, Box 8.
60. *Calendar of Inquisitions Post Mortem,* Henry VII, ii, item 245.
61. Ibid., pp. 160–1.
62. See W. Dugdale (1656), p. 409; also M. W. Beresford, *The Deserted Villages of Warwickshire,* p. 88.
63. F. L. Colville, *Worthies of Warwickshire* (1869), p. 706; also J. H. Round, op. cit., p. 187.
64. M. E. Finch, op. cit., p. 39. See especially Spencer MSS. 1698 and 1699.
65. Spencer MS. 1706. A supplication of *circa* 1519 by John Spencer I to Henry

VIII states that £2000 was paid for Wormleighton alone (*vide* I. S. Leadam, ii. 485).

66. I am indebted to Professor M. W. Beresford and Mr J. G. Hurst of the Deserted Medieval Village Research Group for their help in checking depopulated settlements in the Northamptonshire portion of figure 1.6.
67. F. L. Colville, *Worthies of Warwickshire* (1869), p. 707.
68. About 1502 John Spencer I may have enclosed part of the manor of Wicken in Northamptonshire and evicted people. See I. S. Leadam, i. 285.
69. For an example of both the Statute of 1489 and the Act of 1515 see M. W. Beresford, *The Lost Villages of England*, pp. 104–6; also I. S. Leadam, i. 6–14.
70. *Calendar of Letters and Papers of Henry VII* (eds. S. R. Gairdner and J. S. Brewer), iv (iii), no. 5750. For ease in reading punctuation has been added to the above quotation.
71. Op. cit.
72. William Cope died in 1513 (*vide* I. S. Leadam, ii. 657, footnote).
73. Ibid., ii. 485–7. Earl Spencer MS. of *circa* 1519. The original document is to be found in Earl Spencer Papers, Box 8, folder 15, at Althorp.
74. Public Record Office, *Miscellanea of the Exchequer*, E 164/10/7.
75. I. S. Leadam, ii. 657–8.
76. Ibid., ii. 487–9, Earl Spencer MS. of *circa* 1522.
77. I. S. Leadam, ii. 485–6.
78. A very detailed description of the old moated farmstead in 1522 is given in Early Spencer Papers, Box 8, folder 17, terrier 3.
79. It is intriguing to find that in 1504 John Spencer I had undertaken in first leasing the manor of Wormleighton from William Cope 'within 12 years to build upon the premises as good a mansion as the said William has of late built in a Quadrant within the lordship of Hampton, co. Oxon.' See Spencer MSS. 1698 and 1699.
80. *Letters and Papers, Foreign and Domestic, Henry VIII*, i, pt. 1, item 1494, sect. 28, p. 684.
81. This remarkable tapestry map, size 18 ft 8 in. × 14 ft 5 in., covering the county of Warwick, makes very early use of actual prospects as the cartographic symbol for places. Although the map bears the date 1588 and the incorporated topographic data agrees with that period, the tapestry may be a somewhat later copy of an original. The tapestry map is on display in the County of Warwick Museum, Market Place, Warwick. For further information see P. D. A. Harvey and H. Thorpe, *The Printed Maps of Warwickshire 1576–1900* (1959), p. 5; also J. Humphreys, 'Elizabethan Sheldon Tapestries', *Archaeologia*, lxxiv (1923–4), 181–202; E. A. B. Barnard and A. J. B. Wace, 'The Sheldon Tapestry Weavers and their Work', *Archaeologia*, lxxviii (1928), 155–314.
82. Etchings of Wormleighton House appeared in W. Niven, *Illustrations of Old Warwickshire Houses* (1878), plate 31 facing p. 32.
83. A manuscript in Early Spencer Papers, Box 11, refers to sheep, bullocks and colts received by John Spencer in 1515–16.
84. Op. cit.
85. This small pool was not shown on the map of the lordship of Wormleighton prepared for Lord Spencer by Richard Norwood in 1634 (see figure 1.8), but appears on the estate map of 1734 made by John Reynolds. Both these fine maps are kept in the Muniment Room at Althorp and I am indebted to Earl Spencer for allowing me to consult them.
86. 'Cattell' in this sense would include livestock in general, but particularly sheep and cattle. John Spencer I makes this clear by quoting separate prices for beasts and sheep though both are collectively described as 'cattell'.

87. I. S. Leadam, op. cit., p. 488.
88. The will of John Spencer I shows that he held certain lands in Essex as well as those in Northamptonshire and Warwickshire. To the latter estates shown on figure 1.6 should be added 1 messuage and 60 acres of arable land, meadow and pasture in Leamington. See P.R.O., MSS. C 142/40, nos. 83 and 124.
89. Op. cit.
90. M. E. Finch, Appendix I, Tables E and F.
91. *Calendar of Patent Rolls: Philip and Mary, 1553–4,* p. 265.
92. M. D. Harris, *Some Manors, Churches and Villages of Warwickshire* (1937), p. 165.
93. M. E. Finch, p. 45 and footnote.
94. Spencer, MSS., no. 1879.
95. M. E. Finch, p. 46.
96. Ibid., p. 41.
97. *Vide* Early Spencer Papers, Shepherds' Charges, Box 11, for references to sheep, bullocks and colts in 1515–16, and to sheep and cattle in 1576. See also M. E. Finch, p. 44, footnote.
98. Early Spencer Papers, Box 11.
99. M. E. Finch, p. 44.
100. Ibid., p. 45.
101. J. H. Round, *Studies in Peerage and Family History* (1901), p. 281.
102. See J. E. Thorold Rogers, *A History of Agriculture and Prices in England* (1882), v. 207; E. Kerridge, 'The Movement of Rent, 1540–1640', *Economic History Review,* vi, no. 1 (1953), 16–34.
103. M. E. Finch, p. 46.
104. Letter from George Carter to William, Lord Spencer, in Spencer unlabelled folder.
105. Since writing this account a similar map, also dated 1634, of enclosed Spencer pastures in Radbourn has been found in the County Record Office, Warwick (reference number CR. 732). This would appear to confirm that the Spencers were having their lands accurately surveyed at this time preparatory to making leases on a large scale.
106. P. D. A. Harvey and H. Thorpe, *The Printed Maps of Warwickshire, 1576–1900* (1959), pp. 2–5.
107. Although it is not unusual to find later data superimposed on estate maps, the information on that of 1634 seems to date from one period only.
108. M. E. Finch, p. 48 and footnote 5.
109. M. E. Finch, p. 48.
110. Ibid., p. 178, Appendix V.
111. This map is housed in the Muniment Room at Althorp.
112. See Spencer Account Books for 1777 where payments for sheep washing and 'repair of the Washbrook' are mentioned.
113. W. Hamper, *The Life, Diary and Correspondence of Sir William Dugdale* (1827), p. 83.
114. W. Dugdale, *Antiquities of Warwickshire,* 2nd edition (1730), i. 517.
115. W. E. Tate, 'Enclosure Acts and Awards relating to Warwickshire', *Transactions Birmingham Archaeological Society,* lxv (1943–4), 79.
116. C. Hadfield, *British Canals* (1952), p. 75.
117. Spencer Muniments.
118. Ibid.
119. W. E. Tate, p. 83.
120. The drained bed of the old pool is shown as being under arable use on a 'Map of The Wormleighton Estate, 1856' in the muniment room at Althorp.

121. See Ordnance Survey 2 in. = 1 mile, field sheet No. 227, surveyed some time before 1812.
122. Census Returns for 1801.
123. Enumeration Schedules, Public Record Office.
124. H. C. Prince, 'The Tithe Surveys of the Mid-nineteenth Century', *Agricultural History Review*, vii, pt. 1 (1959), 14–26.
125. *Agricultural Returns for Great Britain*, 1867. Parish summaries for England and Wales are held by the Collection of Statistics Branch, Ministry of Agriculture, Government Buildings, Epsom Road, Guildford, Surrey.
126. For example, see Land Utilization Survey of Britain, 1 in. = 1 mile, sheet 83, surveyed 1931–7.
127. 1924 Rental in Spencer Muniments.
128. 1926 Rental in Spencer Muniments.

ADDENDA TO REFERENCES

Professor Thorpe has supplied the following information for this reprint, updated to July 1973:

Ref. No.

4. The latest synthesis is given in H. Thorpe, 'The Evolution of Settlement and Land Use in Warwickshire', in D. A. Cadbury, J. G. Hawkes and R. C. Readett (eds), *A Computer—Mapped Flora: A Study of the County of Warwickshire* (1971).
33. See also M. W. Beresford and J. G. Hurst (eds), *Deserted Medieval Villages* (1971).
35. See also E. Le Roy Ladurie, *Times of Feast, Times of Famine: A History of Climate since the Year 1000* (1973).
85. During the recent construction of a sewage plant on the lower side of the pool, the small stone-lined pit was unfortunately filled in.

2 The Development of Rural Settlement Around Lincoln

with special reference to the eighteenth and nineteenth centuries

D. R. MILLS

INTRODUCTION

THE study of rural settlement occupies a significant place in geographical literature and the relationship between settlement patterns on the one hand and physical, economic and social conditions on the other has long been recognised. In eastern England the pattern of rural settlement is composed basically of nucleated villages established in pre-Conquest times and of dispersed settlement made at a much later date, mainly in the last two hundred years. While the pattern of this settlement is generally well-known, the conditions under which it came into being are not so well appreciated. This study has therefore been prepared as an attempt to assess and elucidate these conditions as they applied to an area of approximately fifteen miles radius around the City of Lincoln.[1]

EARLY SETTLEMENT

Roman Lincoln was built on the northern side of a gap in the limestone escarpment which runs the length of the county from south to north (figure 2.1). On the western side of this Jurassic cuesta lies a vale composed principally of Liassic clays covered in places by large tracts of Pleistocene river gravels. To the east of Lincoln is another clay vale consisting mainly of Upper Jurassic clays, in the southern part of which these rocks are now partly buried beneath deposits of silt and peat which form the northernmost part of the Witham fens.

The Roman occupation made few lasting impressions on the countryside around Lincoln, except for two major roads and a canal, and the main outlines of the dominantly nucleated settlement pattern were established in the Anglo-Saxon and Scandinavian periods. Few villages were founded after the Conquest, for the great majority of present day villages are recorded in Domesday Book. Reliable plans for

For references to this chapter, see p. 96.

these villages are, however, uncommon for dates prior to 1700, but plans are available for a large number of villages between 1750 and 1850 and these show that the villages were then of a strongly nucleated character. The houses were frequently grouped along either

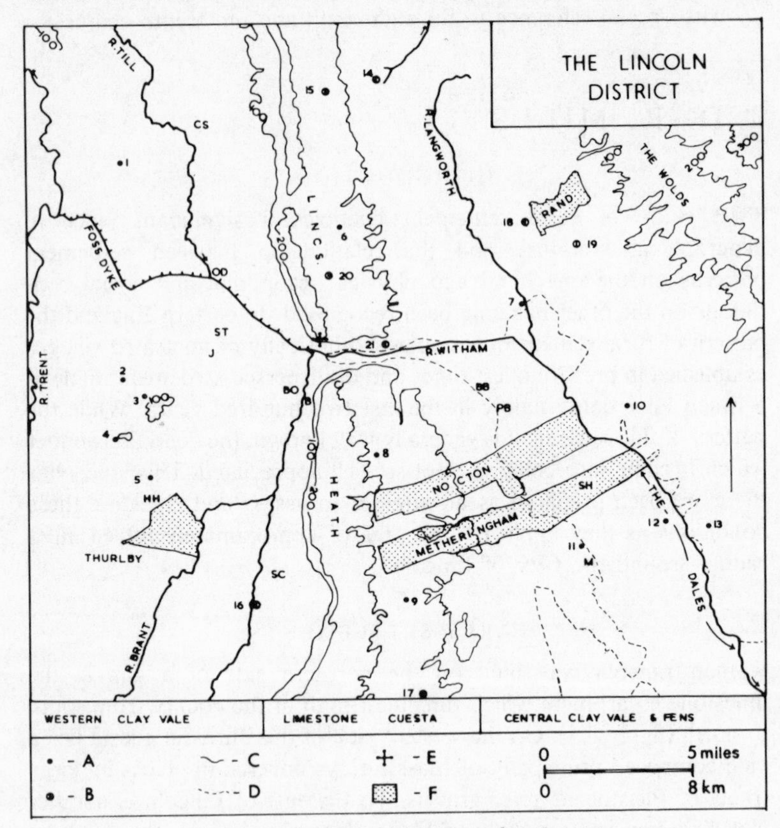

Fig. 2.1 The Lincoln District – location map

A. Monastic settlements represented by dwellings at the present time:
1 Stow Park; 2 Swinethorpe; 3 Eagle Woodhouse; 4 Eagle Hall; 5 Morton Hall; 6 Grange de Lings; 7 Low Barlings; 8 Mere Hall; 9 Temple Bruer; 10 Tupholme; 11 Linwood Hall; 12 Sim Booth Grange; 13 Kirkstead Abbey.

B. Settlements partly or wholly depopulated during the medieval period, now containing a few houses:
14 East Firsby; 15 West Firsby; 16 Skinnand; 17 Dunsby; 18 Bullington; 19 Goltho; 20 Riseholme; 21 Greetwell.

C. Contours at 100 ft interval.

D. Limit of the Witham Fens.

E. Lincoln: position of first Roman Enclosure.

F. Areas of sample townships.

Other Places mentioned in text:
B Bracebridge; BB Branston Booths; BO Boultham; C Canwick; CS Coates-by-Stow; HH Halfway House Inn; J Jerusalem; M Martin; OD Odder; PB Potterhanworth Booths; SC Somerton Castle; SH Sot's Hole; ST Skellingthorpe.

one main street, or two parallel streets, while a second (back) street which contained few or no houses was another common variant.

The sites of these villages appear to have been chosen mainly with an eye to two main requirements, a reliable water supply and proximity to land suitable for arable farming. The areas chosen for cultivation at that time were generally those with deep clay or heavy loam soils, although the settlements themselves were usually placed on an adjacent outcrop of a drier nature. For example, the settlements of the cuesta are situated on the limestone outcrop near its junctions with clay horizons, i.e. in the spring zones of both scarp and dip slopes. In the vales many villages occupy sites on gravels which yield a good supply of water because of the underlying layers of impervious clay. Other villages in the vales are to be found on the modest, but well-marked eminences which act as the water partings between minor streams.

The availability of settlement sites appears to have largely determined the pattern of township boundaries, which is an important subject in relation to the later dispersal of settlement. There are, in fact, two characteristic township shapes; the long narrow townships attached to the villages of the spring zones and the townships of a more compact shape, sometimes almost square, which are found in the clay vales. (See figure 2.1 for examples of each type.) The shapes of the first type were largely due to the fact that suitable settlement sites could only be found in the narrow spring zones which run from south to north; flanking these zones lay the limestone heaths and the damp ground of the fens and the lowest areas of the clay vales. Land could therefore be freely taken in for several miles to east and west, while on the other hand settlements were hemmed in on the north and south by similar villages situated at intervals of about a mile – hence the gridiron pattern of long rectangular townships so common in scarpland England. Generally speaking this gridiron pattern is repeated in the clay vales around Lincoln, except that there the townships form rectangles which are much shorter in relation to their width. This pattern seems to be mainly a response to the rectilinear plan of the minor streams, for where the natural drainage network is more irregular, as in the gravel terrace country south west of Lincoln, the pattern of township boundaries also becomes more irregular.

Prior to the eighteenth century isolated dwellings appear to have been exceptional, but records do exist of various kinds of early dispersed settlement. In late medieval times both monastic houses and their granges were frequently erected at some distance from existing villages and many of them are still represented by isolated farmhouses, such as Eagle Hall and Grange de Lings (see figure 2.1, settlements numbered 1–13).[2] Most of these monastic settlements were situated in the less attractive areas of heath, fen and moor.

A second type of dispersed settlement sprang up on the banks of the River Witham and the Foss Dyke canal. There are, for example, several extant sixteenth century probate inventories of persons who had lived on the right bank of the Witham in the fens between Blankney fen and Billinghay fen, an area known as the 'Dales'. The occupation of waterman is sometimes recorded, but some of the inhabitants of the Dales may have been fowlers, fishermen or shepherds. A similar isolated dwelling near the Foss Dyke, called Odder, is recorded as early as 1509, while there are two isolated 'Booths', whose recorded existence also begins in the sixteenth century, which are situated on the bank of the Car Dyke, a drainage channel of Roman origin (figure 2.1).[3]

Among the settlements mentioned in Domesday Book there are some that have failed to survive to the present day, while others are represented by only one or two farms. These were originally small nucleated settlements, but they must now be regarded as dispersed settlement. This change in the form of settlement came about as a result of the depopulations of the fourteenth to seventeenth centuries, which also removed the 'lost villages' entirely from the map of settlement. In some cases one factor which probably promoted the loss of population was the small size of a township and the fact that it contained only one major soil type. Thus Skinnand and Dunsby, for example, both contained less than 1000 acres, while Skinnand was confined to the Witham clay vale and Dunsby to the limestone heath. On the other hand, some pre-Conquest settlements appear never to have grown to any substantial size and still contain so few houses that they barely deserve the title of hamlet; a good example is Coates-by-Stow which consists of a minute church, one farm and three or four cottages (figure 2.1).[4]

Sometimes purely local circumstances, which were not repeated within the district, led to the dispersal of settlement at an early date. For instance, the warrener's house on the Lord's Moor in Skellingthorpe is recorded as early as 1694 and there is evidence that Somerton Castle has been continuously occupied since the days of its military importance.[5]

THE DISPERSAL OF SETTLEMENT SINCE *circa* 1750

Despite all these minor reasons for the scattering of settlement, many townships in the middle of the eighteenth century contained no dispersed settlement at all and nowhere is it likely that the dispersed population exceeded 5 per cent of the total.[6] Yet by 1851 the situation had radically changed and in a few townships nearly half the population was living outside the villages. Information for this date is derived from the original copies of the census returns, in which the enumerators were required to state the address of each household. Unfortunately many of the enumerators appear to have felt that the name of the township was a sufficient address; in other cases they have not indicated precise addresses very clearly. However, about one return in four is sufficiently accurate for present purposes and table 2.1 has been based on the returns for those townships in the district to which this provision applies.[7]

Other than the large increase in dispersed population, three salient facts emerge from table 2.1: firstly, the high averages of dispersed population (31·0 per cent and 35·4 per cent); secondly, the wide variations from these averages in individual townships; and thirdly, the similarity between the averages for the two main types of

Table 2.1 Proportion of population dispersed in selected townships, 1851

(Note.—The hamlets mentioned are of medieval and not modern foundation)

Part I. Spring zone townships

Township	Population in township. 1801	Population in township. 1851	Population in village. 1851	Population dispersed. 1851	Population % dispersed. 1851
Cammeringham	111	141	79	62	43·8
Canwick	215	210	122	88	41·8
Coleby	301	423	339	84	19·8
Hackthorn	218	258	163	95	36·8
Harmston	235	414	357	57	13·7
Ingham	225	712	370	342	48·0
Nettleham	377	944	627	217	23·0
Nocton	287	510	266	Heath 99, Fen 150 } 249	48·7
Saxby	69	120	90	30	25·0
Spridlington	126	313	262	51	16·2
Welton	380	604	379, Rylands Hamlet 111 } 490	114	18·7
Totals and Average	2542	4649	3165	1484	31·0

Part II. Clay vale townships

Township	Population in township, 1801	Population in township, 1851	Population in village, 1851	Population dispersed, 1851	Population % dispersed, 1851
Aubourn	179	304	219	85	27·6
Cherry Willingham	77	148	134	14	9·4
Doddington	140	175	103	72	41·1
Dunholme	140	411	297	114	27·7
Fiskerton	270	463	303	160	34·8
North Hykeham	254	443	304	139	31·4
Reepham	183	368	260	88	29·3
Saxilby	389	1137	587 } 648	489	43·0
N. and S. Ingleby Hamlets			61 }		
Skellingthorpe	193	584	297	287	49·1
Thorpe-on-the-Hill	190	379	256	123	32·7
Wickenby	119	289	172	94	36·0
Totals and Average	2134	4700	3035	1665	35·4

Sources: Censuses 1801 and 1851, and enumerators' schedules 1851.

township, the average for the clay vale townships being slightly the larger. The last point is particularly significant in relation to the impression gained from a study of the Ordnance Survey Third Edition One-Inch Maps of 1883–8. The impression is that there was considerably more dispersed settlement in the spring zone townships than in the clay vale townships. If it can be supposed that the census and the Third Edition Maps are equally reliable, it must be inferred that the dispersal of settlement continued to a later date in the spring zone townships than in the clay vale townships. Unfortunately there is suitable information on this point for only one spring zone township, Nocton, where the proportion of the population living in dispersed dwellings rose from 48·7 per cent in 1851 to 52·5 per cent in 1891 and 57 per cent in 1901.[8] Only further work over a larger area and upon enumerators' returns at later censuses as they become available will enable a more definite conclusion to be reached on this subject.

Generally speaking, dispersed settlement took the form of farmhouses, sometimes with cottages nearby, situated perhaps a quarter or half a mile from each other and frequently at some distance from a public road. Occasionally the houses are grouped loosely together, as at Jerusalem in Skellingthorpe. This settlement form is more frequently found in the fens where hamlets generally straggle along the bank of the River Witham or along a main drainage dyke, for example Martin Dales and Sot's Hole. It is in the narrow townships stretching for five to ten miles, partly across the cuesta and partly across fen or vale, that the dispersed settlement is most noticeable. For example, the western end of Metheringham township lies on the heath four miles away from the village. The heath had its own school for the children from the farms and cottages which straggle at intervals along or near the lane which leads down to the village. On the eastern side of the village the pattern is repeated for another five miles as the road continues first across a clay upland and then across the fen to the River Witham. In Metheringham fen there are two hamlets known as Sot's Hole and Tanvats, names which are rather quaint, yet typical of these nineteenth century settlements; their size and their isolation from Metheringham village warranted their being given a school and, at a later date, a bus service of their own.

This type of dispersed settlement has sometimes been regarded as a result of Parliamentary enclosure.[9] Although it is true that very large tracts of land in central Lincolnshire, especially on the heath and in the fens, were enclosed by this method between 1765 and 1820, it is equally clear that the enclosure of land was not the only factor responsible for the large scale dispersal of settlement. Thus in the townships which were enclosed before 1750 the dispersal of settlement occurred no earlier than in townships where enclosure was not completed until the passing of an enclosure Act sometime between 1765 and 1850. The enclosure movement was, in fact, only one aspect of the 'agricultural revolution', which must be considered in some detail in order to understand fully the need for a dispersal of settlement at this time.

THE EFFECTS OF THE AGRICULTURAL REVOLUTION

During the fifty years or so beginning about 1765 considerable changes took place in the agricultural methods employed in Lincolnshire, as in many other parts of the country.[10] Drainage improvements were particularly important in the fens where they made possible the conversion of meadow and pasture to arable; they also made it possible to build farmhouses and cottages over a much wider area of fenland and the banks of the new drainage dykes were favourite sites for new roads and buildings. The adoption of the Norfolk rotation of barley, seeds, wheat and turnips made possible the cultivation of the light soil areas of heath and moor, thereby again turning grassland into arable land. Since the reclaimed areas of heath, fen and moor usually lay at the extremities of townships, their use as arable land doubtless prompted the erection of farmhouses and cottages within them.

In general, the agricultural revolution made farming operations more intensive and more complicated, especially during the winter months. For example, hedging and ditching now occupied farm workers for a large part of the winter. Most important were the increased numbers of cattle and sheep which were kept throughout this season. Sheep were kept partly for the sake of their manure and therefore spent the winter 'folded' in the turnip fields. Another method of manuring the soil was the application of cattle and horse dung which accumulated in the covered accommodation of the farmsteads during the winter. The carting of dung and daily visits to sheep folds clearly made it very desirable to erect the farm buildings and dwellings amongst the fields belonging to the farm.

In addition to new farming activities, there were many age old operations which could be carried out more conveniently from farmsteads situated in the fields. One important example was the carrying home of the corn harvest, for until the middle of the nineteenth century threshing was still carried out by the use of flails on a barn floor. Even when machine threshing was introduced it was generally more convenient to carry out the operation in a farmyard than in a field, since water had to be supplied to the engine in large quantities and storage space found for the grain.

Apart from the years 1815–40, agriculture was a prosperous business from the mid-eighteenth century until the Great Depression of the 1870s and 1880s. Capital was therefore available for improvements, many of which had possibly been obvious to farmers for a long time, but had not been carried out for lack of money. Moreover, a new spirit of efficiency entered farming in the third quarter of the eighteenth century and the new farmsteads in the fields were spacious and well-made and generally contained a 'crew-yard', a partly covered yard in which cattle and horses spent the worst parts of the winter. The amount of space required by these new steadings may in itself have been a factor dictating construction in the fields, rather than in the relatively built-up areas of the villages, where however some farmsteads of the new type are to be found.

Despite the inflow of money and ideas, the dispersal of settlement was clearly a gradual rather than a sudden process, for in most townships there were far fewer dispersed buildings shown by the First Edition of the Ordnance Survey in 1824 than by the Third Edition in the 1880s. One of the causes of the relative slowness of dispersal may have been the fact that although money was more easily found for investment in farming, there were many other calls on capital resources, such as enclosure, drainage and fencing.

Another cause may have been the difficulty of re-arranging farm boundaries satisfactorily. In the days of open field farming, the village had been the nodal, if not the central point of most farms, since each of them held land and common rights scattered throughout the township. In principle, enclosure was followed by the creation of compact holdings, thereby reducing the effective nodality of the village. However, in practice, enclosure commissioners in Lincolnshire frequently gave owners several blocks of land in different parts of a township, so that several years or decades may have elapsed before the more or less compact holdings of today were the general rule. (One commissioner complained vociferously about this practice on the grounds of inefficiency (Stone, p. 43: see note 10 in References). Unfortunately enclosure awards seldom give information about the actual occupation of land.) Only when the fields of each farm were grouped together was there any point in building new farmsteads outside the villages.

The overall effect of the many changes in farming methods was a vast increase in the demand for labour, especially in those areas where grassland had been ploughed up in large quantities. Only in the 1840s was labour saving machinery of any importance brought into operation on farms; in the meantime many time-consuming tasks had been introduced into the farm calendar. Consequently there were large increases in population in rural Lincolnshire from about 1770 until about the middle of the nineteenth century and in many townships the population doubled between 1801 and 1851 or 1861 (see table 2.1). The need for extra living accommodation was therefore very considerable and since few of the villages expanded by more than about one-third in the size of built-up area, a large proportion of the population increases must have been housed in the new dispersed dwellings. In fact, had there been no substantial increases in population the dispersion of settlement might not have reached its present proportions.

OTHER REASONS FOR THE DISPERSAL OF SETTLEMENT

In addition to the changes in agriculture, there were other minor factors which promoted the dispersal of settlement after about 1750.

These included the turnpikes and the railways which respectively necessitated the construction of toll houses and crossing keepers' cottages and stations. Inns, too, were sometimes built in isolated positions, generally on main roads where they could cater for passing travellers. A good example is the Halfway House Inn in Swinderby parish which lies on the Fosse Way seven miles from both Lincoln and Newark. In townships where there was a resident landed family, lodges were often built either on the boundaries of the township or at the entrances to the park and were no doubt largely the result of Romantic ideas of landscape gardening. In connection with farming, many windmills were erected, either for milling corn or for drainage purposes and many of them had houses attached.

In the main however the dispersed settlements were, and still are occupied by families whose livelihood comes directly from the land and many of the houses are 'tied cottages'. In fact, the tied cottage system appears to have evolved largely out of a desire to house rural workers as near as possible to the place of their work. On the other hand most of the families engaged in the various service trades and in building continued to live in the villages, which for their purposes remained the most convenient places of business.

CHANGES IN THE GROUPED SETTLEMENTS

Despite the great increases in dispersed settlement, table 2.1 shows quite clearly that these did not absorb the whole of the increase in population in every township. Two other possible explanations must therefore be considered: firstly, that owing to an increase in the size of families there was a smaller number of households per unit number of the population and consequently a smaller demand for extra houses than might otherwise have been the case: and secondly that the rebuilding of villages provided an opportunity to build more houses on the same amount of ground.

Evidence concerning the latter point is difficult to assess. There is no doubt that a great deal of rebuilding was done, for the great majority of houses built before the First World War in Lincolnshire villages betray, by their building styles, that they were constructed in the eighteenth and nineteenth centuries. Moreover, in many villages a sizeable proportion of the smaller houses have been built in terraces of about four to ten dwellings. However, a study of village plans and of One-Inch Maps shows that the extent of the built-up areas of villages did not increase by more than modest amounts. This cartographical evidence does not, however, indicate which buildings were dwellings or how many separate dwellings there were in each building. It is impossible, therefore, to assess with any precision how much of the increase in population was absorbed by the old nucleated settlements and in what manner it was so absorbed. But the major argument stands that the increase in population was one factor promoting the dispersal of settlement.

Judged by their appearance today, and to a certain extent by their size, there are two characteristic types of grouped settlements: the estate village and the freeholders' village. Most of the houses in an estate village were built by the landed family who resided there; they are therefore frequently of similar design and appear to have been built on a pre-conceived plan. The squire's home, generally known as the Hall, lies a little way off, secluded in its park, surrounded by lawns and gardens and therefore safe from the public gaze. The village itself has been made more beautiful by the planting of trees, shrubs and hedges, many of them of evergreen habit. In short, the estate village was a nineteenth century rural version of the 'select quarter'.

Two examples will suffice to illustrate this type of village a little further, especially in regard to the large scale changes which were sometimes carried out by the gentlemen resident in the country. For instance, at Nocton, the church was rebuilt in 1775 because the old one 'stood in inconvenient proximity to the hall'.[11] Although the church remained untouched at Canwick, even more widespread changes were carried out by the Sibthorps (figure 2.2). This family had bought a 'capital mansion house' there in 1730[12] and in 1787 it was able to acquire a more compact block of land owing to the exchanges of plots and closes which took place at the time of the enclosure award. At a later date the Sibthorps bought most of the remaining old enclosures. In the last years of the eighteenth century a much larger mansion house was built and extensive grounds, a park and walled gardens were laid out. For this reason a public road from Heighington to Lincoln was diverted to the south and a row of cottages along this road was pulled down. Only in the 1950s has the road been re-opened to the public and detached villas built on the sites of former dwellings.

The second type of village, that belonging to a large number of small owners, was of a quite different character. It was generally much larger and the density of population in the township was much higher than the average for the district (for example, Metheringham and Mar-

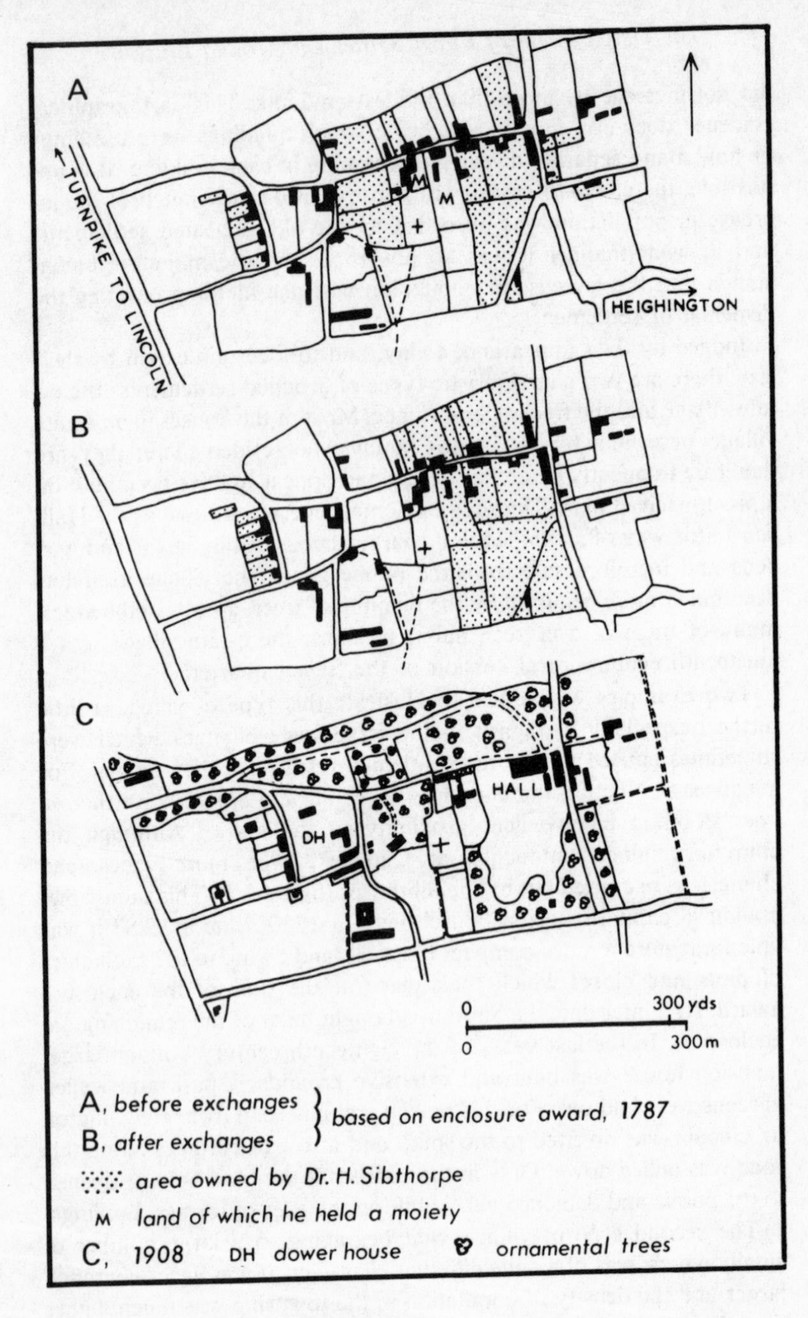

Fig. 2.2 Canwick – 1787 and 1908; changes due to Sibthorp influence

tin), whereas the population density was almost always well below average in a squire's township. This difference was largely due, not to variations in soil or husbandry, but mainly to the differential operation of the Poor Laws.[13] Up to about 1860 each parish or township had to maintain its own poor by means of a parish poor rate and it was therefore to the advantage of landowners and occupiers to restrict the working population and thereby reduce the numbers of potentially destitute persons. This restriction was most effective where a squire owned all or most of the land in a township and had control over the building of cottages. It was least effective where there was a large number of owners and occupiers, forming a large leaderless vestry which was unable or unwilling to discourage the building of cottages for 'poor' people.

Amongst the freeholders in such a township were many tradesmen, such as blacksmiths and saddlers, and shopkeepers such as grocers and beer retailers. Occupations of this kind were much less well represented in estate villages, partly because there was a smaller population and therefore less trade, but also, no doubt, because it was the policy of controlling landlords to limit the number of tenancies given to tradesmen who needed their own labourers and assistants, persons always potentially dependent on poor relief. Another important factor was that tradesmen and shopkeepers appear to have sprung in many cases from the ranks of the yeomen, or small landowning farmers. Thus, in many freeholders' villages the 1851 Census and nineteenth century directories reveal the presence of men who were, for example, 'publican, carrier and farmer of 30 acres' or 'tea dealer, agricultural merchant and farmer of 140 acres'. Such self-made men were noticeably absent from the estate villages where there was little opportunity to own small amounts of land, those precious assets of the small entrepreneurs.

The freeholders' village, therefore, was larger than the average, it contained many small workshops and business premises and owing to its piecemeal development its streets were full of houses built in a variety of styles (and sometimes of materials) and frequently arranged in the most haphazard manner. Here and there would be a rather larger house, but seldom the great house of a landed family; absent were the cypress trees and yew bushes and flowering shrubs, and the overall effect was that of the workaday world.

While at either extreme the estate village and freeholders' village stood in great contrast to each other, there were also many villages which represented a compromise between the two dominant elements of rural society. In some cases most of the land was owned by an absentee landlord, or a corporate body such as Christ's Hospital, London, who were lords of the manor at Skellingthorpe. Here the farm tenancies were generally very large ones, but the absence of a great house and family allowed the inhabitants much greater freedom in parochial affairs. In other cases the land was owned by a few substantial families who appear to have adopted a 'middle of the road' attitude to the question of poor relief. Today, as in the nineteenth century, one may therefore encounter a great variety in the outward appearances and in the social structures of villages in central Lincolnshire.

More recently, since the First World War, another element has entered rural society, that is, the overspill of urban population from Lincoln. Alongside the eighteenth and nineteenth century houses of redbrick or stone, there are many villas of the suburban type in those villages which are conveniently near the City, and two former villages, Boultham and Bracebridge, have been enclosed within the City boundary by the extensions of the early twentieth century. But despite the changes of the twentieth century, including the decay of the landowning class, it is still possible to distinguish in the field the mixture of settlement types which the changes of the eighteenth and nineteenth centuries brought about.

SOURCE: *East Midland Geographer*, no. 11, June 1959.

REFERENCES

1. This article is based largely on the writer's unpublished M.A. thesis, entitled *Population and Settlement in Kesteven, circa* 1775 – *circa* 1885, University of Nottingham, 1957 (1958). For an interpretation of township boundaries see D. R. Mills, 'Regions of Kesteven devised for the purposes of agricultural history' in *Reports and Papers of the Lincs. Architectural and Archeological Society*, 7 (1), 1957, pp. 60–82.
2. Monastic orders were often given grants of demesne land which could be enclosed without undue complications (see *Victoria County History, County of Lincoln*, II, pp. 202–4, 206, 211, 212–13 and 239). Sites of monastic houses on figure 2.1 are based on *Victoria County History, County of Lincoln*, II; Mrs F. L. Baker, *History of Riseholme* (1956) pp. 18–20 and C. W. Foster and T. Longley, *The Lincolnshire Domesday*, Lincoln Record Society, Vol. 19 (1924) pp. xlvii–lxxii.
3. Lincs. Archives Office: information for Odder from Hathey Account Book of Bishop's Possessions; for Branston Booths from inventory *circa* 1566.
4. Nos. 14–21 on figure 2.1 are depopulated settlements based on Foster and Longley, loc. cit., and M. Beresford, *The Lost Villages of England* (1954) pp. 361–4.

5. Information on Coates and other villages north of Lincoln from D. R. Mills, *Settlement Patterns and Population in the Till Basin,* unpublished B.A. dissertation, University of Nottingham, 1952; LAO, LD 71/4 and T. M. Blagg, *Somerton Castle,* paper read to the Thoroton Society of Notts., 20 May 1933, p. 1.
6. Based on A. Armstrong's One-Inch map of Lincs., 1776–8 and on many maps of individual townships.
7. Public Record Office, HO 107/2104–6. (See also below, chapter 10, for another example of the use of these records. Ed.)
8. Information for 1891 and 1901 from H. Green, *Lincolnshire Town and Village Life,* Lincoln Public Library (1901–4) p. 23.
9. A Demangeon, *Problèmes de Géographie Humaine* (Paris, 1952) pp. 199–200.
10. Major sources of information for this section are: Joan Thirsk, *English Peasant Farming, the agrarian history of Lincolnshire from Tudor to recent times* (1957); T. Stone, *General View of the Agriculture of Lincolnshire* (1794); D. R. Mills, 'Enclosure in Kesteven', *Agricultural History Review,* VII(1959) 82–97.
11. K. Norgate and M. H. Footman, 'Some notes for a history of Nocton', *Reports and Papers of the Associated Archeological Societies,* 24 (II), 1897–8, p. 368.
12. A. R. Maddison, *An Account of the Sibthorpe Family* (Lincoln, 1896), p. 27.
13. D. R. Mills, 'The poor laws and the distribution of population, *circa* 1600–1860, with special reference to Lincolnshire', *Trans. Inst. Brit. Geogrs.*, 26 (1959) 185–95. See also Chapter 8, below.

3 Dispersed and Nucleated Settlement in the Yorkshire Wolds, 1770–1850

M. B. GLEAVE

THE eight decades with which we are concerned in this paper witnessed remarkable changes in the agricultural system of the Yorkshire Wolds. In 1770 the major part of that area was still being worked by means of the open field system or some variation of it. Each township had its arable fields, worked in common, and its pasture which was frequently the highest area, most remote from the village nucleus. The homesteads and farmsteads were concentrated in villages and hamlets. Outlying farmsteads were the exception rather than the rule, and in each case were associated with partial pre-parliamentary enclosure in the townships concerned. By 1850 parliamentary enclosure had taken place, affecting over 70 per cent of the area. The expanses of open arable and pasture had been replaced by smaller hedged fields and the Norfolk four-course rotation had been introduced at the expense of the earlier methods of rotation. These innovations resulted in the decline of fallowing and in increased agricultural potential and returns. Furthermore, the compact holdings which replaced the scattered strips in the former open fields were often remote from the existing village centres. The geographical and economic centre of these holdings was no longer in the nucleus. A rash of new outlying farmsteads, which originated in the period 1770–1850, reflects this new state of affairs.

The study of post-enclosure dispersion, with which we are concerned here, has not been neglected by settlement geographers. H. Thorpe,[1] working in Denmark, reported it several years ago, whilst D. McCourt,[2] considering the breakdown of the run-rig system in parts of Donegal and County Londonderry, further corroborated the existence of this phenomenon. The result of Thorpe's work in Denmark shows that prior to enclosure all the lands of the township of Østerstillinge, in western Zealand, were worked from farmsteads in the nucleus and that there were no isolated settlements in the township. After enclosure the larger portion of the township lands, consisting of both large farms and smallholdings, was worked from dispersed

For references to this chapter, see p. 115.

farmsteads. A smaller portion, again consisting of large farms and smallholdings, was worked from farmsteads which remained in the nucleus and, in addition to these, a number of agricultural labourers' cottages remained in the nucleus. By 1893 two-thirds of the settlements were outside the village, whereas in 1769 all the houses were either grouped around the green or located on it. Similarly, McCourt, after investigating the breakdown of the run-rig system in parts of Donegal and County Londonderry, concluded that dispersion of settlement was almost complete after enclosure and that the hamlets associated with the run-rig system declined as the result of this dispersion. In the case of the Wolds, however, dispersion of some of the farmsteads rarely implied decline of the old village centre. Although post-enclosure dispersion was common in Denmark, Northern Ireland and the Yorkshire Wolds, one should stress that, in the Wolds, it was not accompanied by decay of the existing villages as a cursory glance at the Ordnance Survey Six-inch map will confirm. The aim of this study, then, is to investigate the new farmsteads which followed in the wake of parliamentary enclosure in the Yorkshire Wolds and to consider the village nuclei during the same period, bearing in mind the findings already published for other areas at a similar stage in their settlement history. To fulfil this aim I have chosen two examples typical of the general trend and have treated them in depth.

Middleton-on-the-Wolds, which lies on the dip-slope of the Wolds, is an elongated township, extending from 450 ft O.D. in the west to 67 ft O.D. in the east, having a mean length of five miles and a maximum width of one and a half miles (figure 3.1). The chalk surface is dissected by two dry valleys floored with chalky gravel and in the lower parts is covered by a thin layer of boulder clay. The village, clustered around the church and pond, is situated on a patch of glacial sand and gravel in the floor of a dry valley about 80 ft higher than, and a mile and a half distant from the nearest surface water (figure 3.2).[3] The pre-enclosure field system was remarkable for its adjustment to the surface configuration. About one-third of the township, lying farthest west and embracing an area where the soil was thinnest and the relief most extreme, was Wold. The remainder was laid out in six arable fields, three west of the village and three to the east. The village itself is sited where two small valleys meet and continue as a single one, with the result that the three western fields extended across the width of the township, their boundaries following the valley floors.

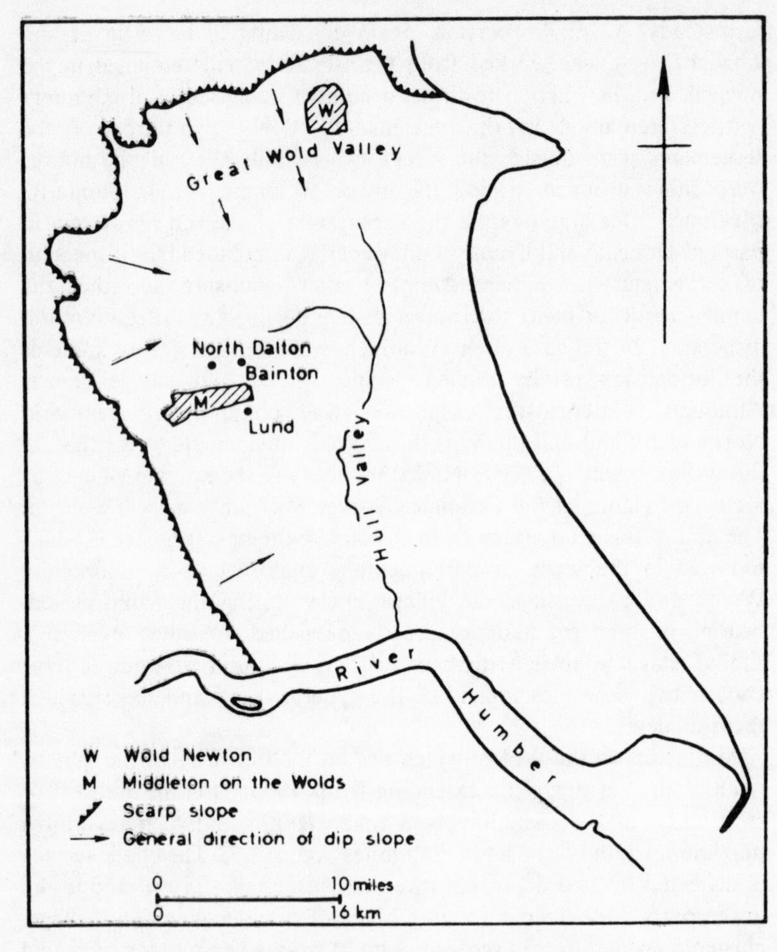

Fig. 3.1 The Yorkshire Wolds: key diagram

The boundary of two of the eastern fields also followed the valley floor, the third, Little East Field, being situated beyond Swan Close Field. Little is known about the method of working the fields, but from evidence in neighbouring townships it seems reasonable to assume that the individual holdings were distributed in small parcels of land throughout the fields. The tofts and crofts represented the only enclosed land in the township and all the farmsteads and cottages were clustered in the nucleus about the pond and church. There were no outlying farms in the township before parliamentary enclosure.

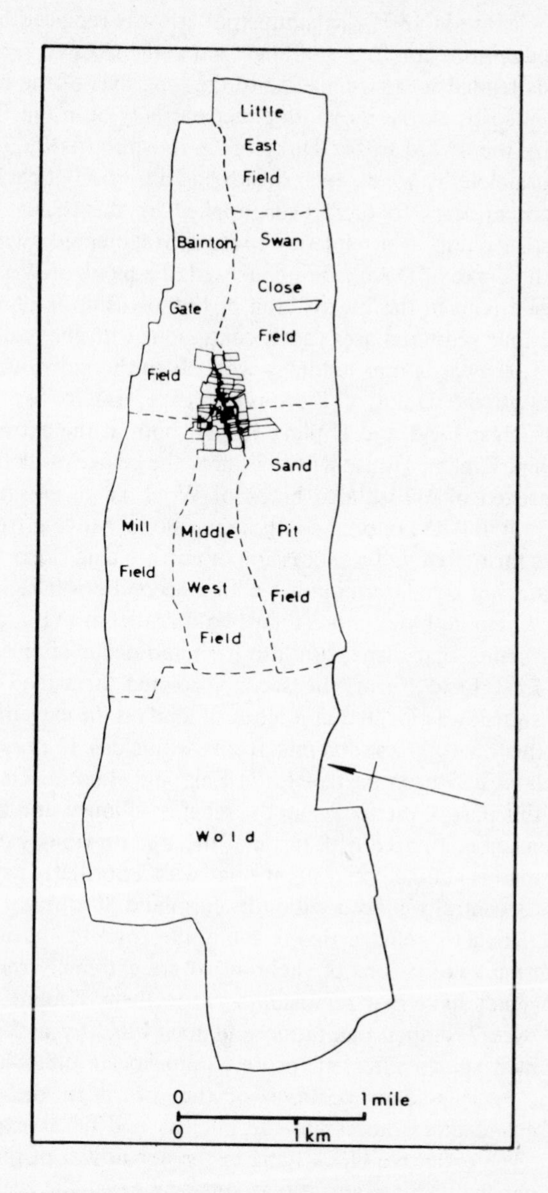

Fig. 3.2 The township of Middleton-on-the-Wolds before enclosure 1803

After enclosure in 1805 this simple pattern was replaced by one of hedged fields, more compact holdings and some isolated farmsteads. The awards tended to be transverse to the long axis of the township, occurring in strips across its width either partially or in full. This is illustrated by the award to the Duke of Devonshire (figure 3.3).[4] The medieval principle by which each owner had a portion of each type of land surface appears to have been applied by the Inclosure Commissioners, resulting in a tendency towards fragmented awards. The award to the Duke of Devonshire consisted of a block of Wold land, a block of field land in the lowest area of the township, a block in the centre and four scattered areas each contiguous with the nucleus. The subdivision of awards into holdings was left to the individual owner. The award to the Duke of Devonshire gave rise to two outlying farmsteads, East Field and Kipling House, both at the extremities of the township. Kipling House was built near the centre of its farmland, which consisted of the isolated block of Wold, at an altitude of approximately 430 ft O.D., on a south-facing slope. Moving from north to south its farm area had a succession of north-facing slope, ridge top and south-facing slope, terminating with a second north-facing slope. As it was a remote block more than two miles from the nucleus it is hardly surprising that dispersion into it should occur after enclosure. Similarly East Field Farm, the second isolated farmstead resulting from this award, was located in a block of land on the extreme eastern border of the township about a mile from the nucleus. In pre-enclosure days this land had been part of Little East and Bainton Gate arable Fields. In this part of the township the relief is subdued and the slopes are gentle when compared with those of the area previously described. The farmstead is situated on a slight ridge with a northerly aspect. It is more or less centrally placed within its farmland at a height of about 115 ft O.D. and to achieve this it shuns the road to the nucleus.

The internal subdivisions of each award are extremely regular and both farmsteads have dew ponds adjacent to them. Kipling House is protected by a T-shaped plantation and East Field by a shelter belt, both of which served after enclosure to ameliorate difficult climatic conditions. Four smaller portions of the award to the Duke of Devonshire had direct access to the nucleus and never experienced dispersion. The extensive block lying to the north-west of the nucleus and with reasonable access to it was similarly never the scene of dispersion although it had no direct access to the nucleus. The award to Sir Mark Sykes exhibits similar characteristics. Those close to, and

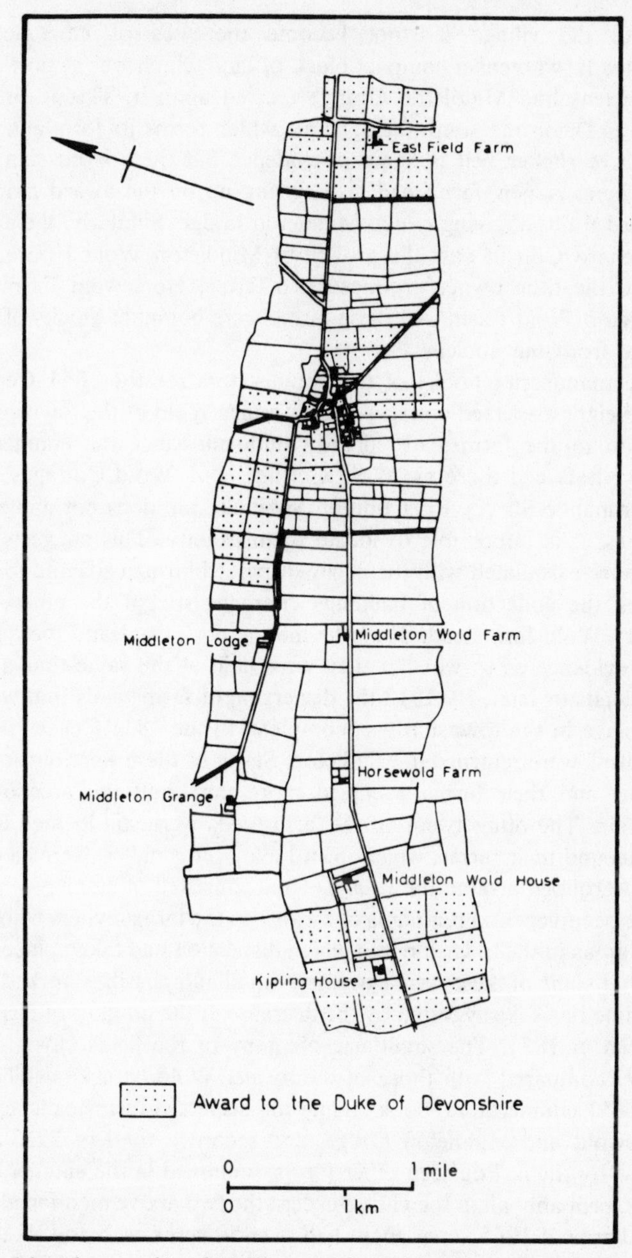

Fig. 3.3 The township of Middleton-on-the-Wolds after enclosure circa 1818

around, the village did not become the sites of new isolated farmsteads, whereas a compact block of land which was remote from the nucleus had Middleton Grange erected upon it. This is sited at 355 ft O.D. on the south-facing slope which forms its farmland. The protective shelter belt is again in evidence but there is no sign of a pond here. A new farmstead also sprang up on the award made to Richard Railton, giving rise to Middleton Lodge. Similarly, the award to Richard Consitt saw the growth of Middleton Wold House, and that to the tithe owner produced two farms, Horsewold Farm and Middleton Wold Farm. All these farms were compact blocks of land remote from the nucleus.

The manuscript books of the enumerators for the 1851 Census[5] record eight dispersed cottages in the former Wold of the township, in addition to the farmsteads already outlined. Since the enumerator merely described these as 'Wold Cottage' and 'Wold Cottages', and the Ordnance Survey First Edition Six-inch map does not name any cottages, it is impossible to locate them exactly. This suggests that they were associated with the newly dispersed farmsteads and formed part of the collection of buildings characteristic of the nineteenth-century Wold farmstead. The tithe map is not extant and there is no other evidence as to whether they were built at the same time as the farmsteads or later. By 1818 the dispersion of farmsteads that was to take place in the township was complete. In the 1831 Census thirty-one farms were returned in Middleton. Seven of these were outside the nucleus and their farms occupied more than half the area of the township. The other twenty-three farmsteads were still located in the nucleus and their farms, which must have been smaller, were all close to and grouped around the village. They consisted of small awards to owner occupiers and remnants of awards to the large owners who held other areas in the township into which dispersion had taken place. The fact that some of these were extremely small and possibly worked on a part-time basis is suggested by the decrease in the number of farms to nineteen in 1851. The small size of many of the fields close to the village, compared with those of the former Wold, is also significant. The 1851 enumerators' books name the dispersed farmsteads, except Horsewold and Middleton Lodge, and record a total of 2233 acres farmed by them. Fourteen other farms, unnamed in the enumerators' books, probably all in the village except the two above mentioned, had a total area of 1065 acres. Eight had over 50 acres each and six under 50 acres each, the largest being 200 acres and the smallest 20. From a

Land Tax Assessment of 1832[6] comes evidence that these smaller farms, with the farmstead remaining in the village, may have been fragmented. William Railton, who in 1851 farmed 35 acres, was owner and occupier of land assessed at six shillings and one penny in 1831 but also rented land assessed at five shillings from Richard Railton. Similarly, Thomas Dooks farmed 65 acres in 1851 and was owner and occupier of lands assessed at two shillings and sixpence and ninepence-halfpenny respectively in 1831. Four other examples can be cited for the earlier date, but by 1851 the farms concerned had changed tenant or owner so that their size is unknown. While these parcels of land may have been adjacent, they were not necessarily so, and this may, therefore, be evidence of fragmentation. If fragmentation did occur it would be a further incentive to continued location of the farmstead in the nucleus. (See Chapter 10, p. 220 for further E. Riding evidence on this point.)

Comparison of the Census Returns of 1801 and 1851 indicates that the nucleus underwent considerable growth during the period apart from the development of these new agricultural settlement units. In 1801 there were forty-six houses in the township, all in the nucleus. By 1851 the number had risen to one hundred and thirty-three. Taking into account the seven isolated farmsteads and the eight cottages associated with them, something in the order of seventy-one houses were, therefore, built in the nucleus during the period. Close study of the maps for 1803 and 1851 (figure 3.4)[7] indicates where the bulk of this new development took place. The open area around the green and mere was encroached upon and the central 'island' was further built up. Development occurred on both sides of Back Lane, in the old enclosures on Lund Road and on the northern edge of the peninsular-like extension at the end of which was the mere. At the eastern end of the village redevelopment took place in the old enclosures on both sides of the Bainton Road. In addition there was general development in depth. All the new buildings with the exception of North End Farm, a large farmstead on the road to North Dalton, were erected within the framework of the old enclosures.

Of the seventy-one houses built in the nucleus between 1801 and 1851 only one was a new farmstead. During the period seven farmsteads moved out of the village, their farms accounting for more than two-thirds of the farm acreage of the township, leaving fourteen smaller farms in the nucleus. The agricultural dominance of the nucleus had now passed to the isolated farmsteads. It is impossible to

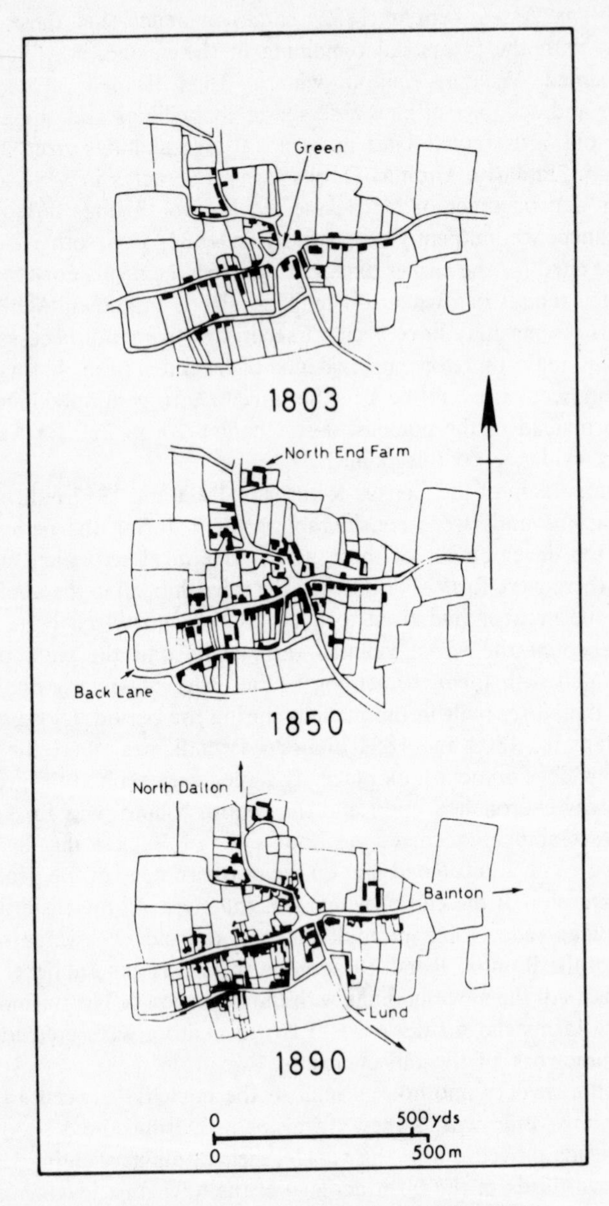

Fig. 3.4 The village of Middleton-on-the-Wolds

say whether the function of the nucleus changed in the period but it can be argued that it must have been modified. Certainly by 1851 forty-eight agricultural labourers were still living in the village in cottages with their families whilst only fifteen lived in dispersed cottages.[8] The unmarried agricultural labourer force lived in the farmhouse. Thirty-six lived on dispersed farms and seven on farms in the village, which reflects the contrast in size and remoteness of the dispersed farms and those in the nucleus. The largest part of the agricultural labourer force, however, continued to live in the village after the dispersion of the farmsteads.

In addition to the labourers' cottages and the remaining farmsteads, the village housed people following a variety of occupations. Some were concerned with the material needs of the community, some provided skill to enable increasing agricultural efficiency, others attended to the physical and spiritual welfare of the community whilst others, ranging from 'a late scavenger' to a Chelsea pensioner, had retired. The figures for non-agriculturally employed persons can be broken down, on the basis of their occupation, into seventeen craftsmen, seventeen tradesmen, five professional people and eleven retired. Between them the craftsmen could provide for most of the agriculturalists' needs for buildings and machinery, whilst the requirements of food, drink, footwear and clothing could doubtless be met by the village tradesmen.[9] Not included in these figures are the unmarried daughters and wives entered in the enumerator's book as 'dressmaker', or the daughter of Henry Bowser, the tailor, draper and grocer, whose occupation is recorded as 'straw bonnet maker'. The rector, doctor and three teachers comprised the five professional people living in the village.

It is difficult to judge for which class of the community the large increase in the number of houses in Middleton between 1801 and 1851 was intended. As there was a nominal decrease in the number of farmers between 1831 and 1851 it must have been due either to an increase in the number of agricultural labourers or of the non-agriculturally employed or, alternatively, to an increase in the number of both. The latter seems most likely. It is impossible to assess the proportion of the increase for which each of these classes was responsible. That it was due to movement into the village, not only from neighbouring townships but also from farther afield, by these two classes can be confirmed by evidence from the enumerators' books.

The master bricklayer, his wife and two children were natives of

Leconfield, a village on the fringe of the Wolds, south of Middleton. His third child, eight years of age, was born in the neighbouring village of Lund, whilst the fourth, five years old in 1851, and the fifth were born in Middleton. The family must have moved from Lund to Middleton more than five years but less than eight years prior to 1851. It seems likely that his brother and another employee who lived with the family came at the same time. Of the heads of households, an equal number originated in Middleton and other Wold townships, two from other East Riding townships and thirteen from elsewhere. Of these five came from other parts of Yorkshire, three from Lincolnshire whilst a master shoemaker was born on board ship in the Mediterranean! All classes appear to have been equally mobile except for farmers, most of whom were born in Middleton and only two of whom originated outside the Wolds.

The farm servants, unmarried men who lived in the farmhouse, are not considered in these figures but show a similar pattern of origins. Thus Nathaniel Shaw Brough, who farmed East Field in 1851, was born in Elloughton, a village at the southern edge of the Wolds, but of his nine farm workers three were born in Middleton, three in other Wold villages, two in towns on the margins of the Wolds and one at Welwick in the south-east corner of the county. Similarly, John Garret, farming Kiplingcote House, employed house servants born in Barmby, Lincolnshire, and Thornton, Yorkshire. Five of his labourers were born in Wold townships, four in towns on the Wold margins and one came from Ireland. (As the name Barmby does not occur in Lincolnshire gazetteers of the time, we must conclude that the census enumerator misspelt one of several similar place-names, a not uncommon problem in this kind of document.)

The township of Wold Newton, the second example, was enclosed in 1772. The bulk of its surface consists of the floor and south-facing slope of the Great Wold Valley whilst a smaller section in the north forms the north-facing slope of a dry valley (figure 3.1). The surface is of chalk, except where this is overlain by gravels in the valley floor. The variety of land types results in this case from slope and aspect rather than from differing geological outcrop. This difference is reinforced by the probable agricultural history of the two parts of the township. The south-facing slopes nearest the village are likely to have formed the infield before enclosure whilst the steeper north-facing slopes remote from the nucleus probably formed the outfield. The pre-enclosure pattern was fairly simple, two fields with all the houses clustered in the nucleus (figure 3.5).[10] The pasture was apparently in the flatts in the fields, but none is recorded. Each award in the township had a share of both north-facing and south-facing slopes and by 1818 dispersal had occurred into those awards not making contact with the nucleus. The two awards to Hutchinson (senior) both made

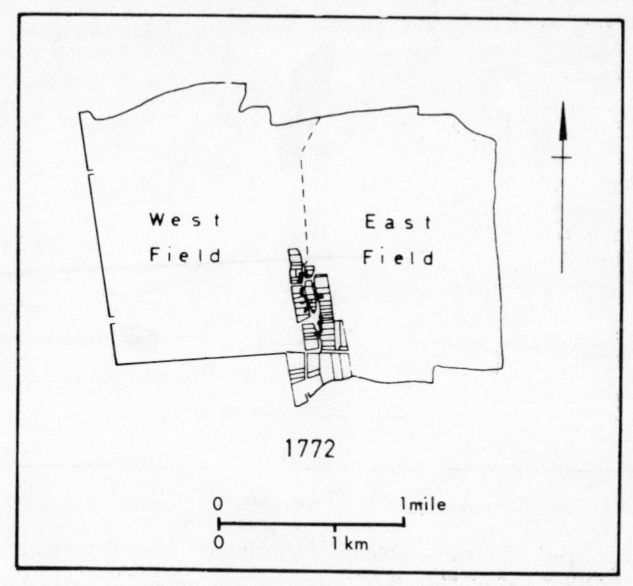

Fig. 3.5 The township of Wold Newton before enclosure 1772

contact with the nucleus by means of acute-angled turns, and early dispersion did not take place into them. By 1850 two further isolated farmsteads had been established, one in the award to Brown in which Mill Farm had earlier been established; the other into the award to Coulson which also had no contact with the nucleus (figure 3.6).[11]

After 1850 no further dispersion took place; those awards making contact with the nucleus continued to be farmed from the village and Wold Newton was similar in this respect to Middleton. The newly built farmsteads also exhibit similar features to those in Middleton. Each was sited on a south-facing slope and the shelter belt and pond were common. The internal subdivisions were, once again, regular. The evidence for this township poses problems of interpretation which makes it difficult to assess with certainty the area of the township

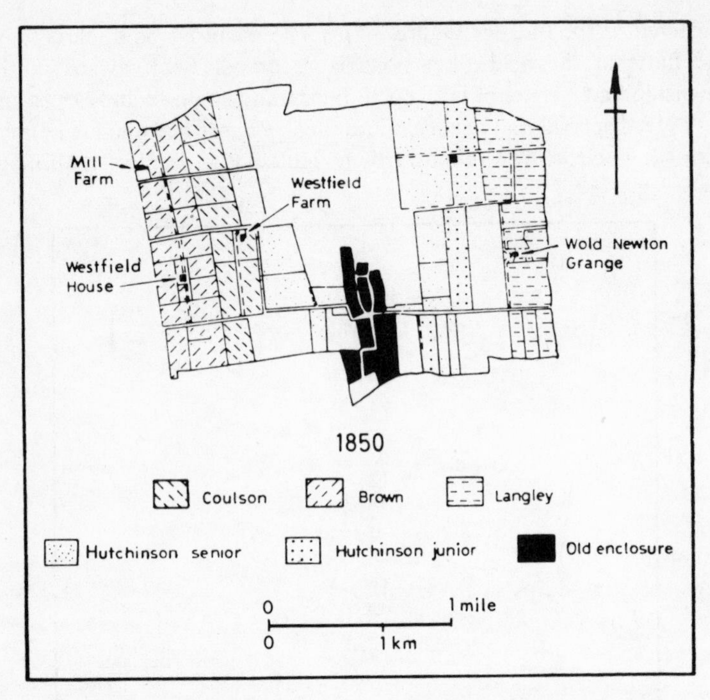

Fig. 3.6 The township of Wold Newton after enclosure circa 1850

worked from the new isolated farmsteads compared with those remaining in the nucleus. The enumerator's book[12] names Westfield Farm, and Westfield House, both dispersed farmsteads, having farmland totalling 555 acres. Judging from its position in the record, coupled with evidence from the first edition of the Ordnance Survey Six-inch map, there was also an unnamed farm of 100 acres with a dispersed farmstead. The total area worked from the new farmsteads was thus 655 acres. There was one other dispersed farmstead, identified as Wold Newton Grange, but the acreage of its farm cannot be determined. Five other unnamed farmsteads, all in the village, worked a total area of 995 acres. The proportion of land still worked from the nucleus in Wold Newton after enclosure was thus considerably larger than in Middleton. Of the farmsteads remaining in the nucleus the largest had 500 acres of land, the smallest 80 acres, considerably larger than in Middleton. Nevertheless there is still evidence of fragmentation of some of these holdings. Thomas Gibson was the occupier of land totalling 500 acres in 1831, owned by Thomas Hagyard assessed at two pounds eight shillings and threepence and by John Thorpe assessed at seventeen shillings and sixpence. Similarly George Knaggs occupied land owned by Francis Dowslin and John Thorpe assessed at one shilling and eight pence and one shilling and four pence respectively.[13]

Like Middleton-on-the-Wolds, Wold Newton also grew rapidly in the period, the number of houses recorded having increased from seventeen in 1801 to fifty-four in 1851, of which only five were outside the old enclosures. Six new farmsteads and cottages were built in the central 'island' (figure 3.7).[14] On the main street there was considerable building in the centre and development in depth with two additions in the old enclosure at the northern end of the village. Almost all the development along the Back Lane took place in the period and there was one new farmstead at the southern end of the village by 1850. Since 1850 the pattern has remained remarkably stable. As in Middleton, the majority of the agricultural labourers living in Wold Newton occupied cottages in the village. There were no cottages on the dispersed farmsteads, which probably reflects the shorter distances between the nucleus and the farthest margins in this township. Ten agricultural workers lived in the farmhouses of the dispersed farms and sixteen lived in the village farmhouses. The latter number may need reducing in view of the lack of certainty of interpretation already indicated. Most of the houses in the village were occupied by agricultural labourers and a few by young married women with children, probably the wives of agricultural labourers working away on remote farmsteads in the Wolds. There were seven craftsmen, including an agricultural implement maker, blacksmith, two wheelwrights, a carpenter and a miller. There were also six tradesmen, a shopkeeper, a tailor and sub-postmaster, a master tailor, cordwainer and two carriers. Journeymen and apprentices appear to have lived with their master in the same way as unmarried farmworkers. There were also a schoolmaster, the vicar and retired people living in the village.[15] The origin of the inhabitants of Wold Newton was, as in Middleton, largely local, the village itself and the Wolds providing the vast majority. The social classes also exhibit similar origins, the farmers being local whilst the craftsmen and tradesmen tended to come from farther afield.

The events taking place in the two townships chosen were characteristic of all townships in the area in which parliamentary enclosure took place. For example, the twenty-four houses recorded in

1801 for East Heslerton, all of which were in the nucleus, had increased by 1851 to forty-two of which only three were dispersed farmsteads. Weaverthorpe had thirty-one houses in 1801, all in the nucleus, but by 1851 the number had increased to one hundred and twenty-five, of which seven were dispersed farmsteads. Thwing in

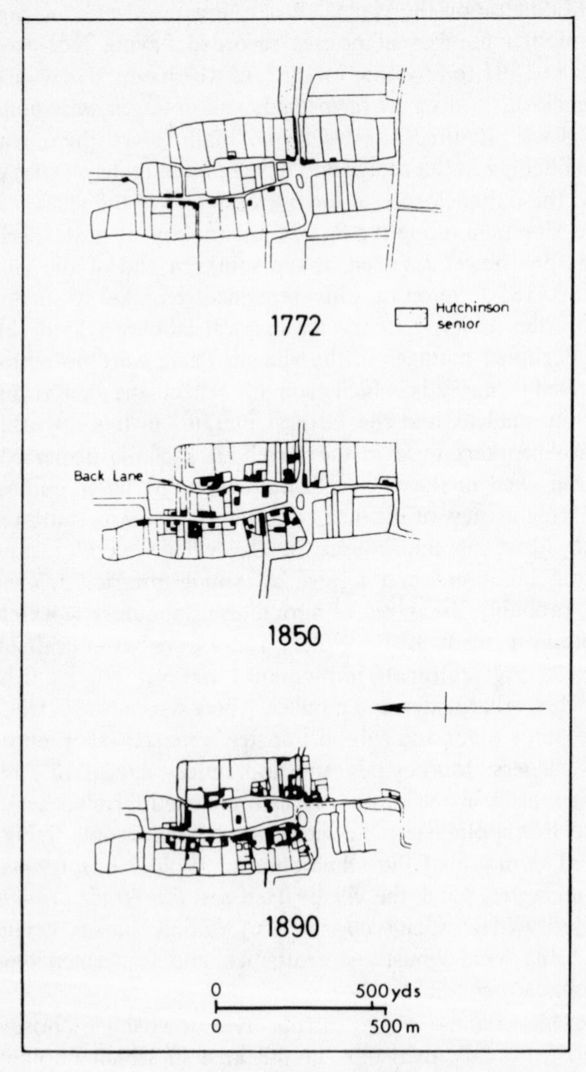

Fig. 3.7 The village of Wold Newton

1801 had forty houses in the nucleus and one early dispersed farmstead; by 1851 the number had increased to sixty-nine and five respectively. In each case the growth of the nucleus took place within the confines of the old enclosures.

The Census Reports record one hundred and forty-four townships and coupled-townships for the Wolds as a whole. In 1772 there were approximately one hundred and ninety-five isolated farmsteads. Some had resulted from shrinkage of village and hamlet; others from monastic granges which continued to function as farms after the Dissolution; and others were the result of dispersion into areas enclosed by agreement before parliamentary enclosure became the normal procedure. By 1843 the number had risen to approximately eight hundred and thirty-five. Meanwhile only five out of the one hundred and forty-four townships registered a decrease in the number of houses between 1801 and 1851 and in none of these was the decrease more than three. Eight townships showed neither increase nor decrease and the remaining one hundred and thirty-three showed increases, including ten which had more than three times as many houses in 1851 as at the earlier date. It seems clear that the effects of dispersion and of parliamentary enclosure with the changes which they made possible had no untoward effects on the nuclei as was the case in certain other areas. The nuclei experienced a period of consolidation marked by extension of the built-up area and replacement of existing buildings. Architecturally the face of many Wold villages appears to be entirely of early and mid-nineteenth century date, which agrees with the documentary evidence.

Whilst most of the occupants of the increased number of houses were of local origin, that is either from the township in which they lived or from other townships within the Wolds, there was appreciable movement into the area from the market towns on the fringes and to a lesser extent from other parts of the country. That the bulk of this influx was in the labouring class and in the trade and craftsman class rather than among the agricultural tenant may reflect the difficulty of working the thin, stony soils of the Wolds successfully or of conservatism on the part of the landlords in preferring local men. The period following enclosure does not appear to have resulted in the buying up and working of farms by people from outside the Wolds. It seems reasonable to suggest two groups of factors responsible for the changes which the settlement pattern underwent after enclosure, the first social, the second economic.

First, rural society in the Wolds was as widely stratified as at any time before or since. In award after award large portions of the township were allotted to a handful of large landowners and smaller lots to a few more. The agricultural labourer and the cottager were general in the Wolds before parliamentary enclosure and the yeoman class was of tenant farmers rather than owner occupiers. The Inclosure Commissioners, where awards were sufficiently large, tried to give a share of each type of land surface to the owners. This resulted in fragmented awards, the subdivision of which was left to the owner, whereas the awards to smaller owners were usually block awards, close to the nucleus. In this way it was ensured that the majority of farmsteads would still be in the nucleus after enclosure even if they did work a smaller portion of the township area relative to that worked from the dispersed farms.

Secondly, the ploughing up of large tracts of sheep walk, so bemoaned by Arthur Young, coupled with the introduction of clover and root crops with the Norfolk four-course system and the decline of fallow acreage, must have necessitated an increased labour force. With the beginning of mechanisation in the earlier part of the century and its subsequent increase in importance, there developed a new range of occupations serving the agriculturalist and these would place a location in the nucleus at a premium. The importance of these non-agricultural occupations varies from township to township, but seems to have a loose correspondence with size of population. In the smaller villages 100 per cent of the males over nineteen years of age were employed in agriculture. In Kirk Ella it was lowest, only 24 per cent, although the majority of townships fall within the 65 to 85 per cent range. Considered in this light it is hardly surprising that in this area the expansion of the nucleus was in most cases more strongly marked than movement away from it. But one should stress that this paper is concerned only with the settlement pattern in an extremely restricted area and further work in many other areas will be necessary before one can say that the conclusions reached have a general application within the English lowland zone. The really distinctive feature of the Wolds was the combination of large farms, few owners and rapid expansion of population. Few other areas have the same combination of factors and therefore few other areas can be expected to have the same post-enclosure development of the settlement pattern.

SOURCE: *Transactions of the Institute of British Geographers*, No. 30, 1962.

REFERENCES

1. H. Thorpe, 'The influence of inclosure on the form and pattern of rural settlement in Denmark', *Transactions and Papers,* 1951, Institute of British Geographers, 17 (1951), 113–29.
2. See D. McCourt, 'Surviving open field in County Londonderry', *Ulster Folk Life,* 4 (1958), 19–28; 'Traditions of rundale in and around Sperrins', *Ulster Journal of Archaeology,* 16 (1953), 69–84; 'Infield and outfield in Ireland', *Economic History Review,* Second Series, 7 (1955), 369–76.
3. Based on the *Enclosure Award Plan, Middleton* (1805), Registry of Deeds, Beverley.
4. Based on the *Enclosure Award Plan, Middleton* (1805), and on *Ordnance Survey Six-inch Map,* Sheet 177 (1851).
5. Public Record Office No. HO 107/523/3.
6. East Riding Record Office, Beverley.
7. Based on the *Enclosure Award Plan, Middleton* (1805), *Ordnance Survey Six-inch Map,* Sheet 177 (1851), *Ordnance Survey Twenty-five-inch Map,* Sheet 177/13 and 177/16 (1890).
8. Enumerators' Books for the 1851 Census, Public Record Office No. HO 107/523/3.
9. The complete list of craftsmen and tradesmen in Middleton, 1851, is: two master blacksmiths and four journeymen, three millers, one master bricklayer and two journeymen, one saddler, one rope-maker, one carpenter and two joiners. Two carriers, five tailors, five shoemakers, two grocers, two publicans, one cattle dealer, one tinner, plumber and glazier and one tailor, grocer and draper.
10. Based on the *Enclosure Award Plan, Wold Newton* (1772), East Riding Record Office, Beverley.
11. Based on the *Enclosure Award Plan, Wold Newton* (1772), and *Ordnance Survey Six-inch Map,* Sheets 126 and 127 (1851).
12. Public Record Office No. HO 107/524/3.
13. *Land Tax Assessment* (1831), East Riding Record Office, Beverley.
14. Based on the *Enclosure Award Plan, Wold Newton* (1772), *Ordnance Survey Six-inch Map,* Sheet 127 (1851), and *Ordnance Survey Twenty-five-inch Map,* Sheets 127/1 and 127/5 (1890).
15. Public Record Office No. HO 107/524/3.

4 The Social Study of Family Farming

W. M. WILLIAMS

IN general the objective study of English country life has been much neglected and our view of it is obscured by a sentimental or romantic outlook which is a peculiar characteristic of the English. It is true that certain aspects of country life have been carefully investigated for many years. Agriculture, the basic industry of the countryside, has been given a great deal of attention and much is known about farming techniques and economic structure. The rural landscape has been studied by geographers who have, for example, analysed its evolution or shown how patterns of settlement and land use can be related to such factors as relief, soil, climate or other aspects of the physical environment. Thus we know in some detail about the geographical background to East Anglian cereal growing or to sheep farming on the Lakeland fells as well as the most efficient methods to use in these areas, the effects of using new fertilizers or modern machinery and the economics of livestock husbandry or wheat production. Unfortunately, these studies have become more and more specialised and their relevance to each other has become increasingly difficult to discern. Even more serious, the *social* study of farming has been almost completely ignored, and very little indeed is known about the social organisation and structure of the farming community or, for that matter, of country folk as a whole.

The present situation is, therefore, that we have a reasonable amount of information about farming and the rural landscape, but that we know very little about farmers. This state of affairs can only be described as deplorable, since it is the farmer, in the course of generations of occupying and cultivating the land, who has created both the present pattern of English agriculture and much of the rural landscape. Clearly there is need for sociological study and also for investigations which take as their starting point the relationship between farmers, as a social and economic group on the one hand and the land they occupy on the other. It is the study of this relationship – between society and the land – which is the particular field of the social

For references to this chapter, see p. 133.

geographer, and it is here, in the context of English country life, that he has the opportunity of linking together the specialised studies which have already been made. There are, of course, many aspects of the society – land relationship to be studied and many ways of studying them. Indeed, the first problem is to choose an appropriate topic for investigation in such a little known field. Family farming has been chosen because it is a relatively simple manifestation of the society–land relationship (compared, for example, with a large city, where social and economic life is extremely complex) and therefore one which can be studied with modest resources of information and technique.

FAMILY FARMING IN ENGLAND AND WALES

In the strict sense a family farm is a holding of land, together with a farmhouse and outbuildings, which is occupied by a farmer and his family and which is maintained as an economic unit without the use of hired labour. For the purposes of this study, however, the definition is extended to include those holdings on which hired workers may be employed at certain periods (for example when a farmer's children are still young) to supplement the labour of the farm family. Family farms are relatively uncommon in England, common in Wales and predominant in continental Europe. In France, for example, over two-thirds of all agricultural holdings are family farms. It is by no means easy to discover how many family farms there are in England and Wales or how they are distributed; this information is not given in the 1951 Census nor in the statistics published annually by the Ministry of Agriculture. It is, however, possible to gain an estimate of total numbers and distribution from the Census. In 1951 there were 246,532 male farmers in England and Wales, and 411,305 male agricultural workers. The Occupation Tables of the Census give the numbers of farmers and farm workers by administrative counties which can be mapped in a form showing farmers as a percentage of the total agricultural labour force. It seems reasonable to assume that where the proportion of farmers is high, as in Wales, the West Country and north-west England, there are relatively large numbers of family farms; similarly, where the proportion of farmers is low, as in East Anglia and the Home Counties, there are relatively few family farms. The incidence of family farms increases steadily westwards and northwards. No simple correlations can be made between family farming and size of holdings, type of farming, land classification, etc. For example, small farms tend to be concentrated in Devon and Cornwall, Wales, the Pennines, Cheshire, the Isle of Ely and the Weald.

This method of approach can be pursued further, by taking such units as Rural Districts and examining variations within counties. In this way it is possible to show, for example, that in the Rural Districts of south-west Lancashire, where cash crop farming is dominant, the proportion of farmers falls to between 35 and 45 per cent, which is well below the figure for the county as a whole but still above the proportions in Rural Districts of the Holland Division of Lincolnshire, where, in another area of cash crop farming, the figures range between 31 and 35 per cent.

Studies on this scale are valuable in so far as they provide information which may serve as a useful background to more detailed investigations. However, given our present lack of knowledge they necessarily involve a considerable degree of approximation and speculation. They raise a large number of questions which can only be answered by detailed studies of small sample areas, using quite different techniques. The remainder of this study is devoted to an analysis of such an area and an indication of the methods used in its study.

'ASHWORTHY': THE GEOGRAPHICAL BACKGROUND

The area chosen is a large parish in North Devon, a county where family farming is well-developed. In the Rural Districts of North Devon farmers and their families make up between 55 and 60 per cent of the agricultural labour force. The parish is a particularly good example of family farming, since 70 of its 75 farms are of this type and farmers with their families account for 85 per cent of all farm labour.

Nature has not been particularly generous to the farmers of Ashworthy. The land surface is composed of irregular ridges and steep-sided valleys; the soils, derived from the slaty shales of the Culm Measures, are heavy, deficient in lime and phosphates, and poorly drained. In many parts there is a thick clay sub-soil lying only a few inches below the surface; here the land may be waterlogged for weeks or even months on end. The climate is equally unfavourable. The annual rainfall exceeds 40 in. a year and, since summer and early autumn are wet, hay making and corn harvesting are often difficult and prolonged. Strong and persistent winds are common just before and during the harvest, while the combination of a moderately high rainfall and cold, ill-drained soils makes for a relatively short growing season.

These natural conditions are closely reflected in the landscape and in the type of farming. The broken land surface, with its sharp changes of slope, gives rise to small fields; the substantial banks and hedges which surround them are an essential part of the drainage system, since they often separate wet and dry land. They also provide shelter for stock against driving rain. The poverty of the soils, and their sharp variation in quality over short distances, militates against large farms, while the steep slopes and irregular relief make certain kinds of farm machinery unsuitable or difficult to use. The wet climate encourages livestock husbandry and the absence of a hot, dry summer makes arable farming unprofitable and very uncertain. Most of the farm land is under grass; cattle, for beef or milk, are the mainstay of the economy.

There is, therefore, a general relationship between the natural environment, the landscape and the economy, which provides, as it were, a set of broad limiting conditions to human activity. Within this broad framework the people of Ashworthy have farmed for centuries and, in order to do this, they have developed ways of occupying the land and of ensuring continuity from one generation to the next; these ways reveal certain regularities which enable one to speak of a *system* of land holding.

THE LAND HOLDING SYSTEM

An examination of land holding is a particularly useful point of departure for studying the relationship between society (i.e. the farm families) and the land, simply because it is a formal, institutionalised expression of this relationship. Any system of land holding is made up of three main elements: the field pattern, the occupation of land and the ownership of land.

(1) *The field pattern*

The pattern is the way the land is divided into territorial units of different size and shape. In Ashworthy there are two kinds of pattern, products of different agricultural traditions. The first, which covers most of the parish, is composed of small irregular fields clustered around isolated farmsteads; it is characteristic of many areas of early enclosure in western Britain (figure 4.2). The second, which is only found around the hamlets, consists of a distinct grouping of long, narrow fields, in turn surrounded by small regular fields (figure 4.3). This is almost certainly a survival of a former 'infield-outfield' system,

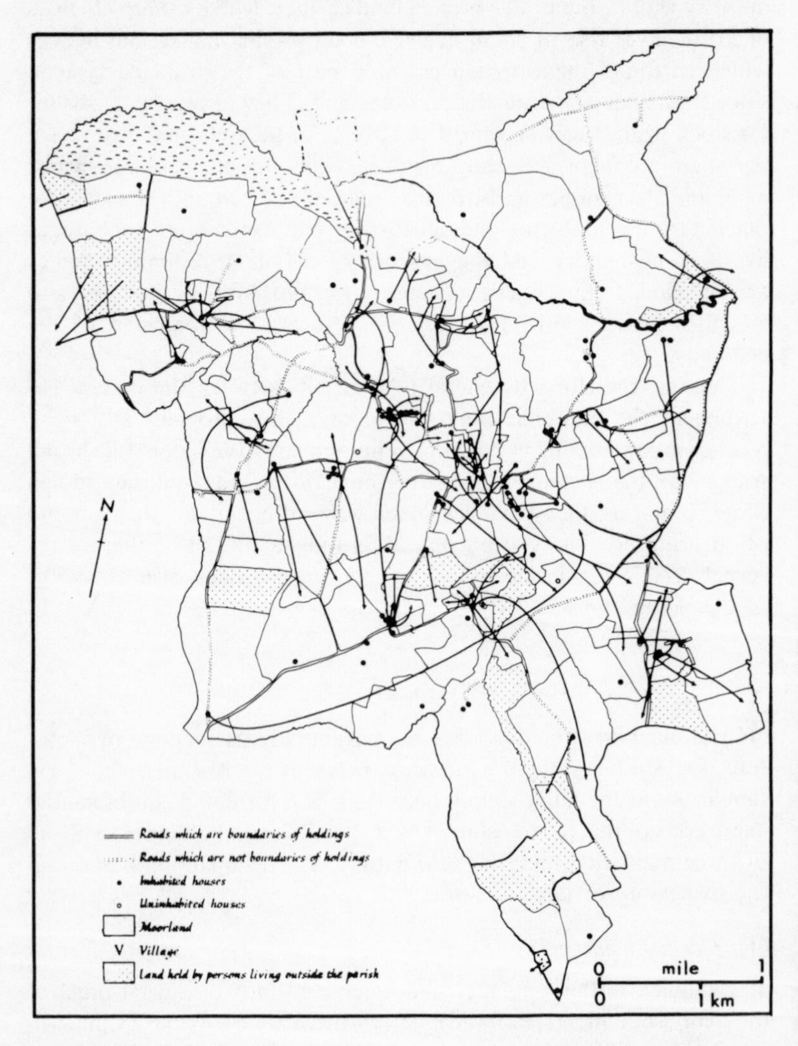

Fig. 4.1 Ashworthy: landholding 1959

Fig. 4.2 Aerial photograph of small, irregular fields associated with early enclosure in Western Britain
(Royal Air Force. Crown Copyright Reserved)

Fig. 4.3 Aerial photograph of long, narrow fields, probable survivals of a former infield-outfield system
(Royal Air Force. Crown Copyright Reserved)

in which the long fields were in open strips of arable land, cultivated continuously, around which the enclosed small fields were periodically in arable strips or in pasture.

The field pattern is, therefore, long established and has changed little. It owes its stability partly to its close relationship to the natural environment – which, of course, changes only slowly itself – and partly to the physical difficulty of altering the field boundaries.

(2) *The occupation of the land*

The individual fields are grouped into holdings or farms occupied by one or more individuals or families. In Ashworthy (see figure 4.1) the farms may be composed of adjoining fields to make a compact holding or may be divided into fragmented blocks of one or more fields some distance apart from each other. Thirdly, there is the common land where occupation is not defined territorially, but according to a system of rights attached to particular farmsteads. The total geographical pattern of occupation is extremely complex and has been characterised by a remarkable number of changes during the last hundred years or so. Fields have been added to some farms at the cost of others; amalgamation has brought about the disappearance of some farms, while new holdings have been created by improving parts of the common land or by subdividing existing farms. In many parts of the parish fragmentation has appeared, disappeared or reappeared at irregular intervals. These changes have been far too numerous and too detailed to be described here; there were, for example, seven major changes in 1959 alone.

(3) *The ownership of land*

The pattern of ownership has changed in detail almost as much as the pattern of occupation. Farms, parts of farms and even single fields have been bought and sold so frequently that no two consecutive years in this century show exactly the same picture. In general, however, there have been two distinctive phases in the history of land ownership. In 1841, the year of the Tithe Survey (figure 4.4), Ashworthy was divided into a few owner-occupier farms, five estates ranging in size from 300 acres to over 1000 acres, a small number of tenant farms not in estates and 2700 acres of common land. During the last half of the nineteenth century one of the estates, owned by the Bishop family, was steadily enlarged, mainly at the expense of the smaller estates. In the same period well over half the common land was enclosed. By 1918 (figure 4.5) the smaller estates had disappeared, leaving the Bishop family as the only large landowner in the parish. Many of the farms of the smaller estates became the property of owner-occupiers, a change which foreshadowed the second phase. The Bishop estate was sold in two parts, in 1920 and 1932; the owner-

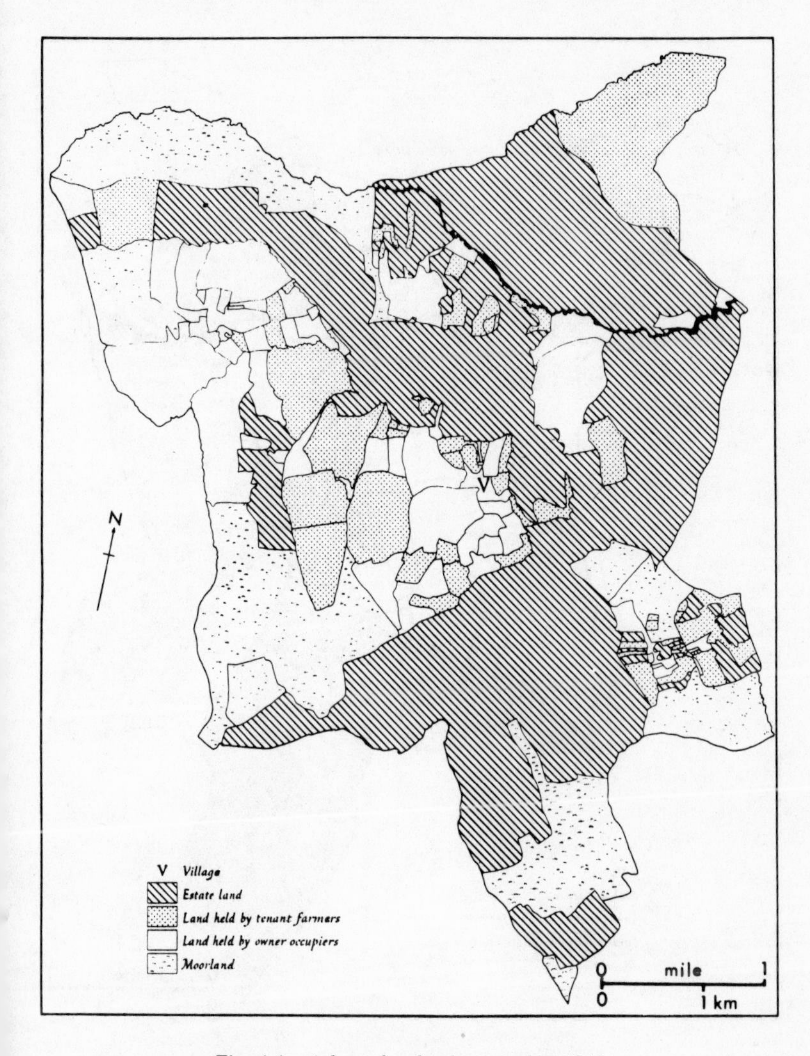

Fig. 4.4 Ashworthy: land ownership 1841

occupier farm became dominant (figure 4.6). This general change is, of course, typical of many parts of the country.

Taken as a whole, therefore, the most striking characteristic of the land-holding system is the way in which it has been subject to piecemeal, irregular changes over a long period. The field pattern and

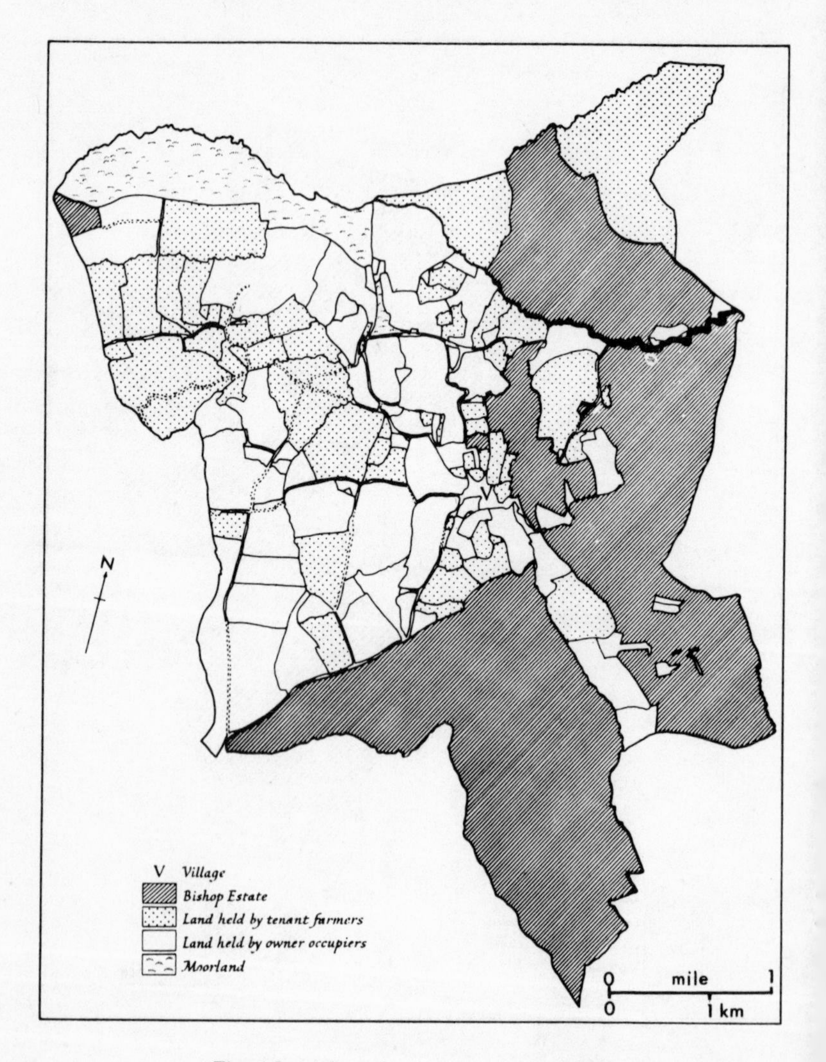

Fig. 4.5 Ashworthy: land ownership 1918

therefore the landscape, has not changed radically but otherwise land holding is 'unstable'. Only a small proportion of the parish has been occupied and cultivated by the same families for more than one generation; there are hardly any farms which have the same layout today as they had at the beginning of the century and many have been changed several times.

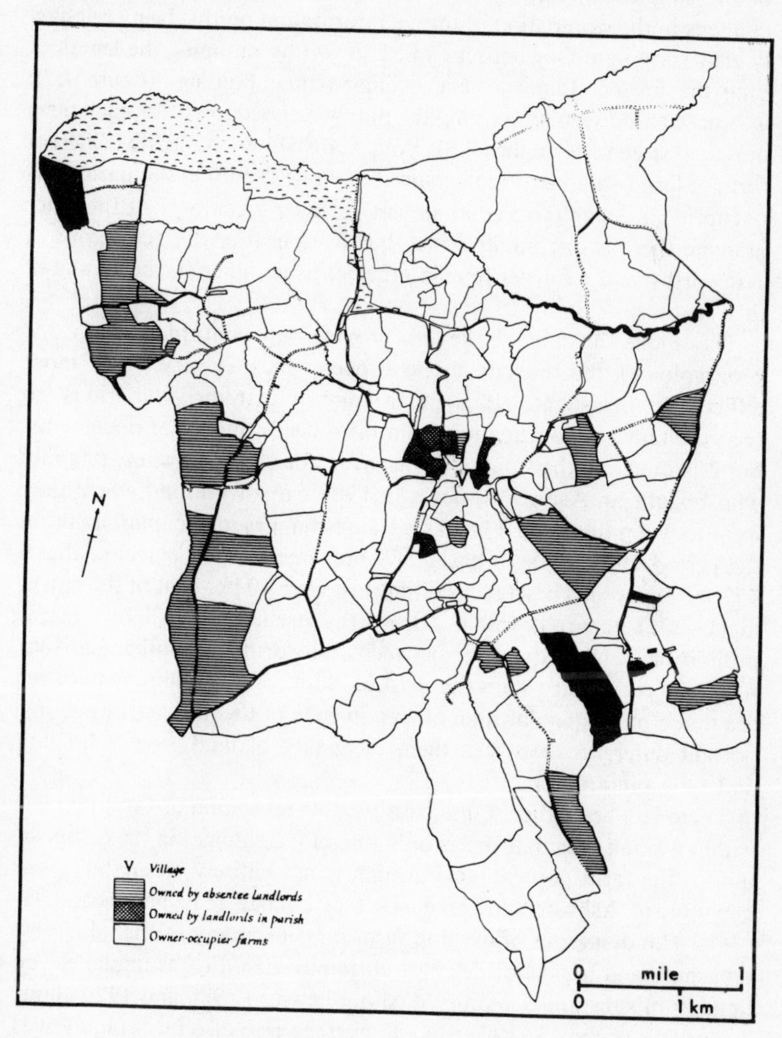

Fig. 4.6 Ashworthy: land ownership 1959

CHANGES IN FARM FAMILIES

Parallel changes have taken place in the farm population, but these are much more difficult to measure. The most striking change in Ashworthy is the movement of farm families from one holding to another, both within the parish and between it and other parishes. One of the simplest methods of illustrating this movement is to examine changes in the occupation of farms, information on this being relatively easy to obtain. One aspect can be shown by mapping the length of time the present families have occupied their holdings (figure 4.7); another can be seen by plotting the number of occupiers for each farm during this century (figure 4.8). Both maps show, in slightly different form, a large volume of movement. Only one family in the parish has occupied the same farm continuously for over a century. At the other extreme there is one family which has lived in four different farms in Ashworthy and a further four in other parishes since the beginning of this century.

The maps do not, however, provide any information on the geography of the movement, an aspect which is very much more difficult to investigate. It is fairly easy, if extremely laborious, to record changes in occupation from farm deeds and other documents, but it is quite another matter to discover, for example, where a family who bought an Ashworthy farm in 1909 came from and where they went to when they sold it in 1913. Using changes in occupation during the period 1900–59 as a basis, 589 movements took place: of these, 477 were traced. They revealed that just over 40 per cent of the movement (205) occurred within Ashworthy itself, and a slightly larger proportion (218) took place between Ashworthy and other parishes within an eight mile radius (figure 4.9). Some of the adjoining parishes are much more popular than others, in spite of the absence of any important differences between them in quality of land, size of holding and type of farming.

There has been, then, quite considerable migration of farm families within a small area, but this is only one of the changes in the composition of the farm population. Farming is not entirely a hereditary occupation in Ashworthy. Three kinds of change may be discerned:

(1) The dying out of existing farm families, many of them long established, and a general decrease in family size. For example, eleven families of substantial yeomen died out between 1900 and 1920 alone. According to the 1851 Census the average size of a farm family was 5·1 people: in 1959 it was 3·4 people.

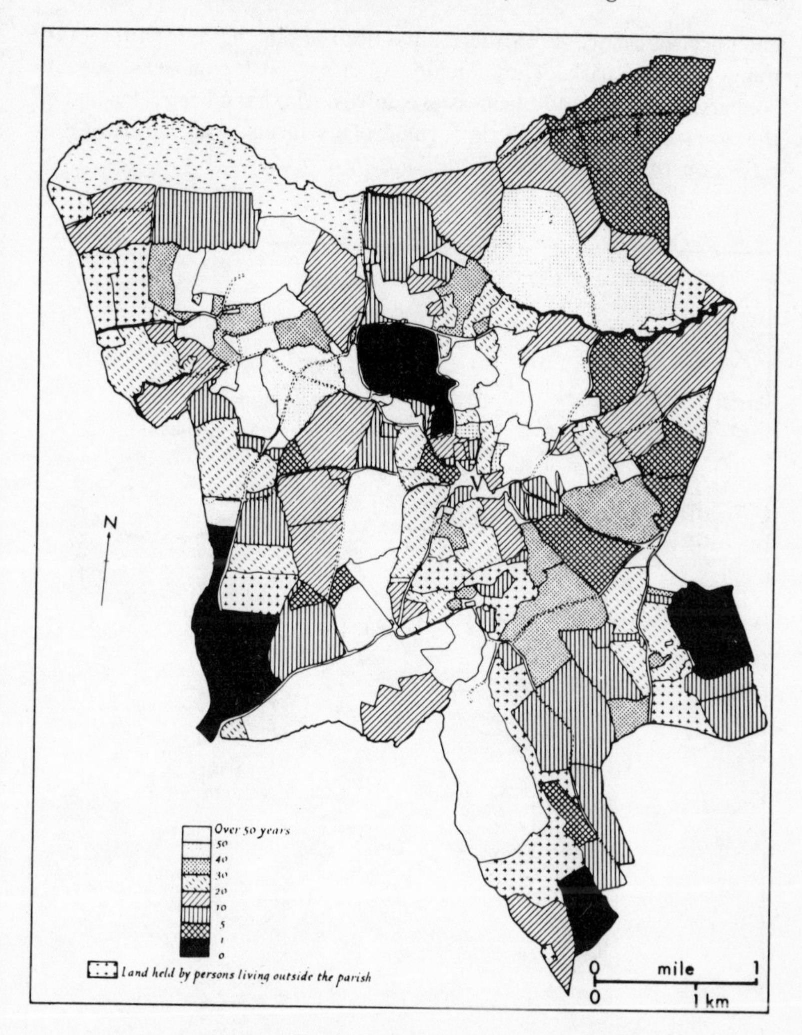

Fig. 4.7 Length of occupation (in years) of present farmers

(2) The entry into farming of labourers and small holders by means of the 'agricultural ladder'. Twenty-two of the seventy-five farmers at present in Ashworthy were once farm labourers or are the descendants of men who were farm labourers during the last hundred years.

(3) The entry into farming of men from other occupations, particularly since 1945. Nine of the present farmers fall within this

category, but since 1945 there have been about thirty such men farming in the parish. They include doctors, civil engineers, regular soldiers, solicitors and business executives, who have been attracted to this area by the relatively low value of its farms, which in turn is a reflection of the poverty of the land.

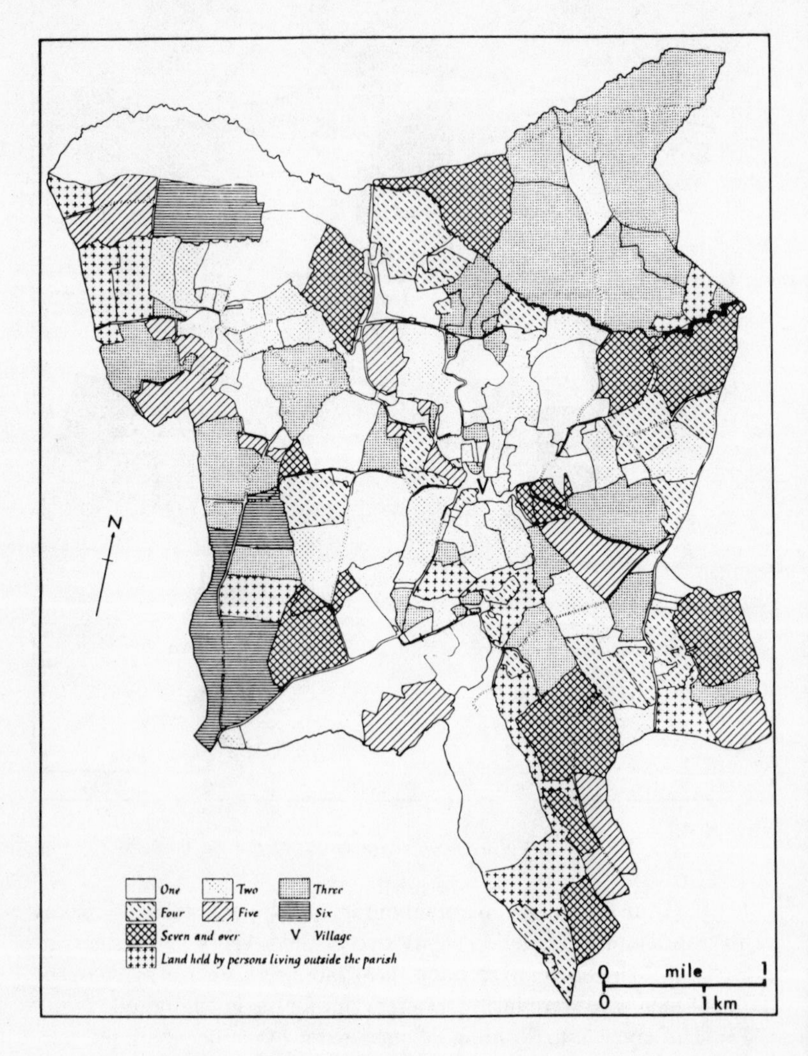

Fig. 4.8 Number of occupants in each farm, 1900–59

When considered as a whole, the changes in land holding and in the farm population reveal an essentially fluid situation which has persisted for many years. It flatly contradicts the widely held view of the remote rural areas as places where the same families cultivate the

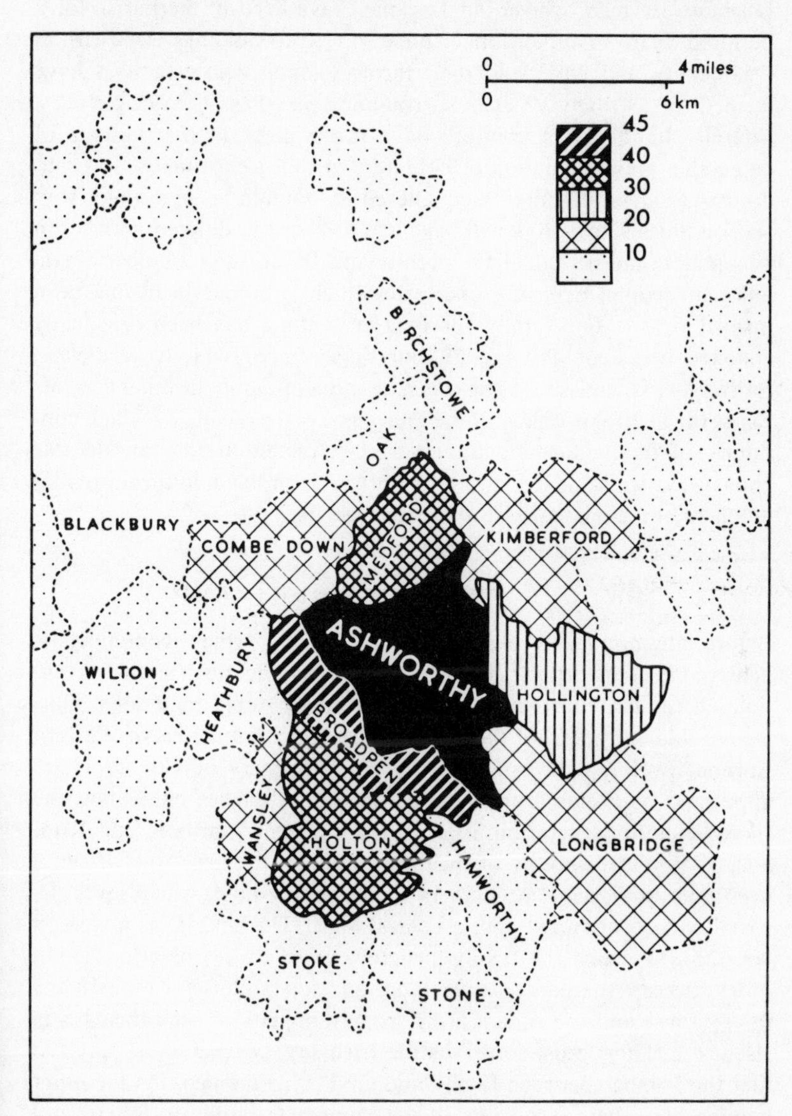

Fig. 4.9 Number of movements of farm families in and out of Ashworthy, 1900–59

same fields for generation after generation and where economic and social change takes place very slowly. In Ashworthy a number of farm families have died out and have been replaced by others, some of local origin, some from as far away as Sussex, Cumberland and Durham. Farmers whose families may have lived in the parish for a hundred years or much longer have moved to holdings elsewhere in the locality and have sold their farms to men whose families have farmed for as many years in surrounding parishes, or to neighbours. Literally hundreds of changes have taken place in the patterns of ownership and occupation of holdings, so that a farm chosen at random will almost certainly have altered its boundaries in a major way several times since 1800, will have had four or five different families in occupation and perhaps have been owned by an equal number of still different people. Even the one farm which is unique in having been farmed by the one family for over a century has been drastically changed in extent and layout four times since 1841. Nevertheless, Ashworthy is, and always has been, an area of family farming and this raises the central problem of the analysis, i.e. the means by which continuity of family farming is achieved in conditions of considerable change. As we shall see, one solution to this problem in turn provides much of the explanation for the change itself.

THE CONTINUITY OF FAMILY FARMING

Before attempting to explain the means by which continuity is achieved in Ashworthy, it is useful to examine the much simpler situation where family farming occurs in extremely stable conditions. This, we are told, is typical of the peasant farming communities of Western Europe. In Eire, for example, the small farmers of County Clare appear to be a classic instance of the same families cultivating the same fields for generation after generation (see Arensberg and Kimball, 1939). The stability of their way of life is derived largely from a deep and unswerving attachment to the family land, which gives the social and economic system a central logic. The land is, as it were, a constant, to which the family structure must always be adjusted. In order to keep 'the name on the land' one son is chosen to inherit the family farm and the others are normally obliged to seek their living elsewhere. They 'must travel' as the Irish say, i.e. they must leave so that the balance between family and land is maintained. On the other hand, where there is no one in the immediate family to inherit and keep the name on the land, a relative is brought in, perhaps a cousin or a nephew. Kindred provide a safeguard against the failure of the elementary family to produce an heir.

Ashworthy is strikingly different from County Clare. As in much of England and Wales, the deep attachment to the family holding is generally absent. Farmers move from one farm to another or sell one or two fields apparently as a matter of course. In this constantly changing situation continuity is achieved, ideally, by each farmer attempting to set up *all his sons* as farmers in their own right. One son inherits the home farm and the others are found holdings of their own elsewhere, either as owners or tenants. Now this method of ensuring continuity is quite inconsistent with a system based on the principle of keeping farms in the hands of the same family, since there can never be more than an occasional holding available for non-inheriting sons in any one generation. Equally important, this inconsistency is found within Ashworthy itself for, although families may not remain on the one holding for a whole generation or more, under ideal conditions there is a son to inherit on every farm. Thus there is a conflict between the aims of immediate family continuity and the desire to establish non-inheriting sons in farms of their own, and this conflict lies at the roots of the fluid situation which has been described earlier.

The resolution of the conflict is made possible in the first instance by the absence of a deep attachment to the family land. Without it there is no necessity to bring in members of the extended family to ensure inheritance and therefore, since the elementary family is a very imperfect instrument for ensuring biological continuity, there are some farms available for farmers wishing to find holdings for non-inheriting sons. In any one generation there are some families which die out because a farmer remains a bachelor, a man and wife may be childless, or their children may die young.

Some movement of individuals from farm to farm and change in the actual composition of farm families are therefore intrinsic features of the system and give rise to what may be termed 'structural instability'. However, from what has been said earlier it will be clear that there are many other elements which contribute to the total changes. Farmers' sons have had to compete for many years with ambitious farm labourers and smallholders in search of holdings and more recently with the newcomers to farming. The general poverty of the area and in particular the existence of small farms on poorly drained land, which can be bought or rented very cheaply, has encouraged the entry into farming of people from these two very different groups. Changes in the pattern of ownership, especially the break up of the estates, have forced some farmers to leave their holdings and made it possible for others to find them. The more successful farmers have bought larger farms on better land.

In the simplest terms, therefore, the changing conditions in Ashworthy are seen to be a product of a particular means of achieving continuity within an economic and physical environment which encourages movement up the rungs of the 'agricultural ladder'. However, this general statement cannot be used to explain all the changes which have taken place at any given time, because they are obviously in part a result of external factors which occur in an irregular way. In the inter-war period of agricultural depression, for example, many farmers went bankrupt and were forced to leave farming altogether or to move to smaller holdings; in the post-war period the 'new' farmers have appeared. The family farming of Ashworthy is constantly being adjusted to new situations which are a result of being part of the extremely complex social and economic structure of English society as a whole. From this point of view their methods of achieving continuity are, in comparison with those of Ireland, flexible enough to withstand the complex changes which occur.

CONCLUSION

This study has attempted to show, in outline, that an understanding of how family farming works as a system can only be achieved by considering it in terms of the complex relationship between society and the land within a small community. In this way as much importance can be given, for example, to the harshness of the environment and its consequences as to methods of inheritance. In this approach to family farming it is necessary to use the techniques and data of several disciplines, notably of the geographer, the economist and the rural sociologist.

Ashworthy is, of course, a very small area with its own special features and many other sample studies are needed in other parts of England and Wales (including those where family farming is not well developed) before it is possible to generalise with any confidence. There is evidence of at least some comparison with many other parts of the country (see, for example, National Farm Survey of England and Wales, 1946), and we also know that the ideal of finding a farm for all one's sons is pursued by farmers in Wales (see Rees, 1950), Cumberland (see Williams, 1956) and elsewhere.

The importance of studies of this kind needs little emphasis. If the planning of an efficient agriculture is to be achieved, if the technological advances which are transforming British farming are to be sensibly applied, then it seems no more than common sense that we should know something about the people who cultivate the land and the problems they face in ensuring a worthwhile living for their children.

SOURCE: *Geographical Journal*, 129 (1), March 1963.

REFERENCES

This study is a slightly amended version of the Lister Lecture given at the Cardiff meeting of the British Association for the Advancement of Science in September 1963. The field work was supported by a generous grant from the Darlington Hall Trustees and is the subject of an extended analysis in *A West Country Village: Ashworthy*, Routledge and Kegan Paul, 1963. The name of the parish and all personal and place names used in this study are fictitious.

Arensberg, C. M., and Kimball, S. T. (1939) *Family and community in Ireland.*

National Farm Survey of England and Wales (1946) *Summary Report*, pp. 31–5 and Table A9.

Rees, A. D. (1950) *Life in a Welsh countryside*, pp. 146–8, 184–5.

Williams, W. M. (1956) *The sociology of an English village: Gosforth*, Ch. 1.

Part Two
Specialisation in Industry

5 Population Changes over the West Cumberland Coalfield

T. H. BAINBRIDGE

THERE are two contrasting industrial regions in Cumberland, one being centred upon Carlisle and the other occupying the western margin of the county. In the former, variety of industries has been accompanied by steady growth of population which is in contrast to the latter where dependence upon basic trades has resulted in population variations characteristic of such areas. It is the irregularities which first attract attention.

Before studying the changes which have taken place, it will be well to point out that over most of West Cumberland settlements consist of mining communities which are small and scattered, in rural surroundings almost concealed in interdrumlin hollows or river valleys. There are no large mining centres with the possible exception of Whitehaven (21,159—1931), for Workington (24,751) has now had centred upon it the whole of the once dispersed iron and steel trade.

Coal mining was in operation as early as the sixteenth century and during two following centuries the coal trade made very rapid progress. Distribution of collieries at the beginning of the nineteenth century apparently differed but little from the present day. Inland collieries, however, were being worked on a small and primitive scale, generally supplying only local demand. Pits near the sea, and especially in the vicinity of Whitehaven, had made great strides. As a result the port was then the chief one in Cumberland and indeed one of the most important in the kingdom, and had a population of 8742. In 1801 there were about 26,000 people on the coalfield–probably double that of 1688 when an estimate of the people in the various parishes had been attempted. That the coal measures exerted geographical control even at this time is indicated by the fact that about 22 per cent of the population of the county was gathered on the coalfield. As at present, some 60 per cent or more of the people resided in the trinity of ports, Maryport, Workington and Whitehaven, indicating that inland mining settlements were then, as now, relatively small, scarcely affecting the agricultural character of the landscape. In 1801 the coastal belt was the only part with more than 250 persons per square mile. The margin

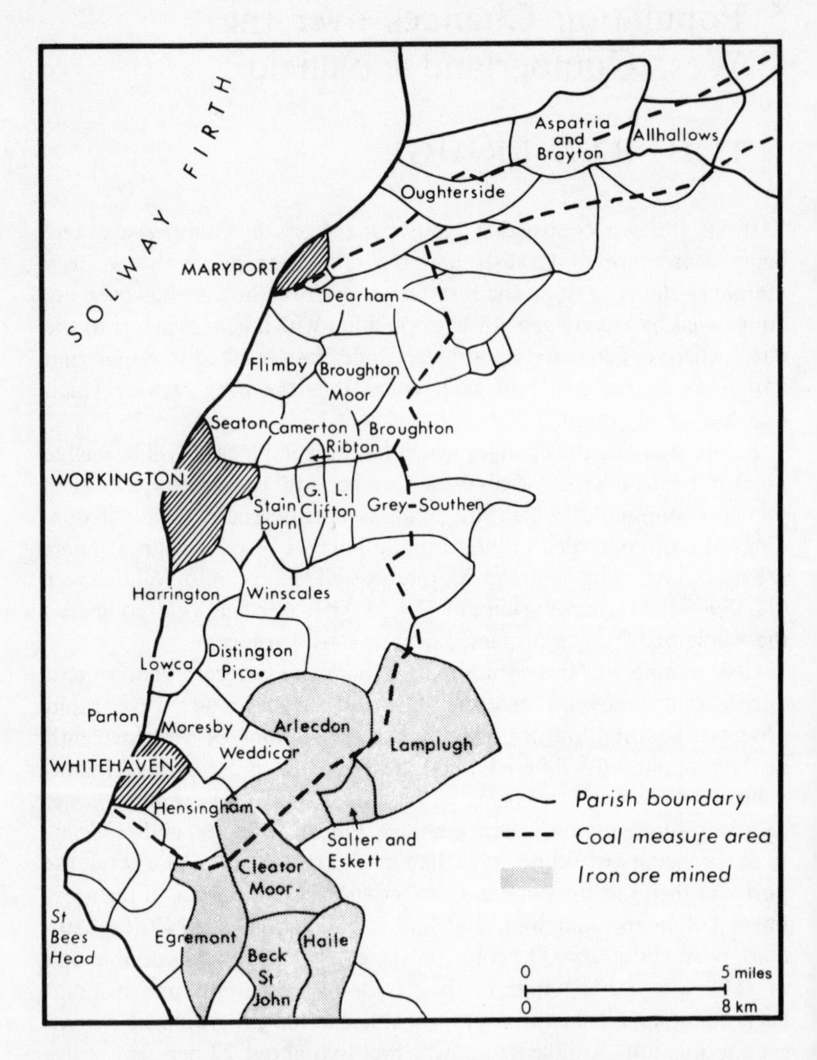

Fig. 5.1 West Cumberland parishes in relation to coal and iron ore areas. In general, except on the more elevated ground to the southeast of the coalfield, the parishes are small. Two of these small parishes, Ribton and Winscales, both without collieries showed a decrease of population between 1801 and 1931. The population in all other parishes increased, the trinity of ports maintaining a supremacy during the whole period

of the coalfield appeared as a zone of discontinuity in the population density, east of which there were fewer than 50 people to the square mile.

Between 1801 and 1831 the population of the coalfield increased by 37 per cent. The greatest development was in parishes near the northern end of the coalfield, the most outstanding being Aspatria, where population was more than doubled. Mr Joseph Harris of Greysouthen embarked upon coal mining there in 1822, when he sank a pit in Plumbland, and worked the Yard Band up to the outcrop. New pits at Dearham were also opened out. In the southern part of the coalfield growth was most marked at Whitehaven, where the population of the port with its suburb Preston Quarter increased by nearly 50 per cent. Developments in the area had been so great and exploitation of the Main Band so keen, that in 1814 nearly a quarter of a million tons of coal were obtained from the Whitehaven Collieries and some of it was from workings about a mile under the sea.

The second quarter of the nineteenth century is not marked by any great change in growth of population on the coalfield, for between the years 1831 and 1851 the increase was about 20 per cent, whereas between the latter year and 1881 the increase was over 75 per cent, and was most rapid in the decade 1871–81.

During the third quarter development was general, but especially great in the northern area and relatively most important in the Derwent Valley where expansion was evident at Seaton, Broughton and Clifton. By this time the coast line and Derwent Valley railway lines were in use, and influence of the former is reflected in the fact that in 1867 the maximum coal shipments took place from Maryport. At the time natural increase was not sufficient to account for the rapid development and there was substantial migration into the industrial area. A large part of it came from neighbouring agricultural areas which showed a decline in population.

New settlements appeared during this period, as for instance the very typical mining village of Pica in the southern part of the parish of Distington. Here on open moorland at an elevation of between 550 and 600 ft, 70 houses were built when in 1880 the Moresby Coal Company completed its Oatlands Pit to a depth of 108 fathoms and obtained coal from the Main Band. An additional 20 houses were built in the early part of the present century; the 90 houses accommodate the 390 people who now live in the village.

The fact that there was greatest expansion in population between the years 1871–81 is due to the intimate relationship between the coal trade and the iron and steel industry, which enjoyed a boom period in that decade. By that time too, numerous branch railways had been opened and mineral traffic was thus encouraged. Although output of pig iron reached its maximum in 1882 there was still expansion in the coalfield, most marked in the northern mining settlements. By the early nineties, saturation point had evidently been reached and the 80,000 or so people on the coalfield remained relatively stable in numbers only because of outward migration.

In early years of the century there was a decline in population in many northern villages (Aspatria excepted), offset by increases in other parts, as for instance Great Clifton and Distington (which includes Pica already mentioned).

The post-war period following 1918 was one which showed further declines. After the maximum number of miners (12,000) had been employed in 1924, only Great Clifton, Moresby and Whitehaven of the mining centres showed an increase of population in the decade 1921–31.

Over the whole coalfield total population has increased threefold during the 130 years for which returns are available. Only two settlements showed phenomenal growth relative to the others—Aspatria (tenfold increase) and Flimby (eightfold), both

Table 5.1 Parishes – Actually *within* the coalfield

A		B	C
Parishes, the populations of which have expanded at the average for the whole coalfield; that is, population has increased ×3 or more.		*Parishes, the populations of which have increased but not doubled.*	*Parishes, the populations of which have actually decreased.*
Allhallows	c	Stainburn	Ribton
Aspatria and Brayton	c	Greysouthen	Winscales
Dearham	c	Weddicar	
Flimby	c		
Broughton (GT)	c		
Seaton	c		
Workington	c		
Gt. Clifton	c		
Harrington	c		
Parton			
Moresby	c		
Hensingham			
Whitehaven	c		
c – Colliery		*Agricultural* *No collieries*	*Agricultural* *No collieries* *Both quite small*

towards the northern end of the coalfield. As at the beginning of the nineteenth century the three ports dominate the coalfield.

It is of interest to notice that in Cumberland there are only four towns and three of them (Whitehaven, Workington and Maryport) are on the coalfield; the other one is the county town, Carlisle.

Not one settlement has shown continuous increase in population; all have fluctuated. The two parishes of Ribton and Winscales, both quite small agricultural areas without collieries, have now fewer people than in the early years of last century.

Movements of the people have been mentioned, but the matter has been complicated by cessation of colonial emigration. It is a strange fact that whilst many thousands of Cumbrians have left their own district (during the last 50 years or so some 130,000 people have left Cumberland) and have emigrated amongst other places to New Zealand, South Africa and Canada, yet efforts to transfer miners to Kent and other areas in England have not been successful. Further complications result from mechanisation with consequent reduction in the number of men needed (output of 1923 and 1930 similar; 11,767 employees in former year, 9701 in the latter; 1943 – 5570 employees) and reduction in the number of collieries operating.

The net result of these factors has been a large residue of unemployed lingering in districts where mining cannot absorb it again, most evident in northern settlements where collieries outside the coal measures outcrop have quickly yielded their coal and are now closed. Aspatria after its period of ascendency is now one of the most hard hit of the mining areas, three mines having closed down in the last 10 years. Dearham in the same district has also been similarly affected. The most depressed area was Maryport, where in 1932 nearly 50 per cent of the insured workers were unemployed. Mining is not, however, wholly accountable for the tragic state of affairs. In the town blast furnaces, a brewer, a tannery and railway engineering shops have been closed down. Two factors have also killed what was once the most prosperous port of Cumberland: first the closure of the Aspatria collieries which exported through Maryport and second, the opening, in 1927 of a large modern dock at Workington.

In the southern part of the coalfield, whilst the depression was great, it was never so continuously severe as in the Maryport area. Some small mining villages like Pica suffered when the local colliery closed, although a number of the men obtained work in a neighbouring colliery.

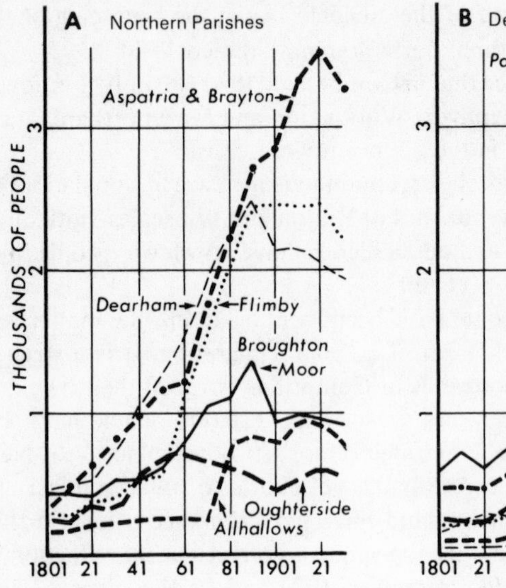

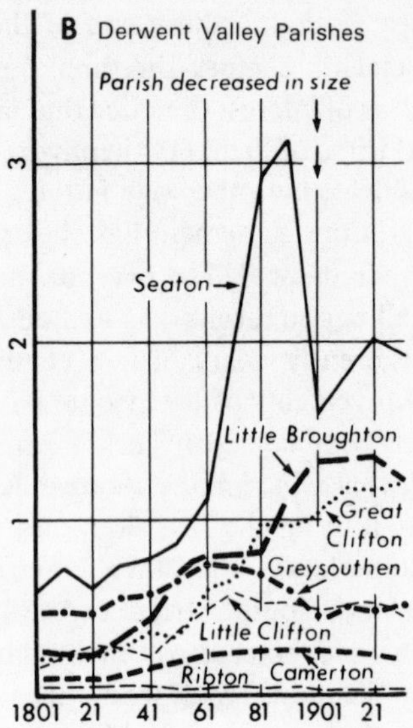

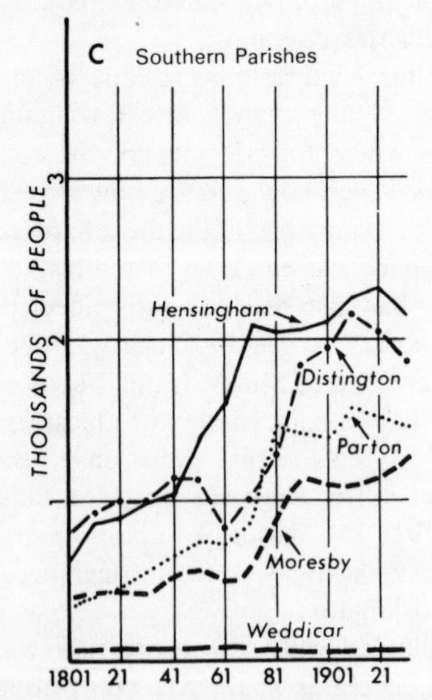

Fig. 5.2 West Cumberland coalfield – population changes – 1801–1931. Maximum population over the coalfield coincided with the boom period in the allied iron and steel industry. In recent years migration has greatly decreased because of the introduction of light industries and there is now work for women and girls

Fluctuating conditions have prevailed within recent years at Whitehaven, not because of the exhaustion of coal, but because of several changes in ownership of the collieries and imposition at one time (1932) by the Irish Free State government of a tariff on coal. Whitehaven is an outstanding example of a community dependent on a single basic industry, coal mining, allied to coal exporting. The four local collieries, almost on the water's edge, have given employment to over 3000 men and the record annual output was in 1927 when 881,000 tons of coal were raised. Yet a few years later, all these men were idle because of external factors beyond their control.

The central portion of the coalfield has been most stable in recent years, not only because of coal mining but because Workington now has centred upon it the whole of the iron and steel trade which was once dispersed throughout West Cumberland. It is in the region too, that there is most likelihood of expansion in coal mining. A new colliery (The Solway Colliery), has been sunk near the steel works, and in 1936 there was opened a battery of ovens with a weekly output of 5000 tons of coke. Other developments have characterised Gillhead and Flimby, and whilst as we have seen, some northern collieries have been closed, boring is taking place with a view to further exploitation. Hope is not abandoned, therefore, of expansion in industry but it will need to be very great indeed to absorb even a small proportion of the 30 per cent or more of the insured workers who were unemployed over the whole area. Diversification of industry is, however, being attempted, the most notable example being development of the Solway Trading Estate at Maryport.

PATTERN OF MINING SETTLEMENTS

It remains to examine the pattern of the mining settlements. Very few are of the dispersed type. The majority consist of single streets, sometimes quite long as at Aspatria, or of single rows of houses built near to road junctions, exemplified by Broughton Moor or Pica. In such places houses are removed from the collieries, but at Great Clifton the village is, so to speak, in the colliery yard. Similarly at Lowca the two or three rows of terrace houses are quite near the workings, and within easy range of fumes from the large smouldering refuse heap. This village with about 955 inhabitants in approximately 180 houses is perhaps the best example of spasmodic growth, and can usefully be compared in plan and architecture with the uniformity and compactness evident in Pica. Twenty-four houses were built about 1905 and 10 years later 22 cottages were condemned and replaced by 30 houses, whilst as late as 1926 a further 40 houses were erected. The older houses are generally low and single storied, but in the later stages of development double storied houses were provided. One feature of the mining villages should be noted and that is their fine situation within view of the Solway Firth and the Lakeland Mountains. Finally, the Cumberland coal miner has maintained his contact with the land through the relative isolation of the villages and his own arable and cultivated patch of ground. This last feature has probably been accentuated by the lack of amenities in the villages. Until recent years the church or chapel was often the sole social centre, and before the Cumberland Bus Company extended its services to the villages, communication was not easy; the nearest railway station was in most cases a considerable distance away. (For a more recent study of the iron-ore settlements south of the coal field, see above in the Introduction, pp. 20–25.)

SOURCE: *Economic Geography*, 26, 1949.

6 The Model Village at Bromborough Pool

J. N. TARN

MODEL villages were almost a commonplace during the middle years of the last century. They usually developed as a result of rapid industrial expansion in the first few decades of the century, when perhaps a small mill or factory, sited in the centre of a growing town, found that there was insufficient room on its existing site for the expansion which prospering sales demanded. A few farsighted owners saw in this the opportunity for a fresh start in country outside the town where expansion could take place freely for years to come, and when they moved sufficiently far out of the town it became necessary to provide housing for the operatives. One, at least, of these communities inspired the popular imagination, and there can be few today who have not heard of Sir Titus Salt, the discoverer of alpaca, who moved his mill from Bradford to a site almost on the moors in Airedale. It was such an isolated position that he was obliged to build housing, but more than this, he desired to establish a 'model' community. There were of course several others, less well known, such as Akroydon near Halifax built by Sir Edward Akroyd, and on the opposite side of the town, a rather smaller development at Copley. As examples of town planning these model communities tended to reflect the standards of their times: Saltaire, for example, was a closely knit series of regular streets clinging to a hillside without open space or private gardens except for small greens in front of the library, the institute and the almshouses; the houses at Copley were built on the back-to-back principle leaving very little space between the two rows, which formed an alley rather than a street.

For some reason little attention has been paid to one of the smallest, but nevertheless one of the most interesting model villages built at about the same time at Bromborough Pool on the Wirral peninsula by Price's Patent Candle Company. Yet of all the organised housing developments associated with industrial enterprises, this was perhaps the most advanced from the point of view of planning, and certainly the most spacious.

For references to this chapter, see p. 154.

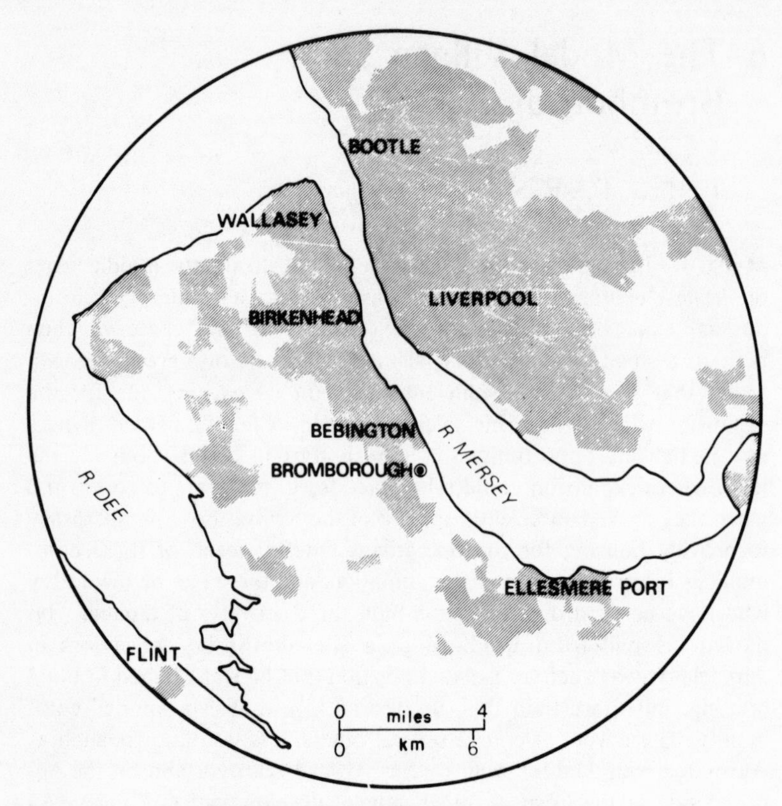

Fig. 6.1 Bromborough Pool: location map

GROWTH OF THE INDUSTRY

The firm of Price's was founded in 1812 by William Wilson. Its early history was typical of the rapid industrial growth which often took place during the early years of the last century. Wilson set up in London with a capital of only £100 as a merchant importing Russian goods and specialising in tallow, from which he began to make candles at the Belmont Works in Battersea. The business which he started was converted into a joint stock company in 1847, and today it still trades under the same name, an internationally famous firm.

Candle making was a very rudimentary business when the Wilson family began work at Belmont, and they soon began to refine the processes of distilling the fatty acids used in candles, eventually producing white non-odorous stearine. The other major by-product of distilling the fatty acids, a liquid called oleine, they turned into a successful lubricant for use in the manufacture of wool. It was the production of these 'cloth oils' which led the firm to take an interest in the North West, for palm oil was one of the principle imports from West Africa to Merseyside, and since the main market for the lubricants would be in the nearby manufacturing towns of Lancashire and Yorkshire, it seemed sensible to establish a plant for the extraction of oleine and stearine near Liverpool.

The search for a site on which to build the new works ended in 1853 when a plot of land was purchased at Bromborough Pool on the Wirral side of the Mersey estuary. It was a rather isolated site, some five miles from Birkenhead and thirteen from Chester, but one well-suited to the industrial processes of Price's, since it was situated on a small creek (which gave the name Bromborough 'Pool') into which the crude cargo could be brought and discharged, and from which small ships were able to take the finished products to Birkenhead or Liverpool. The only real disadvantage was that the nearest housing was two miles away, and any sizeable source of labour considerably further away. It was necessary, therefore, to establish the nucleus of a small village community while the factory was being built if the venture was to be a success. For this reason, just as at Saltaire, the Wilsons were obliged to consider a housing development as an integral part of their initial plans.

The Wilson family were not typical nineteenth century industrialists in the Dickensian sense; as a family, they combined a considerable degree of business acumen with a philanthropic attitude towards their workers. These qualities were peculiar to a certain number of industrialists in the last century, and it seems to have been a Victorian characteristic that a hard business sense was by no means incompatible with a high regard for social responsibilities. The Wilsons, in addition, came from Lanark, and their attitude to industry and society were very much in the tradition of Robert Owen, who, of course, had founded the mill community at New Lanark. The Wilsons were neither so idealistic nor so radical as Owen, but they appeared to share many of his fundamental convictions. In addition to the village at Bromborough they had a scheme for the erection of eighteen dwellings for the Belmont workers in London during the late eighteen-fifties, but this did not materialise, largely because of difficult economic conditions prevailing in the metropolis in the years after the Crimean War.

DEVELOPMENT OF THE VILLAGE

When the decision to establish the new works had been taken, and the land purchased, development of the site started at once, the first houses going up at the same time as the factory. The company provided the houses and also saw to it that the basic amenities of the little community were established; a building was provided which served as a meeting room and school and a teacher was appointed to supervise the education of the children. A small isolation hospital was built in case of epidemics; a necessary precaution in an age when cholera and typhoid were frequent causes of death, and the company arranged for a doctor to visit the village each day. There was no church at this time, but services were held in the school room, and there was a resident chaplain to conduct services each Sunday and hold daily prayers in the works; a feature of life at Bromborough which did not disappear until the First World War.

The works were commissioned in 1854 and within three years four hundred and sixty people were living in cottages adjacent to the factory. Both the works and the village were planned by Julian Hill, the company's London architect, and presumably to him, as much as to the Wilsons, we owe the layout of the housing, which for the period was unique, and certainly a great advance on the more famous work by local Bradford architects at Saltaire. Bromborough is in every sense a garden village, with the cottages laid out in short terraces of four with wide spaces between each block and ample gardens at the back as well as at the front. The open space known as the Green was established at the start, overlooked by two pairs of rather grand managerial houses; off it on one side York Street and Manor Place were laid out and the first working class houses were built there. At the same time the lodge was built and the cooperative store, another of the unusual ventures still continued which were inspired by James Wilson, the representative of the family at that time most interested in the social aspects of the new venture.

Each cottage had a sitting room, kitchen and scullery on the ground floor, and upstairs either two large bedrooms or one large and two small ones. Five of the cottages in York Street were rather larger and had four bedrooms. They were all of modest size; a typical small cottage in Manor Place, for example, had a sitting room of 12 ft by 10 ft 8 in., a kitchen 9 ft 5 in. by 7 ft 1 in., and a scullery 8 ft by 7 ft 6 in. The two bedrooms upstairs were respectively 10 ft 9 in. by 12 ft 2 in. and 9 ft 5 in. by 8 ft 7 in. In appearance the houses were quite simple, constructed in brick with plain arched doorways and traditional sash windows. The pitched roofs were of slate, hipped at either end and with very large chimney stacks rising out of the ridge; over the off-shoot at the rear there was a lean-to roof if there was a single storey scullery, or a little gable if the off-shoot was two storeys high. The architectural style, therefore, was plain and straightforward; there was no decoration or unnecessary ornament on any of the buildings, and their character stands very much in the early nineteenth century vernacular tradition.

There were 48 houses occupied by 1856, with a population of 318 people, many of whom were children. The following year the first stage of the village was completed, and the total number of cottages had risen to 76 containing 460 people. They must have been very crowded at first; the number of people per house was given as 6·63 in 1856, but it fell slightly to 5·55 by 1859 and it remained fairly constant at that level for the remaining part of the century. Today, of course, it has fallen to about three people per cottage in common with any other housing estate.

When the first houses in Manor Place were completed they attracted the attention of the *Illustrated London News,* and the following favourable notice appeared in its columns: 'The fresh-air, open space and cottages give the factory at Birkenhead a great advantage over the parent works. The cottages will attach the people much more closely to the place. The little gardens are very popular; and, considering the short time of occupation and the nature of the soil, their appearance is generally very creditable.'

The village was also known to Henry Roberts, the most active architect and chronicler of the housing movement during the period between 1840 to 1860. In *The Improvement of the Dwellings of the Labouring Classes,* published in 1859, he briefly notes the progress which had been made by that time: 'At the manufactory of Price's Candle Company, Bromborough Pool Works, near Birkenhead, seventy cottages have been built by the company for their workpeople on three different scales, varying in rents from 3*s.* 6*d.* to 6*s.* 6*d.* per week.'

Now that the village was established physically, it began to create its own life, and one of the most interesting documents still in the possession of the company, the Minute Book of *The Bromborough Branch of the Belmont Mutual Improvement Society,* gives a clear account of the activities which took place in the village. The rules said

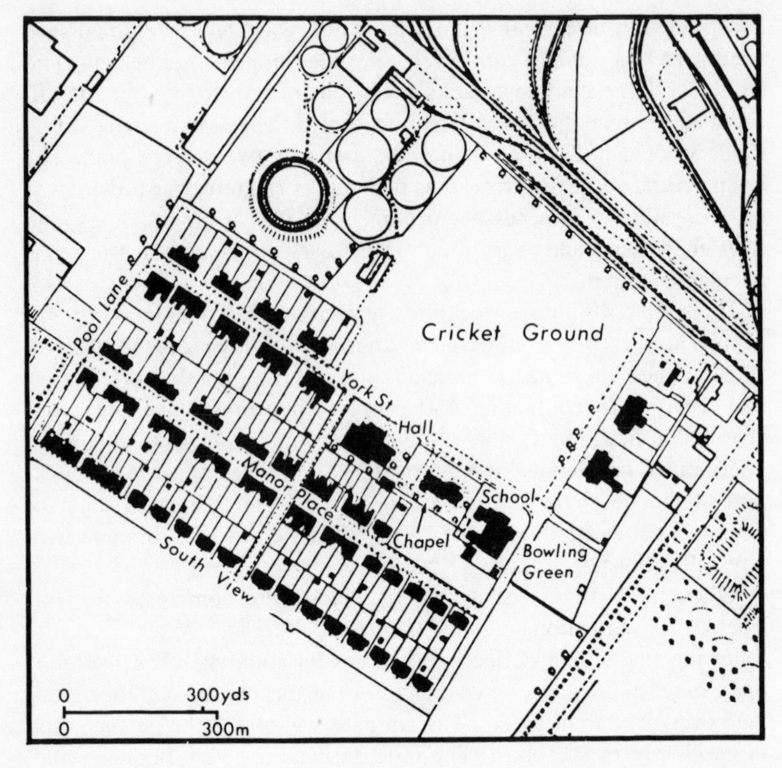

Fig. 6.2 Bromborough Pool: a plan of the model village

that: 'The object of the Society shall be to supply the workmen in the employ of Price's Patent Candle Company, Bromboro' Pool, with instruction and intellectual recreation, and to promote generally their intellectual, moral and social advancement.'

THE GROWTH OF VILLAGE ACTIVITIES AND SOCIETIES

It should be remembered that in the middle of the last century a place like Bromborough was isolated, several miles from the nearest town, and, except for those willing to walk at least the five miles in both directions to and from Birkenhead, there were no recreational activities except any the villagers cared to make for themselves. So the *Mutual Improvement Society* was in many ways the focus of village life. It seems to have functioned for about three years from some kind of temporary building referred to as the 'iron house', and then after 1858 from the new multi-purpose school rooms.

The Society came into existence late in 1854, when there was a general meeting to draw up rules, the preamble to which was quoted above. Its rooms were to be open from 6 to 10 o'clock each evening, and books from the library were to be given out for home reading on Tuesdays from 7 to 8 o'clock. An attendant was soon appointed whose job it was to open the rooms at the appointed hour each evening except Wednesday, to display the current papers – putting aside, ready for distribution, those now out of date which had been purchased by members – attend to the fires, set out the chairs and tables and keep order during the evening. At the correct time, or at 9 o'clock if no members were present, he was to extinguish the lights and lock up.

Papers taken at that time included *The Times, Northern Daily Times, Illustrated News, Punch, The Builder, Chamber's Journal* and *Dicken's Household Words.* Later the *Gardeners' Chronicle* and the *Cottage Gardener* were taken for a trial period to find out which was the more popular, and subsequently the former was given up. By 1862, *All the year Round, Good Words, Leisure Hour, Cornhill,* and *Once a Week* had been added to the list, all of which had been discontinued five years later in favour of the *Manchester Examiner, Public Opinion, British Workman* and the *Quarterly Rivew;* these last, perhaps, reflecting a slightly more radical outlook as the century advanced.

The library formed an important part of the society's activities – a collection of some 700 volumes was built up by the end of the century. Very soon it was found that one hour a week was insufficient time for members to select books, and after 1855 it was made possible to change books every evening. Two years later it was agreed that an official be appointed to look after the Reading Room during the winter and care for the cricket equipment during the summer; for these tasks he was paid £10 per annum. There were, in addition, frequent notes of money spent on books; many well known authors were popular in the village – for example, during 1868 the works of Dickens, Trollope, George Eliot, Mrs Gaskell, Kingsley and Wilkie Collins all featured on the purchase list.

In addition to the provision of papers, magazines and books, the Society decided at the outset that it should organise lectures. The fields suggested were quite ambitious, including music, history, astronomy, painting, wit and humour, poetry, chemistry, pottery and electricity. For the winter session in 1856–7 it was proposed to have four special lecturers who would be paid fees and with the assistance of local lecturers it was hoped to have weekly meetings throughout the season. During the winter of 1861–2 a series of lectures was organised dealing with various aspects of life during the first 20 years of the century; subjects like the policies of the empire, military and naval battles, progress in the arts and sciences, manners and customs and literature were covered. Two special lectures were also given that winter on electro-psychology which attracted great interest and attention.

Presumably for those who had difficulty in reading and writing, there were from time to time classes in these basic skills, and there is record of public readings at 1*d.* a session which seem to have been popular. The Society did not confine itself purely to educational pursuits; a brass band was established as early as 1855 for whom the society subsequently purchased instruments, and the same year the Society was responsible for arranging cricket matches on a piece of ground set aside by the company, and for which it provided the necessary equipment. Support for the activities seems to have come willingly from the company which agreed in 1856 to subscribe a sum equal to the total amount raised by the Society itself each year. With the money available, in addition to the cricket equipment and the instruments for the band, it was able to lay out a bowling green, and for indoor recreations to provide a stereoscope and slides for use at lectures, a set of chess men and a bagatelle board. From time to time summer outings were arranged and concerts during the winter evenings, at which the Liverpool Choral Society became a frequent performer later in the century. No doubt to facilitate musical entertainments a piano was purchased (on the instalment plan) during 1875.

The people of Bromborough, then, created for themselves all the usual activities which were to be found in a small nineteenth century community. Watched over by a benevolent management, one can imagine the excitement and activity which surrounded such an event as a concert or cricket match. One wonders how men who worked a sixty hour week possessed the strength and energy, in those days of hard physical work, to undertake to organise the variety of activities which took place. Until 1870, however, Bromborough was a small community, just slightly more than 400 people altogether, and it is not surprising therefore, to read that from time to time the membership of the

Society had fallen off, or in 1865 that it was intended either to reform the Society or discontinue it altogether. Nevertheless, more than 10 years later it was still flourishing.

FURTHER EXTENSIONS TO THE VILLAGE

In 1872 the company decided to extend the village, building additional houses first in Manor Place, and then the following year forming a new street, South View, with 12 houses in it, of similar size and appearance to those built in the 1850s. Further housing was erected towards the end of the century, when both South View and Manor Place were extended, first in 1896 and again in 1900. None of these alterations destroyed the original concept of the village as an example of open planning. The number of houses was increased to 100 by the first series of additions during the 1870s and to more than 140 by the turn of the century. Bromborough was then a thriving community with a maximum population, in 1905, of 710 people.

The amenities of a village, which had doubled in size between 1860 and 1900, also required extension. The three most important new buildings were a church, erected to the design of C. Pemberton Leach, at the company's expense, in 1890; a new school, to replace the multi-purpose building erected in 1858, was opened in 1898 and the old buildings was converted into a village hall, a function it had in fact served all its life. Finally, a new cottage hospital was built in 1901.

CONCLUSION

Today Bromborough is no longer an isolated rural community, but the model village still shelters virtually unchanged under the shadow of the expanding factory which has always provided its menfolk with their livelihood. No longer, however, does the factory belong to the original firm, for the nature of the fatty acid processes which are carried out at Bromborough have become so far removed from the production of candles and lubricants at Belmont that the two branches divided in 1936, the Merseyside firm becoming a part of the Unilever group, changing its name to Price's (Bromborough) Limited. The new link was an advantage so far as the history of housing is concerned, for Price's are now linked with another great firm whose founder, rather later in the century, built another model village quite close to Bromborough. Across the busy highway linking Birkenhead with Chester lies Port Sunlight; sophisticated, architecturally pretentious, a much more magnificent concept in every way; but it is doubtful whether such a venture would have taken place if the more modest and unselfconscious villages of the earlier years in the century had not proved a success. It is tempting to believe that the first Lord Leverhulme saw Bromborough as the first garden village and sought to build a better one.

Bromborough's place in the history of the model community should be recognised more widely than it is today, for, although a small village at first, it was in reality the first garden village, with its open spaces, its gardens and planting. In these respects it was far in advance of anything built at that time. Only in the simple unaffected layout of the streets and the vernacular quality of the architecture does Bromborough suggest its early date. In the concept of space and density it was a forerunner of the garden city as expounded by Ebenezer Howard, and for its place in the history of this movement as well as its place in the history of enlightened factory management it merits our attention today.

SOURCE: *Town Planning Review,* 35, 1964–5. The original article contains a series of photographs of house types in Bromborough. [Ed.]

REFERENCES

The author wishes to thank the directors and staff of Price's of Bromborough for much help received in the preparation of this study.

The material for this study has been drawn from the following sources:

Price's of Bromborough 1854–1954 published privately by the Company (1954).

Roberts, Henry. *The Improvement of the Dwellings of the Labouring Classes,* (1859).

A Brief History of Price's Patent Candle Company Ltd. (1891).

The Social Side of a Great Industry (1898).

Illustrated London News, 2 December 1854.

Minute Book of the Bromborough Branch of the Belmont Mutual Improvement Society, 1854–78.

Documents, papers, letters, contracts and drawings in the possession of the Company at Bromborough.

Since this study was undertaken there has been one other useful article published on Bromborough:

Watson, Alan, 'Philanthropy, Prosperity, Practicality: The Price's Bromborough Village', *Progress* (the Unilever Quarterly), L (1964).

7 The Economic Geography of Craven in the Early Nineteenth Century

R. LAWTON

MUCH of the historical evidence for the changing geography of Britain is by nature fragmentary and by occurrence sporadic, much of it local rather than national. Before the full story of that changing geography can be told more of this evidence will have to be examined. This paper is the outcome of the study of such evidence for the Craven district in the West Riding of Yorkshire. The local evidence comes from a militia muster list of 1803 for the Wapentake of Staincliff and Ewcross, and the national evidence from the enumerators' books of the Census of Great Britain for 1851. The analysis and comparison of these data help to shed light on the changing occupational structure – and, through it, the changing economic geography – of the region at a most interesting phase of its development.

THE CHARACTER OF THE SOURCE MATERIAL

The period of the Napoleonic wars saw the initiation of the decennial censuses of population in 1801, and a fresh spate of Acts of Parliament both initiating and amending legislation with regard to the raising of militia and yeomanry regiments.[1]

The muster list of 1803

The muster list dated October 10th, 1803, which provides our earlier evidence was the outcome of a number of Acts, principally one dated July 27th of that year: 43 Geo. III, cap. 96 (27 July 1803), clause VII. The Act required that returns be made to the Deputy Lieutenants of counties of the names of all men between the ages of 17 and 55 years, together with their ranks and occupations, whether married and with children, and whether willing to serve as a volunteer. This information was gathered for each township by the constable of the parish and a schedule was left with each householder for this purpose (table 7.1). From these schedules the constable had to return an annual list of men

For references to this chapter, see p. 180.

between the ages of 17 and 55; and it is as a list of this kind, for the 103 townships of Staincliff and Ewcross, that this Craven muster roll has survived. An extract is shown below (table 7.2). There are full names and occupations; classes one to four are groupings related to age, marital status and number of children. These four classes were: 1st – men of 17 and under 30, unmarried and with no living child or children under 10 years; 2nd – men of 30 to 50, unmarried and with no children under 10 years; 3rd – men of 17 to 30, married with not more than two children under 10 years; 4th – others not included in the above classes. The last column indicates infirm people, apprentices and volunteers. In short, the most valuable material which it gives, from our viewpoint, is a detailed picture of the occupational structure of the male population between 17 and 55 years of age.

Table 7.1 Copy of householder's schedule (43 Geo. III, Cap. 96)

Names	Description	Age	Married or single	Children under 10	Remarks
	E.g. housekeeper, servant, lodger, inmate, etc.				E.g. volunteer, infirm, etc.

Table 7.2 Extract from the Craven muster list: Burnsall cum Thorpe township

Names	Description	Classes				Remarks
		1st	2nd	3rd	4th	
John Blackburn	Husbandman	*				
Timothy Kidd	Labourer	*				
Rev. James Brown	Clergyman		*			
Marmaduke Brayshaw	Cotton spinner		*			
James Horner	Shoemaker			*		Infirm
Isaac Carnil	Farmer			*		
John Lord	Cotton spinner			*		
Thomas Hodgson	Shoemaker			*		
William Horner	Shoemaker				*	
Robert Gill	Blacksmith				*	

The 1851 census material

The censuses of population before 1841 were little more than enumerations of the people. It is true that in the censuses of 1801, 1811 and 1821 the enumerators collected information about occupations, but only on the crudest of bases. All that was required was whether people were employed in (a) agriculture, (b) trade, manufacture or handicraft, and (c) other occupations. A somewhat more elaborate classification under seven main headings was attempted in 1831. But the first census to gather anything like the present detail of information was that of 1841. This collected and tabulated much information concerning not only the numbers of the people, but also their age and sex composition, their occupations and certain limited information about birthplaces. The 1851 census was much fuller and more systematic in terms of information collected and tabulated, especially for occupations and birthplaces. It obtained information on: (1) place of residence; (2) name of person; (3) marital status; (4) relation to head of household; (5) age and sex; (6) occupation; (7) birthplace; and it noted any infirmities (blindness, deafness and dumbness, insanity). It was also organised on a different administrative basis.[2] Since full information about occupations was being collected for a second time, ambiguities and omissions were less likely to occur than in 1841. Moreover the 1851 census was taken after the coming of the railway to Craven[3] when towns were growing rapidly and rural depopulation was becoming widespread, and when considerable changes in the character and distribution of industry were in progress.

In 1851 the information required by the Census Acts was collected by many enumerators serving small districts. The township was the basic unit of this enumeration in rural areas. Unfortunately the published tables relating to occupations (as with those relating to age and sex composition and birthplaces) do not give information for the township, the unit of tabulation being the much larger Registration District. To obtain information for the township comparable with that in the 1803 muster list one must go to the manuscript census returns – the enumerators' books – themselves. These are available only from 1841 when the taking of the census was transferred to the office of the Registrar General. Those for the 1841, 1851, 1861 and 1871 censuses are housed in the Public Record Office.[4] From these books I have extracted the occupations of men between 17 and 55 years of age. This sample is identical with that required by the Militia Act of 1803.

Thus the information is directly comparable, and that taken from the 1851 census affords a check of the accuracy of the 1803 list.

THE RELIABILITY OF THE SOURCE MATERIAL

Since it is not possible to make a direct comparison between the 1803 list and a similar age group for the 1801 census, for no returns of ages were taken in that year, the reliability and completeness of the muster list were checked by comparison between the 1803 enrolled population and the 1801 census returns of male population. A similar comparison between the 1851 occupation sample and the total male population in that year has also been undertaken. Dispersion diagrams plotting for each township the proportion of (*a*) enrolled men in 1803 as related to the total male population in 1801 and (*b*) males 17 to 55 as related to total male population in the 1851 census, have been prepared (figure 7.1). The diagram relating the muster list to the 1801 census shows that while the extreme range of percentages is fairly wide (20·0 to 63·2), the central 50 per cent lies close to the median figure of 40·4 (between 35·1 and 44·2 per cent). The 1851 comparison gives a rather higher percentage sample: the median is 48·8 per cent, the interquartile range 45·9 to 53·0 per cent. In relation to total populations in 1801 and 1851, the percentages of the samples give medians of 19·6 and 25·4 respectively. This discrepancy of some 8 per cent between apparently similar samples is difficult to explain. Perhaps a higher proportion of these male age groups were enlisted in the Army and Navy in 1803 than in 1851, and so were not returned in the muster lists; perhaps there was some evasion of enrolment despite the heavy penalties laid down in the militia acts for this. But careful precautions were taken to cut down evasion to a minimum and these measures seem to have been generally effective. Fortescue (see Note 1 in References) does not anywhere suggest that the enrolment or muster of men from each parish as a preliminary to balloting for militia service was avoided. It was only after the ballot itself that evasion (by substitution, by payment of fines and other methods) to avoid actual militia service began. More fundamentally, the population structure would change in the half-century separating the two. This cannot be accurately checked because of the lack of information about population structure at the earlier date. But the greatest variations are found in those townships where the sample is smallest and where, consequently, relatively slight changes in age structure would have quite a marked effect.

The areal distribution of population density for both muster list and 1801 total and for 1851 sample and 1851 total have been plotted, using the same grades of shading. The densities for the 1803 map are one-fifth of those for 1801, a ratio closely related to the median of the percentages between the two for all townships (19·6). The relationship between sample and total for 1851 is one-quarter, closely related to a median of 25·4. There is a strikingly similarity in the patterns of distribution within each pair of maps (see figures 7.4–7.7).

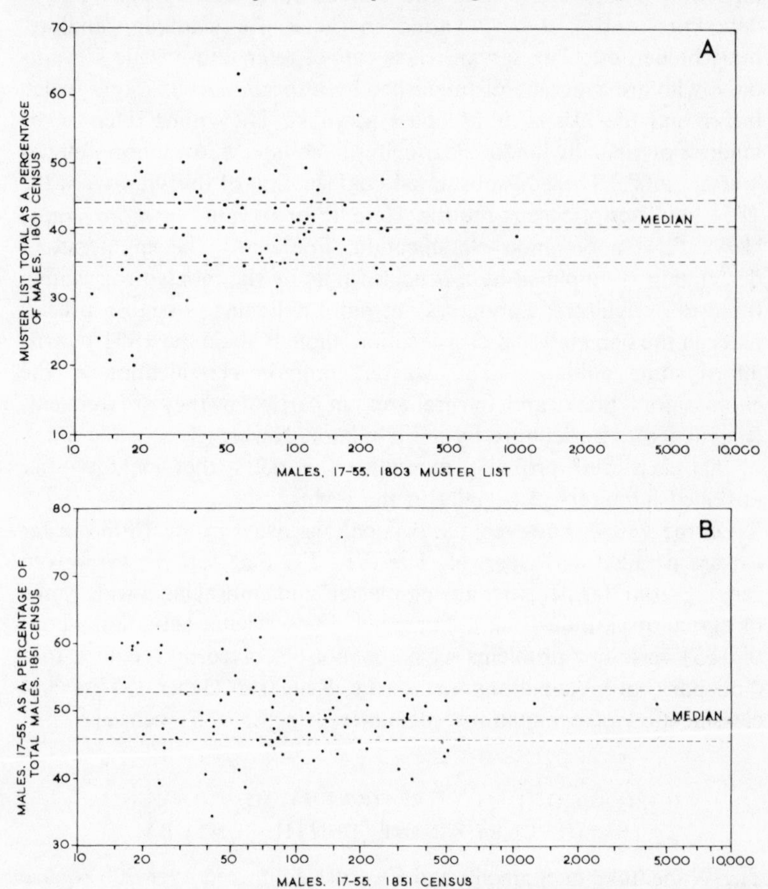

Fig. 7.1 Dispersion diagrams relating the sample analysed to total male population, 1803 and 1851. Each dispersion diagram shows individual values for each township by dots; quartile and median values are indicated by pecked lines. A logarithmic scale has been employed for the horizontal scale to facilitate accommodation of a wide range of figures

The detail and accuracy of the occupational descriptions, especially those of the muster list, are more difficult to assess, since they cannot be checked quantitatively. But the occupation column of the 1803 list is remarkably complete. Only 169 out of a total of 9027 (1·8 per cent) have no specific occupation given, most of whom have some explanatory remark; for example, 40 'apprentices', 83 'infirm'. More perplexing are the entries which cannot be assigned to any particular industrial group. These total 2057, made up of 652 'servants', 1146 'labourers' and 259 of a varied character, for example, landlord, householder, etc. The servant class cannot refer to domestic servants only, who are generally distinguished by a specific occupation – valet, butler and the like – or as house servants. They must refer to the landless or virtually landless agricultural labourer known more fully as 'outservants'.[5] There is substantial confirmation of this view from the 1851 manuscript census returns. Here 'farm servant', or more simply 'servant', is a common classification. Frequently the enumerator's description is amplified by a pencilled note by the tabulator assigning these to agriculture. Labourers are more difficult to assign a precise place in the occupational classification, though again the 1851 returns afford some guidance. This was a common classification in the enumerators' books and, in rural areas in particular, they are frequently assigned to agriculture by the tabulator. Nevertheless, while many of this class were probably agricultural workers, they include other unskilled labourers, especially in the towns.

On the whole, however, the occupations listed in the 1803 muster list are detailed and clear. No less than 237 occupations were given ranging from 'farmer' to 'dancing master' and embracing a wide range of agricultural, industrial, commercial and servicing activities. Those of 1851 raise few problems which cannot be solved by recourse to a dictionary of occupations or to the Registrar General's list and classification of occupations encountered in the 1851 census.[6]

THE ECONOMIC GEOGRAPHY OF CRAVEN IN THE EARLY NINETEENTH CENTURY

The Wapentake of Staincliff and Ewcross embraced over 700 square miles in the Craven region, an area then as now of marked geographical individuality. Contemporary agricultural writers with an appreciative eye for difference in country leave us in no doubt as to the distinctiveness of Craven. William Marshall described it as 'a fertile

Fig. 7.2 Craven: relief and drainage features. The 800-foot and 2000-foot contours are shown by pecked lines

corner cut off from the County of Lancaster . . . well cultivated and rich in soil'.[7] The distribution of population, both at the beginning and in the middle of the century, reflects generally the distribution of moorland and valley, although no detailed correlation with the physical map can be expected since township boundaries frequently cut across the grain of the country to take in both hill and valley within their area (figures 7.2–7.7). In the early nineteenth century the larger populations were to be found in the lowlands, notably in the

Fig. 7.3 The townships of the Wapentake of Staincliff and Ewcross in 1803

Aire and Ribble valleys and in the Ingleton corridor. Bowland Forest and the extensive uplands of Langstrothdale Chase, and the Howgill and Baugh Fells alike had a low population density, punctuated only by dale hamlets and market towns. The concentration in the Craven lowlands, especially in the Aire valley towns and villages around Keighley, was due partly to considerable industrial activity, chiefly in textiles, but elsewhere the basic physical factors were expressed in terms of agriculture: the map of population mirrors closely that of physique.

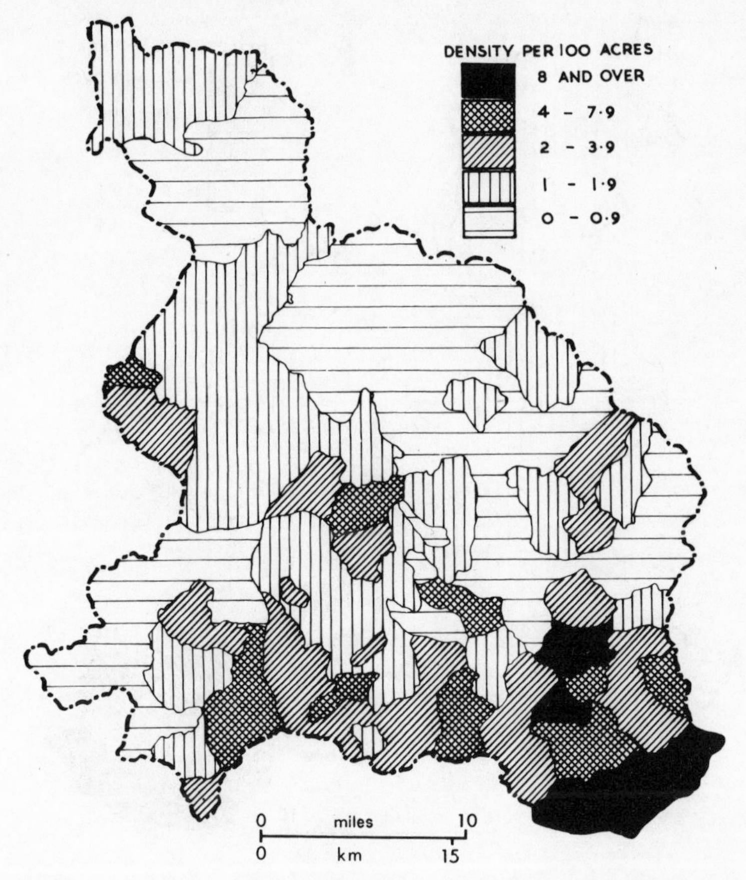

Fig. 7.4 The density of the male population (17–55 years), by townships, based on the muster list of 1803

By 1851 the relative pattern of distribution had not greatly changed, although there had been considerable growth in the townships of the Aire valley, in particular around Keighley. Complementary to this industrial growth in towns and large villages of the area, many purely rural townships showed little change, perhaps even decline, in total population – for example Thornton-in-Lonsdale and Arncliffe, in Littondale. But there are many others where the decline in numbers was not reflected in a lower density grouping. These two contrasting but complementary trends of urban growth and

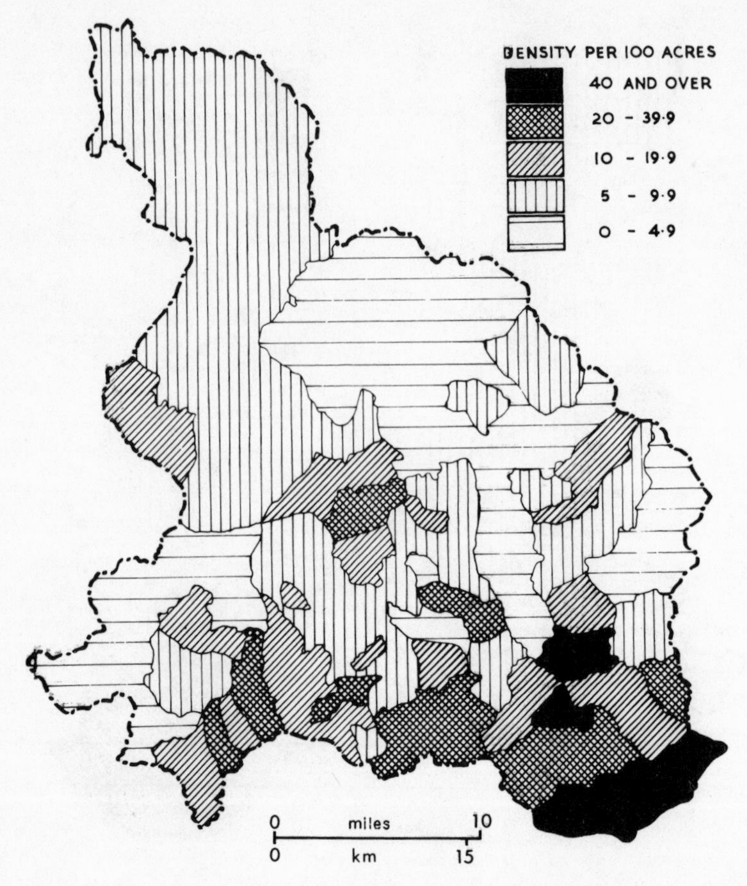

Fig. 7.5 The density of the total population, by townships, based on the census of Great Britain, 1801

rural decline are in common with population trends over much of Britain during this period.[8] The pattern presented in the sample extracted from the 1851 census is similar to that of the total population, and exhibits similar trends when compared with its counterpart from the 1803 muster list.

The maps of agricultural occupations display similar characteristics to those of the total population distribution, and the pattern of distribution is remarkably similar at both dates. With a few exceptions agriculture had kept its importance in 1851, though there were cases

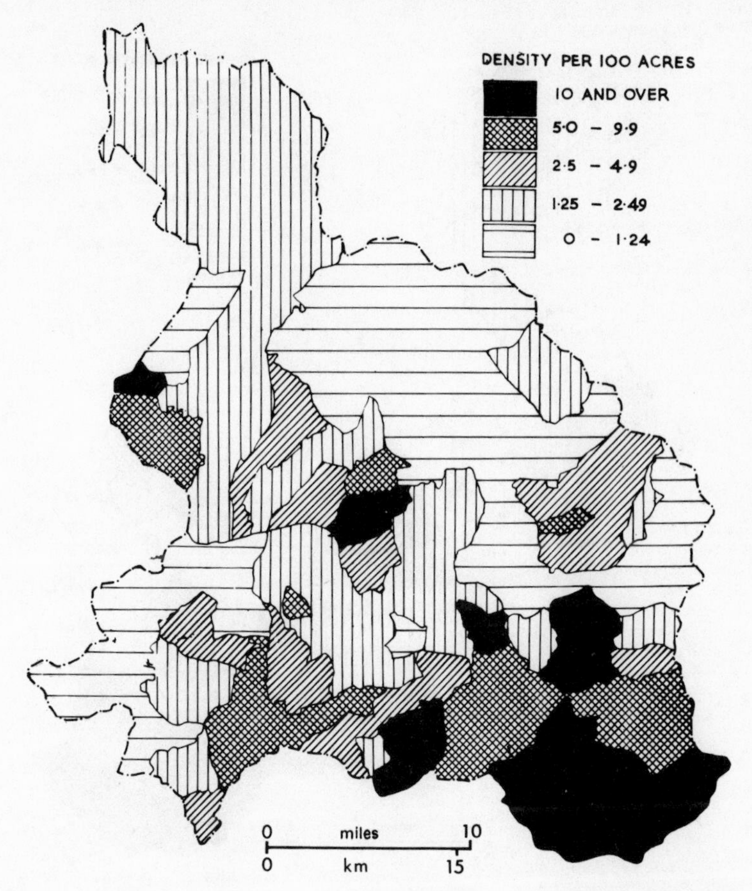

Fig. 7.6 The density of the male population (17–55 years), by townships, based on figures extracted from the enumerators' books, census of Great Britain, 1851

of decrease in numbers of agricultural workers in upper Airedale, upper Wharfedale and adjoining hill areas. Agricultural workers increased in areas where industry was growing very rapidly, though it is true that the proportion they formed of the whole population in such cases tended to fall (see figure 7.11). Thus in Keighley the totals were 213 and 408 in 1803 and 1851 respectively, but the proportion these form of the total sample fell from 23·0 to 9·0 per cent. Conversely, in many rural townships the proportion engaged in farming often increased with the decline in handicraft industry. Nevertheless it would

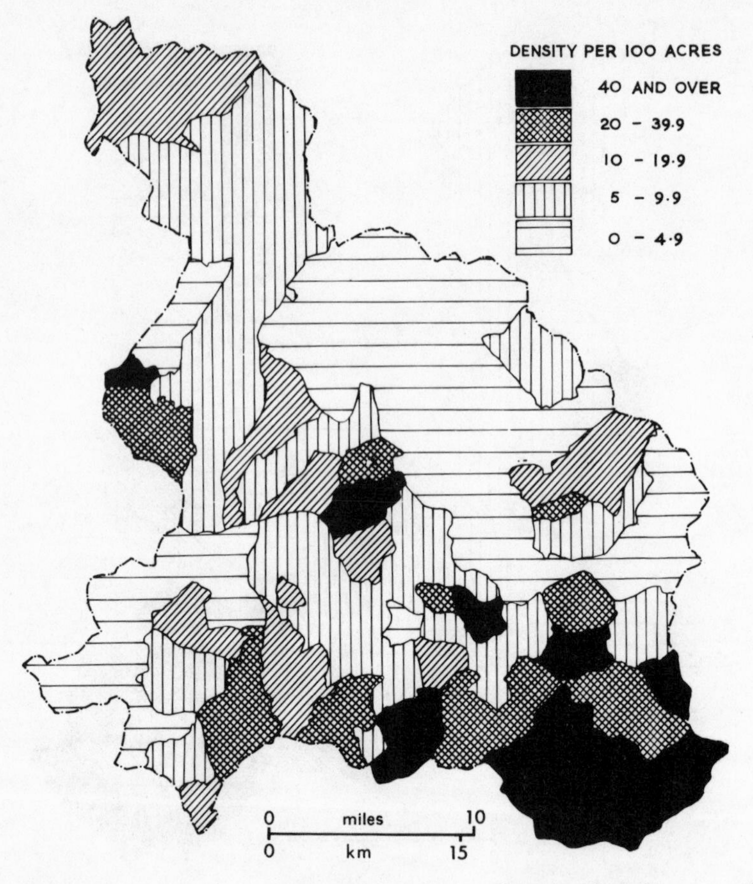

Fig. 7.7 The density of the total population, by townships, based on the census of Great Britain, 1851

seem from the density and distribution of agricultural workers that farming was *everywhere* relatively important. Indeed some contemporary agricultural writers maintained that manufactures were 'of material advantage towards promoting good husbandry'.[9] Unfortunately one cannot discuss to any great degree the *type* of agriculture followed from the occupational descriptions given: farmer, husbandman and yeoman are general terms in both the 1803 muster list and the 1851 census. In 1803 paid farm hands are described as servants or, more simply, labourers: in 1851 they are described as farm labourers (often only labourers) or farm servants (or servants). We know from agricultural writers in each period that the district was predominantly one of grassland farming.[10] Occasionally the mention of 'graziers', 'drovers', 'shepherds', 'cattle dealers' and like pastoral pursuits in both 1803 and 1851 returns point to a grassland stock economy.

This region had a long tradition of mining, principally of lead but also of small pockets of coal. Throughout the period in question lead mining and smelting were important in upper Wharfedale, notably at Kettlewell, Grassington, Hebden (where it was the chief single occupation) and Appletreewick (whose mines had been worked since the Middle Ages)[11] (figures 7.10 and 7.11). These were important alike in 1803 and 1851, but changes in lead working between the two dates are seen in the decline of lead mining in Littondale and the emergence of Cononley in the Aire valley. Coal mining was confined to the small pocket of coal measures preserved along the southern flank of the Craven Fault, especially at Ingleton and Garsdale. Quarrying was locally important in a number of townships and occasionally became of greater significance, as at the lime quarries of Embsay with Eastby.

The character of manufacturing was very varied, as the large range of industrial occupations testify, but in 1851 as in 1803 pride of place was held in most townships by the various textile industries. This was more true in 1803 than in 1851 for by the latter date there was a decline in certain rural townships where it had been mainly a handicraft, 'cottage' industry. Craven was, then as now, an area in which the main textile areas of the West Riding and east Lancashire met and inter-digitated. In 1803, the general distribution of all textile workers was a wide one with relative numbers not dissimilar from those of the total population (figure 7.8). Relatively few townships had no textile workers. To a degree each township had its weavers and the like, indicating a stage in development when the widespread nature of the textile industry had not yet been overthrown. But, beside this basic scatter, there was some concentration of activity, especially in townships of the Aire and Ribble valleys, nearer to the main cotton and wool textile areas. Outstanding among them was Keighley, easily the largest town in the Wapentake, with over half of its occupations concerned with the various textile trades, principally woollen and worsted manufactures. This Aire valley textile area extended upstream through the townships of Kildwick Parish to Skipton where it merged with the relatively unimportant Ribble valley area (for example, Rimington, Bradford, Waddington and Great Mitton).

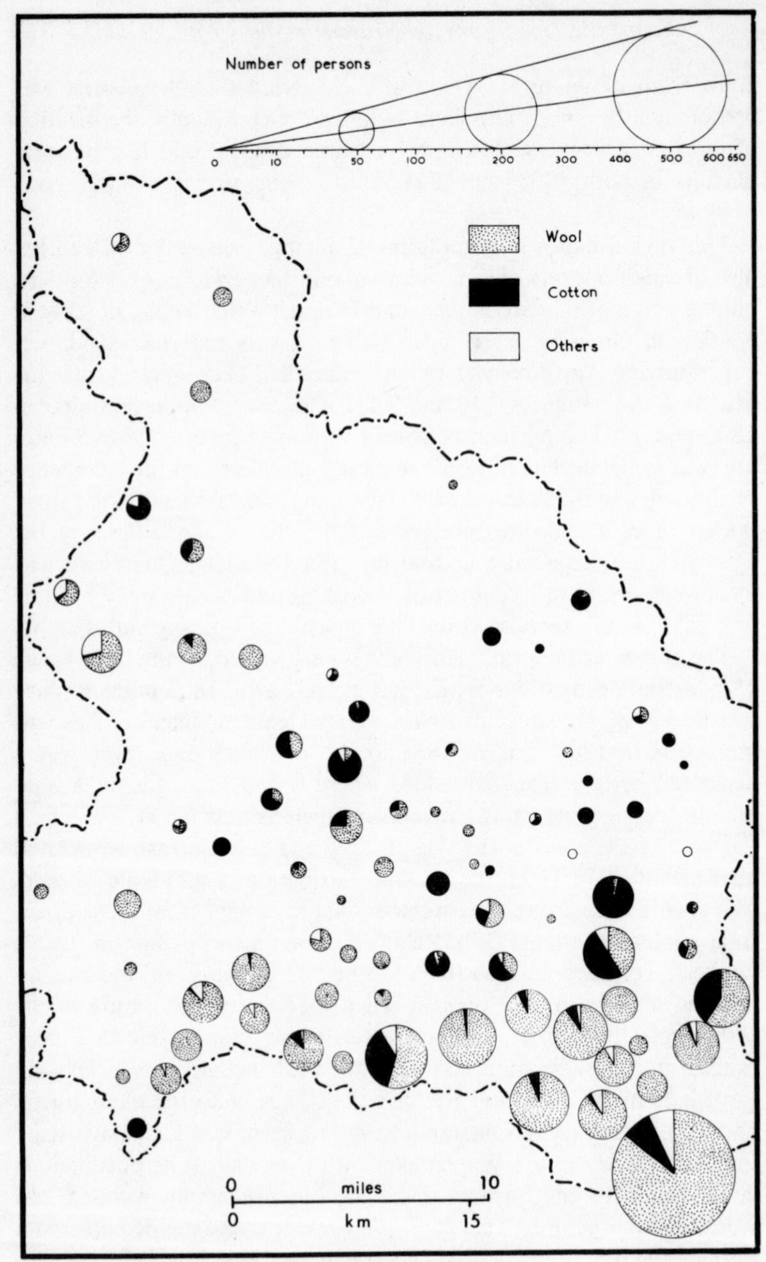

Fig. 7.8 Textile workers, 1803. The total number of textile workers listed in each township by the muster list is shown by a proportionate circle. The percentages engaged in particular textile industries are shaded as in the key

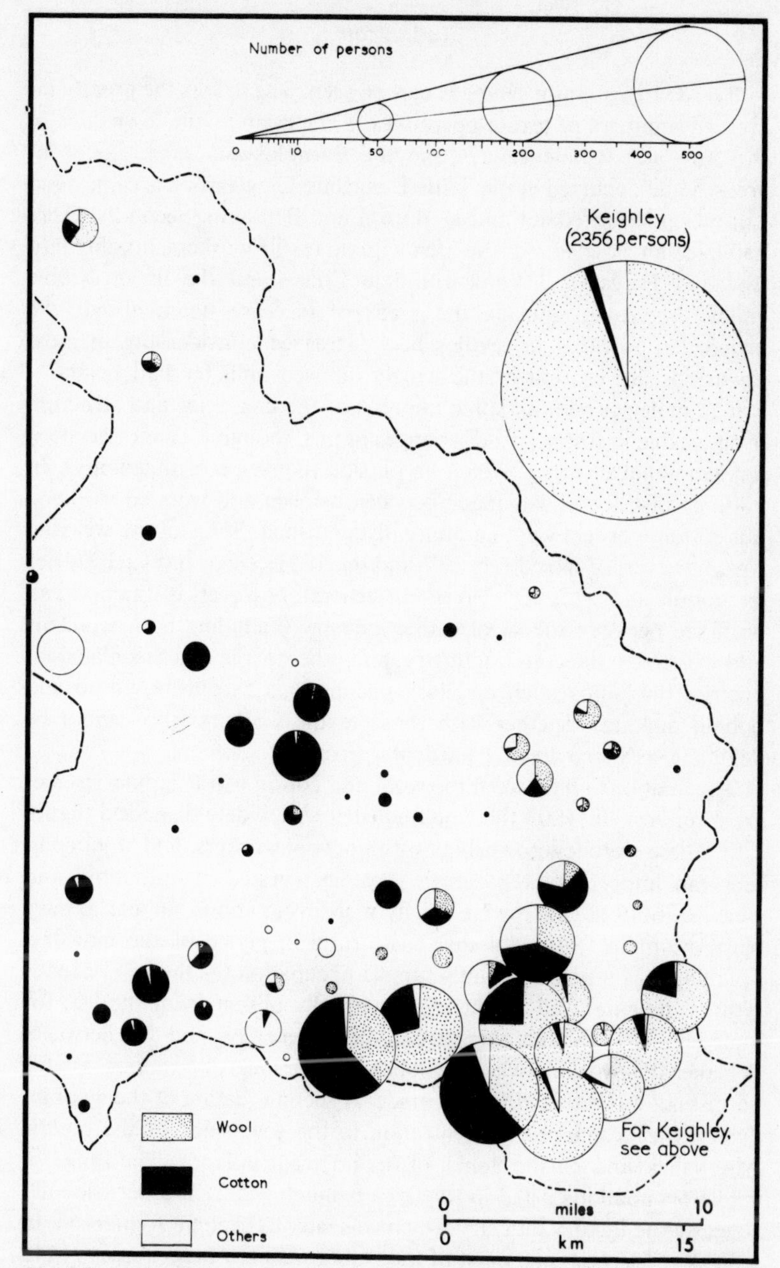

Fig. 7.9 Male textile workers, 1851. The number of male textile workers (17–55 years) listed in each township in the census enumerators' books is shown by a proportionate circle. The percentages engaged in particular textile industries are shaded as in the key

By 1851 two major changes can be seen. The first is the greatly increased numbers of textile operatives in the main textile townships of the Aire and Ribble valleys and the Barnoldswick area. Local increases had occurred in the Settle-Langcliffe-Giggleswick area, around Linton (in Wharfedale) and at Burton and Bentham. Secondly, there had been an extension of the area with no textile workers, notably into Bowland Forest and Langstrothdale Chase and the upper Ribble valley. Moreover, outside the areas of increase noted above, the proportion working in textiles had decreased considerably in most townships: an erosion of the widely diffused industry had begun.

The material permits some analysis of the character and structure of the textile industry and of changes in this, though it cannot account for locational changes (which lie outside the scope of this study). In 1803 no distinction was made between woollen and worsted workers, but cotton workers were carefully distinguished. Some of the weaving was, however, of mixed fabrics[12] and the 1851 census has such entries as 'cotton and worsted weaver'. In general, however, distinction can be made between the wool textile industry (including both woollens and worsteds), the cotton industry, and other textile and associated industries (including such ancillary occupations as dyeing, comb and bobbin making) together with those textile workers who cannot be definitely assigned to any particular group.

The relationship between the wool and cotton textile industries is of great interest. In 1803 the wool industry was widely dispersed (figure 7.8). There were few townships with no wool workers, and wool combing (an important preparatory stage in worsted manufacture) and weaving, both of which were chiefly male occupations, appear to have been the main feature of this basic rural dispersal of the industry. Spinning was a predominantly female occupation (as the 1851 census returns indicate) and is, therefore, virtually absent from the list, for male spinners, though there were such, were few and far between. Whether this weaving was of woollens or worsteds one cannot say, for no distinction of this kind was made. A second feature of the wool industry was a marked concentration in the townships of the middle Aire valley and on the flanks of the adjacent uplands. The range of textile occupations listed in this area is much wider, and occasionally suggests the factory industry which was later to become so marked. In Keighley, for example, most of the textile workers were weavers (446 out of 603), but others ranged from the preparatory processes (for example, wool combing) to the finishing processes (for example, dyeing). There are a number of 'manufacturers' and specific mention of a 'factory engineman'; perhaps we see the factory textile industry in process of development.

The cotton industry at this date displayed marked contrasts with the wool industry in character and distribution. The manufacturing unit was much more commonly the factory: cotton factory superintendents, cotton masters, cotton manufacturers and the like, are named in the list. Nor was there the same wide dispersal of manufacture. Many townships had no cotton workers listed. The chief areas of manufacture were concentrated into fewer townships, mainly along rivers, as around Skipton, in Barnoldswick, around Settle and in the Ribble valley township of Great Mitton. Over 30 years later in 1835, Baines showed that the cotton mills of Craven were mainly water-powered.[13] In those places where cotton was prominent, indeed sometimes dominant, mills were listed by Baines, for example, at Skipton, Addingham, Settle, Kettlewell and Grassington.

There were no areas of specifically cotton or wool textile manufacture but rather an overlap, especially in the Aire valley. Usually areas where cotton manufactures were important were precisely those areas where the textile industry as a whole was most active. Throughout Craven the emphasis was generally on wool, at least so far as the numbers of men employed were concerned, though locally cotton dominated. What their relative importance was in terms of men, women and children employed we cannot say from this evidence alone. The proportion of adult male workers to total workers does not, however, seem to have differed much as between cotton and wool manufacture according to the 1851 census.

By 1851 this picture had been substantially modified (figure 7.9). Although the textile industries were of much greater significance in the area taken as a whole, they had not increased substantially more than the sample of population considered. The total of males on the 1803 list was 9287 and in the 1851 sample 19,206: a difference of 105 per cent. The total of textile workers in 1803 was 2594 and in 1851, 5993: a difference of 131 per cent. The differences for wool and cotton were 99 and 132 per cent respectively. But because of the retreat of textile manufacture from some townships, this growth was concentrated into a smaller area. In 1851 there were more townships without any textile workers, notably in rural townships of scattered settlement where wool combing and weaving had been of some limited significance in 1803. There had been a decline in the Ribble valley townships between

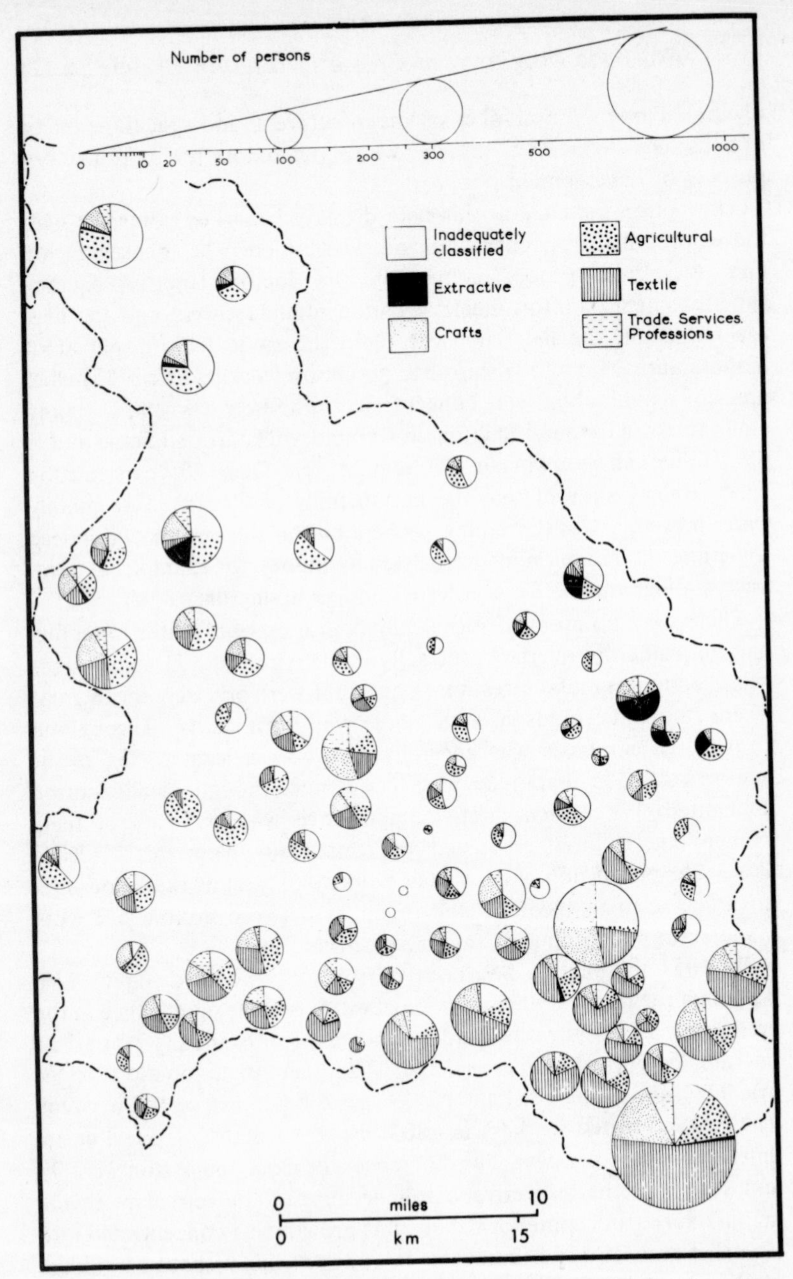

Fig. 7.10 The occupational structure of Craven townships, 1803, based on figures compiled from the 1803 muster list. The enumerated population of each township is shown by a proportionate circle except where the numbers are too small to allow clear reproduction. In a few such cases figures for adjoining townships are combined. The percentages engaged in particular groups of occupations are shaded as in the key

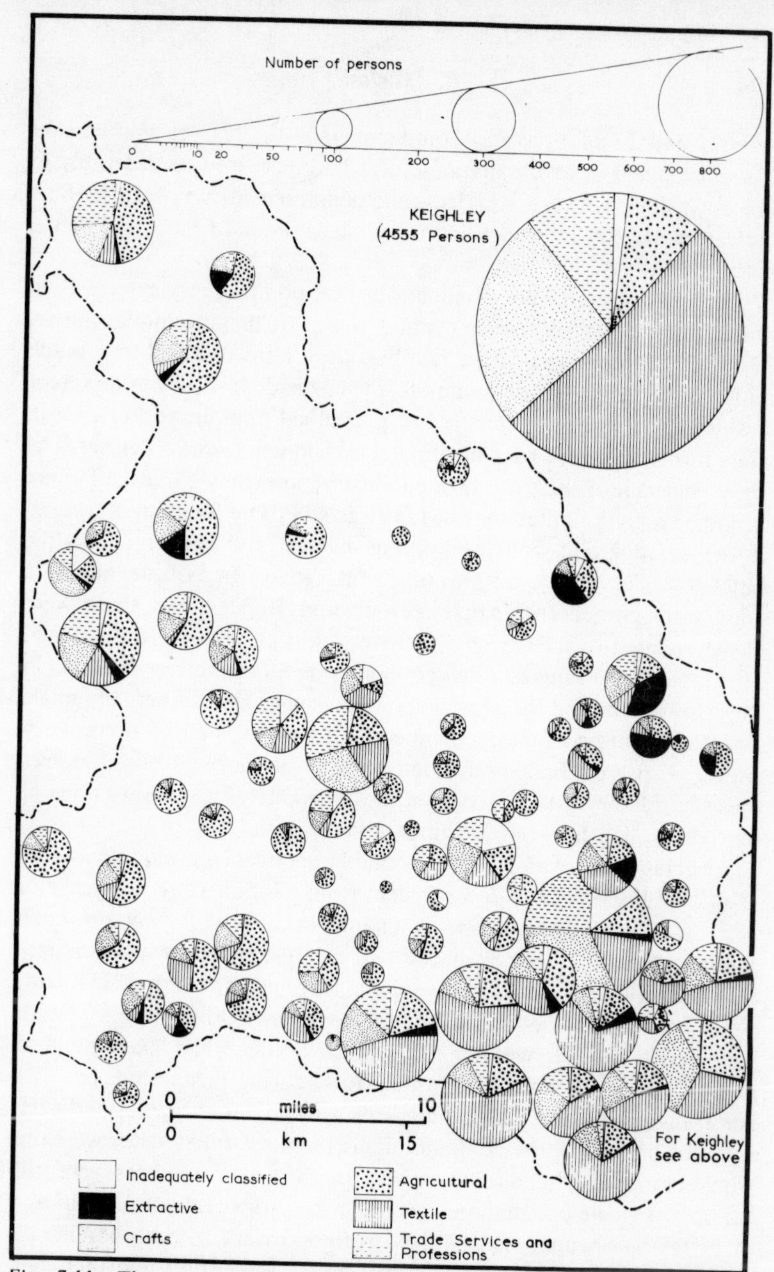

Fig. 7.11 The occupational structure of Craven townships, 1851, based on figures of the male population (17–55 years) extracted from the enumerators' books, census of Great Britain, 1851. The total males (17–55 years) in each township is shown by a proportionate circle except where the numbers are too small to allow clear reproduction. In a few such cases figures for adjoining townships are combined. The percentages engaged in particular groups of occupations are shaded as in the key

Mitton and Long Preston. Complementary to this the numbers of those occupied in textile manufactures had increased considerably in the townships between Keighley and Skipton and westward to Barnoldswick. Lesser increases had taken place around Linton and Settle, and in Bentham.

The changes were not confined to total numbers: the contrasts in distribution of wool workers stand out with diagrammatic clarity. Despite the doubling of their numbers they were confined to a much more limited area. In 1851 many townships had no wool workers. Nor is this explained by the sample being confined to male workers, for in such townships there were no female or child wool workers either. The rural dispersal of the wool textile industry, so prominent in 1803, had become severely limited by 1851. It was still to be found, it is true, as in the weaving and stocking knitting of Dent and Sedbergh. But the latter township also had its wool manufactories. In Wharfedale there were wool combers in Appletreewick and Hebden, but these were closely related to the worsted factory at Linton, as were the worsted weavers of Grassington. Power loom operators were prominent in these townships and the census shows considerable numbers of female and child worsted factory spinners. This conversion of a formerly widely dispersed handicraft industry into a more localised power operated factory industry is seen most strikingly in the townships of the Aire valley between Keighley and Skipton.

Keighley itself was the most notable centre of development. The growth of population – 218 per cent from 5745 in 1801 to 18,259 in 1851 in Keighley township – is mainly accounted for by the great growth of the textile industry, which had expanded proportionately with the growth of population and was as important in the 1851 sample (51·9 per cent) as in 1803 (54·0 per cent). Although this growth was mostly in the wool textile industry, there had been marked changes in its character and organisation during this period. In 1803 some suggestion of the beginnings of a mechanised factory industry could be noted, but the dominant figures in the wool industry were the wool comber and hand loom weaver. In 1851 wool combers were still the largest single occupational group in the sample (about one quarter of all textile occupations) as they were necessary to both handicraft and factory industry. Hand loom weavers were still important, but there were now very many power loom weavers. Moreover, in marginal notes the census enumerators gave details of the total numbers of workers employed by manufacturers. These show that nearly 58 per cent of the *total* population of Keighley were engaged in textile manufacture (compare nearly 52 per cent of the sample taken). Some of these worsted manufacturers employed large numbers; for example, Butterfields had 1413 hands, James Mitchell 1342 and John Craven 1350. Wool combing and hand loom weaving were predominantly adult male occupations. Not a few power looms were tended by women, and spinning and winding were mainly done by the women and children. Moreover, the change over from hand to power loom weaving had been less complete outside of Keighley town and in the older age groups. It is not uncommon to find whole families engaged in the worsted industry, the father as a hand loom weaver, his wife as a spinner and the sons (sometimes children) as power loom weavers. Outside the town a very substantial portion of textile occupations were in wool combing. Similar trends were exhibited by adjacent townships but in some less urbanised areas something of the old relationship between agriculture and the textile industries can be seen. Though by 1851 a considerable part of textile manufacturing was in factories, many farms in textile areas were small and the farmer's family (and 'lodgers') were textile workers. Moreover, dual occupations (for example, farmer and textile worker), formerly much more widespread, are still encountered.

The cotton industry did not show the same dramatic changes after 1803 as the wool industry. The most noticeable changes include the retreat of cotton manufacture from the Aire valley townships, where the growth of the wool industry had been so marked; the confirmation of the supremacy of cotton in and around Barnoldswick and Settle; the localisation of the cotton industry in Wharfedale, chiefly at Linton; and the growth of cotton manufacture to replace wool in the middle Ribble valley and, partially, in Dent, Garsdale and Sedbergh.

The bulk of this cotton industry was a power-driven factory industry,[14] but the unit of manufacture was much smaller than that of the worsted industry in and around Keighley; for example, in Barnoldswick mills employing 119 and 129 workers were noted by the enumerator. In many cases there is direct evidence of the use of steam power in these mills (for example, 'engine tenters' and 'steam power loom weavers'), as in Ingleton, in Settle-Langcliffe-Giggleswick and at Skipton. The division of labour in the industry was not dissimilar from that in the worsted factories. Weaving was the chief male occupation, with women and children important in spinning and winding.

Apart from the factory element in the textile industries most industrial occupations were of the craft type in 1851 as in 1803, though there were some changes in the variety and numbers of these in certain localities. In 1803, milling, baking, joinery and carpentery, smithing, tailoring, shoe making and the like all had a wide dispersal and point to the self-sufficiency of the rural township, even in Craven where townships frequently had small and scattered populations. A few examples will illustrate the characteristics of these craft industries.

Smithing was widely scattered in 1803. Most townships had one smith, and Keighley, with twelve, had the largest number. The smith's craft was one which, in a rural no less than an urban community, was in regular demand; in fact with the demands of agriculture it was often more so. There was no marked concentration beyond that stemming from the unequal distribution of population, though Grassington and Ingleton had a limited importance in this respect, perhaps because of their mining industries.

Milling had a similarly wide and scattered distribution, though limited by the need for water power to townships on the larger streams. Most townships had only one miller, in keeping with the small unit of the milling industry at this date, often consisting of a working master with one or two apprentices or assistants. Most millers were in the more thickly populated area in and around Keighley.

Shoe making and repairing formed one of the most widely dispersed and numerous of the crafts. Almost every township had its shoemaker, cordwainer or clogger. But while there was a basic dispersion of these crafts, considerable numbers were concentrated in the towns and larger villages, notably Settle, Giggleswick and Skipton. Possibly shoe making (as distinct from repairing) was stimulated by the greater orbit of market centres. In addition to its basic dispersal, tailoring also had a greater number of workers in the market towns and larger villages than their own populations warranted.

By 1851 these features relating to the character and distribution of craft industry had not been substantially modified. Milling and smithing were practised in 27 and 59 townships respectively (the same as in 1803), although in both cases there were substantial increases in the total numbers. There had been considerable increases in shoe making and tailoring, with shoemakers in 68 townships in 1851 (58 in 1803), and tailors in 56 townships (compared with 42).

In addition, there were certain local specialisms in 1851, such as paper making in Keighley, Skipton and Settle,[15] a pottery at Burton and nail making in Silsden. One of the notable features of this group of industrial occupations was the rapid growth of a class of mechanics and engineers closely related to power-driven textile industry, and to steam power in particular. From a handful of workers limited to eight townships in 1801, this group had grown to 353 by 1851 and was found in 22 townships, especially in Keighley.

These changes were not uniform throughout the area and there was a tendency for the greatest proportional increases to take place in the larger centres, particularly Keighley, though old-established market towns like Skipton and Settle continued to show most diversity from the point of view of the varied craft trades. They acted, and were to act increasingly, as local centres for certain products. As population in rural areas declined, the village craftsmen began to disappear, though in 1851 this was only beginning to be apparent, and then only in relation to the proportion these formed of the total population.[16] There was also some concentration of commercial, professional and servicing occupations in the towns, where they formed part of the amenities of the local market centre. Here their numbers were greater and the proportion they formed of the total population generally a higher one than in the area as a whole. This was most notable in places like Gargrave, Skipton, Giggleswick, Settle and Sedbergh, especially when these are considered beside a predominantly industrial town like Keighley.

One particular group of service workers, those employed in transport, increased considerably between 1803 and 1851, but in some townships a considerable part of this was due to the presence, in 1851, of workers engaged in railway construction: for example at Bentham (38), Skipton (35), Keighley (22), Giggleswick (22), Clapham (19), Hellifield (12), Long Preston (10) and Settle (10).

Figures 7.10 and 7.11 are an attempt to show the balance of the economy of each township in the area and to give a general picture of the region as a whole. The occupations have been reduced to six categories; inadequately classified (largely, in 1803, the servant-labourer group), agricultural, extractive industry, textile industries, other (mainly craft) industries, and a group including trade and commerce, services and professions.

The principal bases of the economic geography of Craven in 1803 were two-fold: agriculture and the textile industry (figure 7.10). These did not, however, display the separatism which developed between agriculture and industry during the later part of the nineteenth century: they interacted closely and were to be found alongside each other. A considerable proportion of agricultural workers were found in Keighley (the main textile township), while weavers were to be found in practically every rural township. Furthermore, there was a remarkably balanced economy in the majority of places. A wide range of crafts was practised, if not in each township, at least in small groups of townships throughout the area. Local self-sufficiency was still both a necessity and a reality. The occupational structure of a village was not necessarily dissimilar from that of a town, a characteristic true of much of England until the sweeping changes wrought in its economic structure during the nineteenth century.

Within the urban townships there were differences. Keighley, and adjoining townships like Sutton and Cowling, afford a contrast with older market centres like Skipton, Settle and Sedbergh. Keighley, with 54 per cent of the enumerated male population engaged in textile manufacture, had a much less varied character than the others, with proportionately fewer handicraft workers and workers in trade, commerce and transport, and in services and professions. In Skipton, Settle, Sedbergh and Bentham there were much higher proportions in the professions and services, in trade and in craft industry. Some of these other industrial occupations were related to local specialisms, such as paper making at Skipton, but in the main they were related to a wide range of crafts. Keighley, at this date, was much more than the others an industrial centre concentrating on a single main industry. The growing township of Barnoldswick was similar, with over 60 per cent of its occupations in textiles.

By 1851 the economy of such towns as Keighley and Barnoldswick had begun to broaden (figure 7.11). There had been a relative decline in agriculture, especially in Keighley, and a growth in trade, services and professions, and in industrial crafts other than textiles. It is true that some of these occupations were closely related to the textile industry, and had the census returns recorded industry rather than occupation they might well have been returned under textiles. A notable group in this respect in Keighley was the considerable number of mechanics and engineers (247 in all). There had been, moreover, considerable changes within the textile industry as a whole. Many townships in the now dominant textile area of the Aire valley had increased their proportion of textile workers, largely at the expense of agriculture. In the Ribble valley, on the other hand, despite some growth in cotton manufacture most townships were predominantly agricultural, more so even than in 1803. But Settle itself and the adjacent townships of Langcliffe and Giggleswick were exceptions. Settle had increased the proportion of its occupations in craft industry and in trade, services and professions. It was, like Skipton in the Aire valley, the principal market town of Ribblesdale and the Ingleton corridor. Similarly, in Wharfedale, Grassington showed a smaller proportion of agricultural and lead mining workers (though these were still dominant) and a corresponding increase in crafts and trades. Although agriculture was still the predominant occupational group in the dale townships of the Wenning, Greta and Dee valleys, the market towns themselves (Sedbergh, Dent, Burton and Bentham) show a relative increase in other occupations, especially in the craft occupations and in trade, services and professions. Sometimes this was due, in part, to particular local circumstances; thus the 'professional' class in Sedbergh was inflated by grammar school masters and senior pupils, and the industrial class in Burton by the pottery which employed thirty-one people from the sample. In general it appears that in towns and large villages occupations were growing in range and variety and giving rise to rather more diverse occupational structures. But many of the small agricultural townships of the Ribble valley, of Wharfedale and Littondale, and of the uplands were increasingly given over to agriculture and had suffered a decline in population in some cases.

The picture in this relatively small area is one of an economy in the process of change. Towns were growing, notably those associated with textile factory industry. They were acquiring a more significant range of occupations and functions, more like, though by no means so developed as, those of the old market towns which are relatively less dominant in this respect than they had been in 1801. Outside the towns agriculture was more dominant than previously, often in a reduced population. Nevertheless the wide range of occupations followed is still striking to the present day observer.

THE VALUE AND AVAILABILITY OF THE MATERIAL

The general value of this sort of material in relation to the wider question of the changing economy of England is clear. The muster lists of 1803 provide the raw material for detailed sample studies on which a general picture can be built up from regional examples. It is material well suited to precise cartographic analysis, and is of reasonable reliability (so far as can be ascertained) at a date some years before the detailed occupation returns of the censuses from 1841 onwards. These censuses provide from that date a source of comparative material, though we must go to the enumerators' books to extract occupations in the necessary detail for cartographical representation on a township basis. (See Note 4 in References.)

Unfortunately such muster lists are not generally available; we are dependent purely on local survival. Such records are to be sought in local collections and county archives. There is nothing of this type in the Public Record Office: the government was not interested in the raw material from which the militia was raised, but in the end-product, the militia regiments themselves.

SOURCE: *Transactions of the Institute of British Geographers,* No. 20, 1954. The original article has been specially revised by the author for this volume.

REFERENCES

1. For an account of this legislation see Hon. J. W. Fortescue, *The County Lieutenancies and the Army, 1803–1814* (1909), especially pp. 12–119.
2. For an account of the development of the Census of Population for Great Britain down to 1851, see *Census of Great Britain, 1851,* vol. I, Report, esp. lxix–lxxvi; and E. Wrigley (ed), *Nineteenth-Century Society,* Cambridge (1972).
3. See W. T. Jackman, *Transportation in Modern England* (1916), vol. II, p. 820. 'A Reproduction of Collins' Railway Map of England issued about the middle of the 19th century shows that the following lines serving Craven had been completed: (a) Leeds and Bradford-Keighley-Skipton-Lancaster (with a branch to Settle and thence to Lancaster via Hornby); (b) Preston-Blackburn-Skipton. In process of construction were (*i*) the Preston-Clitheroe-Settle-Kendal line, with a branch to (*ii*) Skipton and Askrigg.
4. The enumerators' books are subject to a one-hundred year confidentiality constraint. Since this study was originally written, in 1953, the 1861 and 1871 books have been added to the Public Records. The 1841 and 1851 enumerators' books are in the Home Office Papers (H.O. 107) and those for 1861 and 1871 in the Registrar General's Records (R.G. 9 and 10, respectively).
5. See Sir John Clapham, *A Concise Economic History of Britain,* Cambridge (1951), pp. 209–10: 'When statistical writers began to appear, late in the seventeenth century, they called the members of this agrarian proletariat 'outservants' (as opposed to male and female domestic servants), 'cottagers', or 'paupers'.
6. For a full discussion of such problems see W. A. Armstrong 'The use of information about occupation', pp. 191–310, in E. A. Wrigley (ed) *Nineteenth-Century Society* (Cambridge, 1972).
7. W. Marshall, *Rural Economy of Yorkshire* (1788), vol. I, pp. 2–3.

8. For a fuller geographical analysis, see R. Lawton, 'Population Changes in England and Wales in the Later Nineteenth Century: An analysis of trends by registration districts', *Transactions of the Institute of British Geographers*, XLIV (1968), pp. 55–74.
9. G. Rennie, R. Broun and J. Shirreff, *The agriculture of the West Riding of Yorkshire* (1794), p. 39.
10. Thus 'The management from Paitley-bridge to the western extremity of the county, is almost uniformly the same, and grass the sole object' (Rennie, Broun and Shirreff, op cit., p. 113). Again, Craven is 'an open and hilly country famous for breeding and feeding great numbers of cattle' (J. Aikin, *England delineated* (1800), pp. 59–60). See also the account of a mainly grazing area given by J. Charnock 'On the farming of Yorkshire', *Journal of the Royal Agricultural Society*, 1st series, ix (1849), 300.
11. *Victoria history of the county of Yorkshire*, vol. II (1912), p. 351.
12. Thus there is mention of the manufacture of 'shalloons, calimanoes and all sorts of double goods' at Skipton by Rennie, Broun and Shirreff, op. cit., appendix xi, p. 112.
13. He lists 44 mills in this area with an aggregate water horse-power of 459 and an aggregate steam horse-power of 196 (E. Baines, *History of the cotton manufacture in Great Britain* (1835), p. 387).
14. There were, in aggregate, more power loom than hand loom weavers enumerated in 1851.
15. See A. H. Shorter, *Papermaking in the British Isles*, Newton Abbot (1971).
16. For a fuller account, see W. M. Williams, *The Country Craftsman*, London (1958).

8 The Geographical Effects of The Laws of Settlement in Nottinghamshire:

an analysis of Francis Howell's report, 1848

D. R. MILLS

ON the whole, geographers have not paid much systematic attention to the influence of institutional factors on the evolution of settlement patterns. One exception is the reference by K. C. Edwards to the relationship between great houses and landscape features in the Dukeries.[1] Also in Nottinghamshire, his colleague J. D. Chambers was one of the first regional historians to relate social structure to enclosure history and poor law policy.[2] Enclosure history has long been of interest to geographers for its contribution to landscape evolution. On the other hand, poor law policy has been very largely overlooked. This is, therefore, an appropriate opportunity to bring forward some neglected evidence collected in Nottinghamshire by Francis Howell in 1848.

In the 1840s the poor law system was still adjusting to the tremendous changes brought about by the Poor Law Amendment Act of 1834, which had bound townships together in unions equipped with central workhouses. The townships, however, still remained financially responsible for their own poor. Moreover, Parliament's intention that the vast majority of destitute persons should be put in the workhouses failed to become a reality even in the 1840s. One reason for this failure was the fact that a labourer remained the financial responsibility of his native township, at least in theory, even if he settled permanently in a far distant part of the country. Thus, in two most important respects the 1834 Act left untouched the traditional way of administering poor relief.

The tradition that every person belonged to one place, which was responsible for his well-being, had grown up in the Middle Ages, when it was part of an insurance that the ploughs of a village would always have a ready supply of labour. As the economy became increasingly market oriented and industrialised, this tradition became a restriction on the necessary free movement of labour. The settlement laws of

For references to this chapter, see p. 191.

1662 were a formal recognition of the problem, in that they required townships exporting labourers to issue them with certificates promising maintenance in their home townships should they fall destitute in the places which received them. Thus mobility was permitted, but the theory of belonging remained in force. Unfortunately, good labourers were less likely than inefficient ones to be given the freedom to migrate. This is one of the reasons why there was large-scale evasion of the settlement laws. Indeed, as time went by it became easier to gain a new legal 'settlement' in a place other than one's native township.[3]

There was one way in particular of avoiding the tiresome business of recalling destitute persons to their 'home' township, which was known as 'non-resident relief'. In other words, it was cheaper to send money to the destitute to be spent where they were living. This was obviously not an easy procedure to administer with care. Moreover, it enabled a whole class of paupers to get relief without going to a workhouse, in defiance of the main provision of the 1834 Act. The Poor Law Board were naturally concerned to block the loophole and one of their first measures was to find out the total number of persons in receipt of non-resident relief on Lady Day, 1846. In the whole of England and Wales it came to the very substantial figure of 82,249.[4]

Thus we come to the immediate reason for Francis Howell's fieldwork: to investigate the effects of the Acts of 1846 and 1847. Sir James Graham's Act, following up the Lady Day tally, 'made persons who had been resident five years wholly irremovable; widows, resident when their husbands died, irremovable in the first twelve months of widowhood; and persons chargeable only through temporary sickness and accident irremovable'.[5]

After a period of confusion, during which it was decided that the Act had retrospective effect, there was a flood of applications for relief from persons who had hitherto held back, for fear of being removed to their 'home' township and thence to the workhouse.

As will be shown below, this flood did not affect all townships equally. The afflicted places set up a great outcry of injustice, which led to the passing of Bodkin's Act. This placed *on the unions* financial responsibility for the wandering poor and also the cost of relieving unsettled persons chargeable to the poor rate by virtue of sickness and accident.[6] This Act made the first breach in the principle of financing poor relief through township rates and it spread a fraction of the costs evenly on all townships, in proportion to their rateable value. But it was not sufficient to stem the complaints and Sir Charles Buller, President of the Poor Law Board, was now convinced of the need for an inquiry. Thus Howell and his colleagues were dispatched into the country.[7]

OPEN AND CLOSED VILLAGES

Earlier reports on poor law matters had already recorded a piece of terminology important at this point, i.e. the distinction between close and open townships. Close, or closed, townships were those in which one large proprietor, or a small number of large proprietors, controlled cottage accommodation in order to keep down the poor rates, which fell mainly on their own tenant farmers. Although rural population generally rose rapidly between about 1750 and 1850, the closed villages were often marked off from their neighbours by a relatively stable level of population. In some instances, houses were actually demolished to reduce the labouring population, for example at Ossington.[8] Moreover, the landlords and their tenants and bailiffs took precautions to remove 'bad characters' from their villages. Howell described how Lord Manvers cleared out a gang of burglars from Laxton by pulling down cottages; and reported the complaints of open villages that they were worried about the type of labourers who came to them, quite as much as the number.[9]

Open townships were those of mixed ownership, especially where the presence of a large number of small owners effectively prevented the imposition of a restrictive policy. These villages grew rapidly in the century up to 1850, with uncontrolled expansion of the labour force, both native and immigrant, in farming and often in domestic industries or coal mining. Some of the small proprietors willingly sold land for building purposes to small bricklayers and carpenters, who ran up mean tenements to let at high rents.[10] These stood in contrast to the modest but sound cottage accommodation in the closed (estate) villages, of which Perlethorpe and Budby are two of the best examples in Nottinghamshire. They are still worth a visit today.

As population pressure and poor law problems mounted, the plight of the open villages became quite remarkable. Sir James Graham's Act had caused a sudden increase in the already high poor rates in these villages. For example, in Radford the total expenditure on the poor went up from £1981 in 1844 to £5504 in 1848. At Sutton-in-Ashfield, during the first quarter of 1848, the overseers spent £698 on their own poor, £141 on the newly irremovable poor, and £125 on behalf of the union, under Mr Bodkin's Act of 1847. At Newark, it was reckoned that the Act of 1846 threw 100 to 120 extra families onto the parish.[11]

GEOGRAPHICAL ANALYSIS OF HOWELL'S DATA

In the course of his journeys round the county Howell recorded the status of about 125 villages, in terms of open or closed, either directly or by such strong implication that little doubt is left. The distribution of these places is shown in figure 8.1. He did not visit the entire territory of Nottinghamshire, the areas north of Retford and in the far south of the county being the principal exceptions. On the other hand, the shape of Poor Law Union boundaries led him occasionally into surrounding counties. Within the areas visited there are gaps in the record, the significance of which would concern local researchers, but they do not disturb the firmness of the general conclusions reached in this study. On the whole, it is reasonable to assume that Howell was more consistent in recording closed than open villages. After all, he was collecting information about places and proprietors who were shirking their responsibilities to the country. A comparison with Leicestershire also confirms this impression, for in that county closed villages were less numerous than open villages, while the list derived from Howell's report consists approximately of 50 per cent of each kind.

The implication of figure 8.1 is that virtually the whole of the county was affected by the operation of the laws of settlement in some way or other. Open and closed villages were to be found in all the major physical divisions of Nottinghamshire, and the coalfield, the hosiery and lace districts and even towns up to the size of Nottingham, were all caught up in the effects of this institutional factor. It is beyond the scope of this study to attempt to measure these effects, as compared with the effects of many other factors, such as the history of settlement, soil fertility, husbandry practices, the availability of raw materials, the impact of industrialisation on the region, demographic factors, transport networks and the distribution of land and capital among social classes. A comprehensive survey of mid-nineteenth century Leicestershire, however, indicates that the administration of the poor law, linked with patterns of land ownership, was a sufficiently important factor to demand attention in other parts of the country.[12]

In addition to his information on open and closed villages, Howell also reported on daily journeys between them, unfortunately without stating how many men were involved. From other evidence,[13] however, it is reasonable to assume that the numbers were significant

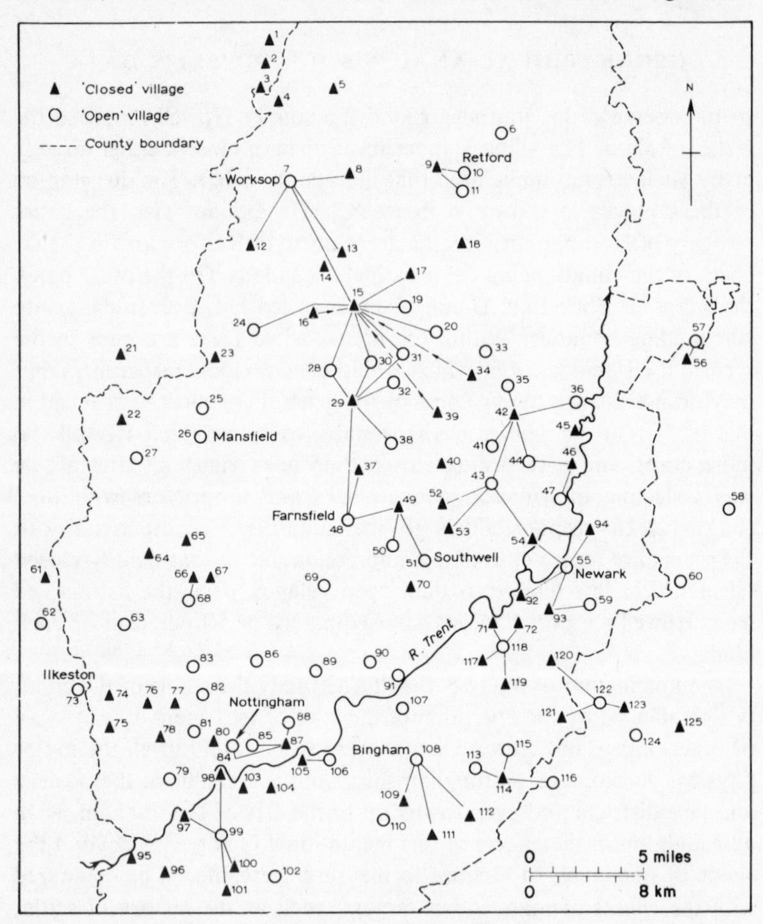

Fig. 8.1 Open and closed villages in Nottinghamshire, as classified in Howell's report (1848)

Notes: Closed villages printed in *italics* in the following list of places.
Nos. 16, 19 and 20 interpolated from *Stanhope's Report of 1867*.
The lines indicate daily movement of labourers from open villages to farms in closed villages.
The three arrows indicate the direction of movement in cases where Stanhope reported movement between pairs of villages both classified as closed villages by Howell (15, 16, 34, 39).
Budby (16) was one of the estate settlements for Thoresby Park (15).

(Fig. 8.1 continued on p. 187)

(Fig. 8.1 continued from p. 186)

No.	*Place*	
1	*Firbeck*	Yorkshire
2	*Letwell*	
3	*Gildingwells*	
4	*Wallingwells*	
5	*Hodsock*	
6	Clarborough	
7	Worksop	
8	*Osberton*	
9	*Babworth*	
10	East Retford	
11	Ordsall	
12	*Welbeck*	
13	*Clumber*	
14	Carburton	
15	*Thoresby Park* and *Perlethorpe*	
16	*Budby*	
17	Bothamsall	
18	*Gamston*	
19	Walesby	
20	Kirton	
21	*Glapwell* (Derbyshire)	
22	*Teversal*	
23	*Sookholme*	
24	Warsop	
25	Mansfield Woodhouse	
26	Mansfield	
27	Sutton-in-Ashfield	
28	Edwinstowe	
29	*Rufford Abbey*	
30	Ollerton	
31	Boughton	
32	Wellow	
33	Egmanton	
34	*Laxton*	
35	Moorhouse	
36	Sutton-on-Trent	
37	*Bilsthorpe*	
38	Eakring	
39	*Kneesall*	
40	*Maplebeck*	
41	Norwell Woodhouse	
42	*Ossington*	
43	Caunton	
44	Norwell	
45	*Carlton-on-Trent*	
46	*Cromwell*	
47	North Muskham	
48	Farnsfield	
49	*Kirklington*	
50	Halam	
51	Southwell	
52	*Winkburn*	
53	*Hockerton*	
54	*Kelham*	
55	Newark	
56	*Swinethorpe* (Lincolnshire)	
57	Harby	
58	Bassingham (Lincolnshire)	
59	Balderton	
60	Beckingham (Lincolnshire)	
61	*Codnor Park*	Derbyshire
62	Heanor	
63	Greasley	
64	*Annesley*	
65	*Newstead*	
66	*Linby*	
67	*Papplewick*	
68	Hucknall Torkard	
69	Oxton	
70	*Halloughton*	
71	*East Stoke*	
72	*Thorpe*	
73	Ilkeston (Derbyshire)	
74	*Cossall*	
75	*Trowell*	
76	*Strelley*	
77	*Bilborough*	
78	*Wollaton*	
79	Beeston	
80	*Nottingham Park*	
81	Radford	
82	Basford	
83	Bulwell	
84	Nottingham	
85	Sneinton	
86	Arnold	
87	*Colwick*	
88	Carlton	
89	Lambley	
90	Lowdham	
91	Caythorpe	
92	*Farndon*	
93	*Hawton*	
94	*Winthorpe*	
95	*Thrumpton*	
96	*Gotham*	
97	*Clifton*	
98	*Wilford*	
99	Ruddington	
100	*Bradmore*	
101	*Bunny*	
102	Keyworth	
103	*West Bridgford*	
104	*Gamston*	
105	*Holme Pierrepont*	
106	Radcliffe	
107	East Bridgford	
108	Bingham	
109	*Tythby*	
110	Cropwell Bishop	
111	Langar	
112	Granby	
113	Whatton	
114	*Elton*	
115	Orston	
116	Bottesford (Leicestershire)	
117	*Syerston*	
118	Elston	
119	*Sibthorpe*	
120	*Cotham*	
121	*Staunton*	
122	Long Bennington	Lincolnshire
123	*Westborough*	
124	Foston	
125	*Marston*	

Baston and *Lostford*, in Basford Union, not located; also St John's, in Worksop Union (possibly St John Throapham, in Laughton-en-le-Morthen, West Riding)

in relation to the total labour force. The patterns of movement shown on the maps indicate that a broad distinction can be made between the mainly industrial areas around Nottingham and Mansfield, on the one hand, and the largely agricultural remainder of the county on the other. The relative absence of movement around Nottingham cannot have been due to any lack of closed villages. There was, for example, a block of them lying to the west of the city (Nottingham Park, Wollaton, Bilborough, Strelley, Trowell and Cossall). We should also note that agricultural labourers went out each day from Nottingham, Sneinton and Carlton to the estate of Mr Masters at Colwick. In the district as a whole, however, the principal occupations were in coal mining and textiles, where the circumstances were different from those obtaining in agriculture.

In mining a large proportion of the capital came from landed proprietors and their lessees, who were in the habit of building cottage accommodation for miners near the pit-head. They took care not to allow this type of settlement into the central parts of their estates, where the great house, the park and the game lay undisturbed.[14] In the hosiery industry the capital came from the urban hosiers and the rural middle class, who were strongest in the open villages. As the industry grew it absorbed the natural increase of population in these villages. As it was excluded from the closed villages, it was inevitable that their population levels would remain relatively stable.[15] Thus mining villages drew on the surplus labour of the surrounding districts, the hosiery villages supported their own population by industrial expansion, and in the agricultural areas the demand for extra labour was often met by daily journeys to work. These are very broad generalisations, but they are supported by other evidence, especially by analysis of some 1851 enumerations in Leicestershire.[16]

The large proprietors and their tenants in the closed townships were much more aware of the burden of the poor rate than many of the tradesmen in open villages and towns, because it fell very heavily on agricultural property. What is more, they were able to do something about it. Despite the inconvenience of having a large part of their labour force resident at a distance from their farms, many proprietors and farmers held back from building cottages at the very time when the new methods in arable agriculture had increased the numbers of labourers required per unit area. The network of daily journeys to work in the agricultural districts will come as a surprise to many town-bound car-borne commuters of today. The morning movement was outwards from the market towns and big villages into the thinly populated large estates. Distances of up to six miles each way were not uncommon, mostly on foot, but sometimes on donkeys. The network was particularly well developed in certain parts of the Dukeries, where the new methods of farming had made it possible to exploit the light sandy soils on a much more intensive basis.

The maps may also be interpreted in terms of social networks. For example, men from Worksop worked on the Thoresby estate alongside men from Kneesall and Laxton, their homes being separated by a distance of 12 miles. Men who lived in Ollerton had a network of personal contacts stretching from Osberton in the north to Farnsfield and Southwell in the south. This is rather different from the townsman's traditional view of the rustic labourer, living and working in one spot all his life. News of good and bad employers would spread very quickly through these channels, which help to explain the relatively rapid turnover of the agricultural work force noticed by the writer in other investigations.[17] By comparison, the men who broke away from the land to become miners or stockingers could live stable lives in a much more self-contained community, usually a town or a large village.

ACTION FOLLOWING THE REPORTS OF 1848

Howell, of course, was chiefly concerned to establish the degree to which Sir James Graham's Act had placed an unfair burden on the open townships. Some places, such as East Retford, reported that they had been relieved by Mr Bodkin's Act and now had no complaints to make.[18] But majority opinion was in favour of a union rating for all poor law purposes. Other reporters passed up much the same message. Thus, in 1848 another Act added to the union's account all 'persons rendered irremovable by reason of five years' residence'.[19] This measure, supported by rising prosperity, satisfied public opinion, but it was not regarded as sufficient by a body of poor law specialists, who kept up pressure for fundamental changes. These came in the sixties when an Act of 1861 made three years instead of five the qualifying period for irremovability, and at the same time altered the principle of payment into a union by a township from one based on pauperism to one based on rateable value. In 1865 a further Act completed the process by making the union the sole unit of administration.[20] These Acts came at the height of the high farming period and, therefore, too late to prevent the operation of the settlement laws from having a long term influence on the distribution of population and the character of places. In the country areas many of the closed villages of 1848 have remained much smaller than their neighbours. The Park and West Bridgford are high quality residential areas today partly because of their earlier history as closed townships adjacent to Nottingham.

In a report written in 1867 the Hon. Edward Stanhope described the continuing movement of labourers each day to work on the Thoresby estate:

> Many of the servants and labourers immediately connected with the establishment, such as stablemen, porters, masons, carpenters, etc., live in the park and at Budby, about one mile from Thoresby; others come from Edwinstowe ($2\frac{3}{4}$ miles), Boughton (3), Walesby ($2\frac{3}{4}$), Kirton ($3\frac{1}{2}$), Ollerton ($2\frac{1}{2}$), Bothamsall ($2\frac{3}{4}$), Warsop (5), Laxton (6) and Kneesall (6). Those from the latter places take lodgings near at hand during the week at 3*d.* a night, and go home on Saturday night. Some of the others, and old men, have donkeys, which they are allowed to depasture in the park; as a matter of course, having to walk a long distance not only interferes with their work, but (to use a common expression) takes the steel out of them.[21]

It is interesting to notice that Laxton and Kneesall both had the characteristics of closed villages in Howell's day. Another change in status, this time the other way round, was recorded by Mellors,[22] when he described how the stockingers were turned out of Papplewick and Linby in the 1840s:

> At Linby the expulsion of the framework knitters caused a diminution of the population from 515 to 271. In other words, the poor were practically driven to live in Hucknall Torkard, and labourers and farm workers had to walk the distance night and morning.... Now look at the revenge Time brings. There was sixty years of occupation, and then the people are expelled, lest they should burden the land and lessen its value. Nearly all the parish [Papplewick] belonged to one owner, doubtless a very good landlord, and his will was, of course, paramount. Hucknall, on the other hand, was an open parish, with a number of freeholders, and there have always been the means of obtaining allotments, or of purchasing land. The value of the land continued to increase in Hucknall because of the growth of population and industry.
>
> For a rural walk, however, commend me to Papplewick....

SOURCE: *East Midland Geographer,* vol. 5, 1970.

REFERENCES

1. K. C. Edwards, *The land of Britain, part 60: Nottinghamshire* (1944), pp. 499–501.
2. J. D. Chambers, *Nottinghamshire in the eighteenth century* (1932, republished 1966, particularly pp. 142, 152, 168, 172, 266–7.
3. This passage is based mainly on: A. Redford, *Labour migration in England, 1800–1850* (1926); T. Mackay, *A history of the English poor law* (1899), especially vol. 3, pp. 340–64; and S. Webb and B. Webb, *English poor law history, part II: the last hundred years* (1929), especially pp. 419–34.
4. T. Mackay, op. cit., p. 350.
5. Ibid., p. 351. The Act was 9 and 10 Vic., c. 66, 1846.
6. Ibid., p. 352. The Act was 10 and 11 Vic., c. 110, 1847.
7. Their work is contained in *Reports to the Poor Law Board on the operation of the laws of settlement and removal of the poor,* presented to both Houses, 1850. There is a copy in Nottingham University Library. The reports also covered Suffolk, Norfolk, Essex, Reading Union of Berkshire, Surrey, Sussex, Dorset, Hampshire, Somerset, Bedfordshire, Berkshire, Buckinghamshire, Oxfordshire and Northumberland. Mr P. Grey of Bedford College of Education is working on Bedfordshire and Mr J. Walton of the University of Keele on Oxfordshire.
8. Ibid., p. 132.
9. Ibid., p. 130–1.
10. Ibid., p. 129.
11. Ibid., p. 126, 138–9. It is interesting to notice that 1847 was the only year in which there was a nationwide collection of parochial data on poor rates: *Return showing population, annual value of property, expenditure, rate in the pound, total number of paupers relieved* (B.P.P., 1847–8), 735, LIII, 11.
12. D. R. Mills, *Landownership and rural population with special reference to Leicestershire in the mid-nineteenth century,* unpublished Ph.D. thesis, University of Leicester, 1963; and D. R. Mills, 'Has historical geography changed?', in Open University, *New Trends in Geography,* IV, Unit 14 (1972) pp. 58–77.
13. J. A. Sheppard, 'East Yorkshire's agricultural labour force in the mid-nineteenth century', *Agr. Hist. Rev.,* 9 (1961), 43–54.
14. Based on fieldwork and D. R. Mills, op. cit.
15. D. R. Mills, op. cit., and D. M. Smith, 'The British hosiery industry at the middle of the nineteenth century', *Trans. Inst. Br. Geogrs.,* 32 (1963), 131–6.
16. C. T. Smith, Population, *Victoria County History of Leicestershire,* III (1955), p. 151.
17. D. R. Mills, op. cit.; investigations into family history; the records of hiring fairs; and in novels of the period, especially those of Thomas Hardy.
18. Howell's Report, p. 142.
19. T. Mackay, op. cit., p. 354. The Act was 11 and 12 Vic., c. 110, 1848.
20. T. Mackay, op. cit., p. 355–6. These Acts were 24 and 25 Vic., c. 55, 1861; and the Union Chargeability Act, 28 and 29 Vic., c. 79, 1865.
21. *Commission on the employment of children, young persons and women in agriculture* (B.P.P., 1868), appendix to part 1 of the first report.
22. R. Mellors, *In and about Nottinghamshire* (Nottingham, 1908), pp. 326–7.

Part Three
Mobility

9 Rural Depopulation in Nineteenth Century England

R. LAWTON

MUCH of the population growth in the rapidly expanding towns and industrial regions of nineteenth century England was initially promoted by migration from rural areas (Redford, 1926). Later, population in these industrial areas was largely self-sustaining, a youthful population structure contributing to a high rate of natural growth, but the increasing proportion of Englishmen who were town-dwellers also pointed to the draining of population from the countryside (table 9.1).

Table 9.1 Urban and rural populations in England and Wales, 1801–1971

	Population (in millions)			Percentage	
	Total	Urban	Rural	Urban	Rural
1801	8·9	3·1	5·8	34·8	65·2
1811	10·2	3·7	6·4	36·4	63·6
1821	12·0	4·7	7·3	39·2	60·8
1831	13·9	5·9	8·0	42·5	57·5
1841	15·9	7·3	8·6	45·9	54·1
1851	17·9	9·0	8·9	50·2	49·8
1861	20·1	11·0	9·1	54·6	45·4
1871	22·7	14·0	8·7	61·8	38·2
1881	26·0	17·6	8·3	67·9	32·1
1891	29·0	20·9	8·1	72·0	28·0
1901	32·5	25·1	7·5	77·0	23·0
1911	36·1	28·2	7·9	78·1	21·9
1921	37·9	30·0	7·9	79·3	20·7
1931	40·0	32·0	8·0	80·0	20·0
1939	41·5	34·2	7·3	82·4	17·6
1951	43·8	35·3	8·4	80·8	19·2
1961	46·1	36·8	9·2	80·0	20·0
1971	48·6	38·0	10·6	78·2	21·8

Based on estimates from the censuses for 1801–41, places recorded as towns in the censuses for 1851–71, and, for 1881 onwards, for Rural and Urban Sanitary Districts then Rural Districts and Urban Districts, County and Municipal Boroughs. 1939 figures are Registrar General's estimates.

For references to this chapter, see p. 218.

In the last hundred years population has grown only in those rural areas where the extension of urban influences has created adventitious population, living in the countryside but working in the town (Stevens, 1946; Vince, 1953). The earliest phases of this flight from the countryside are obscured by lack of precise demographic data. In the late eighteenth and early nineteenth centuries much of the rural increment was retained; the increased demand for farm labour in newly enclosed and reclaimed land alike more than compensated for local losses due to the extinction of small farms and removal of landless labourers (Johnson, 1905). In many areas, especially those far from the large labour markets, the effect of the old Poor Law was to retain population in the countryside, especially in the 'open' villages which were the source of much agricultural labour and later of farm gang labour (Hasbach, 1908; Mills, 1959; see also above, Chapters 2 and 8). In addition, increasing employment in craft industry, workshop and mine gave diversity to the rural economy of many parts of an industrialised countryside (Clapham, 1939; Lawton, 1954).

Thus, a peak of population growth was reached in 1811–21 in England and Wales, and this was also, almost without exception, the decade of greatest increase throughout the rural areas (Williams, 1880). But by the early railway age rural populations were, at best, growing slowly. The proportion of urban dwellers exceeded rural in 1851, even in the conservative understatement of the census, and the numbers of rural population declined absolutely as well as relatively after 1861. Thus, from the mid-nineteenth century, population in many rural areas was decreasing while all were suffering heavy losses by migration. P. A. Graham (1892), noted 'The country parishes are doing more . . . than merely sending their surplus inhabitants to town, they are being depleted', and also commented that 'the movement is confined to no one locality, but is to be observed in every agricultural district which lies remote from towns'. The general decline of rural populations in Europe after 1851 was analysed by G. B. Longstaff (1893) who, by a study of rural districts in the corn growing counties of Essex, Suffolk and Norfolk and in the grazing counties of the south-west, showed that in England quite different types of farming were equally affected.

In summarising these trends T. A. Welton (1900) commented on the uniformity of losses among the 'rural residues' of the population. In a subsequent analysis using Welton's method A. K. Cairncross (1938–9, 1949 and 1953) showed that aggregate rural losses were remarkably general and constant throughout the period 1841–1901 but fell in many areas between 1901 and 1911, partly in response to dilution of rural populations under spreading urban influences, partly due to the arrest of the prolonged agricultural decline of the 1870s to the 1890s.

Table 9.2 Net migration in towns, colliery districts and rural residues of England and Wales, 1841–1911

	Net gain (+) or loss (–) in thousands							
	1841–1851	1851–1861	1861–1871	1871–1881	1881–1891	1891–1901	1901–1911	Total
Towns	+660	+517	+533	+605	+138	+521	–321	+2652
Colliery districts	+83	+103	+91	+84	+90	+85	+114	+651
Rural residues	–443	–743	–683	–837	–845	–660	–295	–4507
(*a*) northern	–159	–229	–254	–263	–349	–237	–152	–1644
(*b*) southern	–284	–513	–430	–574	–496	–423	–142	–2863
England and Wales	+300	–122	–60	–148	–617	–54	–502	–1204

Based on A. K. Cairncross (1953).

The 'northern' rural residues are for Wales, Hereford, Salop, Stafford, Warwick, Worcester, Leicester, Nottingham, Derby, Cheshire, Lancashire, Yorkshire, Durham, Northumberland, Westmorland and Cumberland; the 'southern' rural residues are for the remaining rural counties of England.

The substantial total net gain, 1841–51 is due largely to immigration from Ireland during and after the potato famine.

THE FRAMEWORK OF ANALYSIS

Not all contemporary observers were agreed upon the degree of depopulation. Confusion often arose because of the difficulty of defining rural population from census data, and also from analysing trends for overgeneralised administrative units. Thus, in his controversial discussion of 'alleged depopulations' in rural England, W. Ogle (1889) drew an overoptimistic picture largely because he discussed the problem for county units from which only the towns of over 10,000 inhabitants were excluded. Ogle also argued that the term 'depopulation' should be reserved for those districts where numbers were 'diminishing absolutely' and should not include areas of relative decline due to loss of population by migration.

Fortunately it is possible to compare total, natural and migrational components of population changes in England and Wales from 1841 by using census tabulations for Registration Districts of births, deaths and changes in total numbers, from which may be derived figures of net migration. The Registration Districts, though far from homogeneous in size, are small enough to permit reasonably detailed regional analysis. Created under the Civil Registration Act of 1837 from the Poor Law Unions of 1834, the principle followed in rural areas had been to group parishes around a market town (Lipman, 1949). Though they all contained some urban element, in many country districts the town was small and shared the fortunes and reflected the population trends of the surrounding area. Nevertheless, near industrial areas rapidly growing populations were by mid-century spilling over into adjacent rural Registration Districts and new towns were still returned under the historic centre on which their District was based, as with Middlesbrough in Guisborough Registration District and Barrow in Ulverston. Thus it is impossible to analyse total, natural and migrational trends in which urban and rural elements may be clearly separated. Even when the basis of enumeration of births, deaths and net migration was changed in the 1921 census to local authority areas (County Borough, and Urban and Rural District), the same basic problem of definition remained.

G. B. Longstaff had drawn attention to the problem of those who 'though *in* the country are not *of* it' and sought to remedy the difficulty by excluding urban population, though he noted that many of the smaller country towns were part of the 'rural organism'. Welton (1900) sought to remove urban populations from his analysis by excluding towns of over 1000 in 1801. A. L. Bowley (1914) considered that the problem could be resolved in three ways: by using administrative units; by analysing occupational structure; or by density. His view was that the index of density was the most practicable and stringent test and he concluded that most Rural Districts with a population of under 0·3 persons per acre could be regarded as truly rural. The results obtained by applying the method to Registration Districts may be compared with Welton's formula (table 9.3).

In the discussion following his paper Bowley's definition met with general approval, but it raises a number of difficulties. Adapting the method to the Registration Districts of 1911, it can be shown that despite nearly halving of the proportion of rural population as defined by administrative areas (table 9.1), there were many districts in which the residual rural population at the critical density of 30 per 100 acres accounted for less than half of the total population of the District (figure 9.1). Many such districts could claim to be 'urbanised' to some degree, for example in West Cumberland, south-eastern Northumberland, Cleveland, much of the West Midlands, the Home Counties and the Weald.

Table 9.3 Rural population in England and Wales, 1841–1911

	After Welton (1900, 1911, 1913)[1]		After Bowley (1914)[2]	
	No. in 000s	Per cent	No. in 000s	Per cent
1841	5783	32·6	—	—
1851	5919	33·1	—	—
1861	5845	29·0	4939	24·5
1871	5856	25·8	4936	21·7
1881	5668	21·8	4764	18·3
1891	5534	19·1	4625	15·9
1901	(6611	20·3)	4454	13·7
1911	(6961	19·3)	4581	12·7

[1] Welton's figures are based on the exclusion of places over 1000 in 1801 for the figures to 1891; the definition adopted for 1901 and 1911 is less stringent.
[2] Bowley's definition (1914) is based on the more stringent test of excluding areas with a density over 30 per 100 acres.

Other methods, based on an analysis of occupations, were used by S. W. E. Vince (1955) to define rural population. His general conclusion was that the primary rural population (that engaged in agriculture, horticulture and forestry) has formed a steadily diminishing proportion of the total rural population in modern times, and that in the nineteenth century it fell from an estimated half in 1831 to about one-third of the total rural population in 1911. The primary rural areas, with over 40 per cent of their population engaged in primary pursuits, agree broadly with Bowley's rural areas as defined by population density, though in both low density and high density areas the proportions of primary population suggest the need to take account of both criteria. Mrs Isobel M. L. Robertson (1961) has shown that truly rural areas have diminished and are now confined to a few regions remote from large cities, occasionally in intensively farmed cash crop areas (for example, the Fenland), but more commonly in thinly peopled marginal farming regions such as mid-Wales, south-western England and the northern Pennines. Her conclusion was that by 1951 'three out of four Rural Districts are rural-urban' and that 'As an instrument for study of purely rural population, the Census . . . is insufficient', a sentiment which the student of nineteenth century population would endorse.

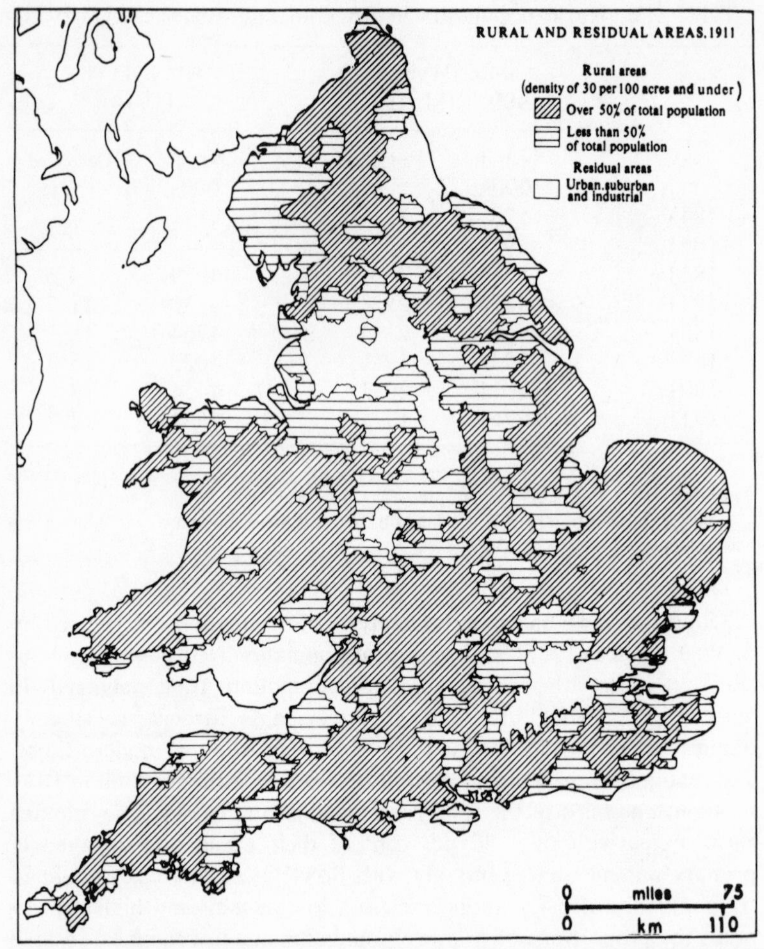

Fig. 9.1 Rural and residual areas, 1911. Registration districts are classified as rural or residual by population density. Based on Bowley (1914), Appendix II. *and the* Census of England and Wales, 1911

RURAL POPULATION TRENDS, 1801–1911

Despite the difficulties of defining rural and urban Registration Districts, these provide the only reasonably detailed territorial framework for a discussion of components of population change in England and Wales in the nineteenth century. First used by the Census in 1851, in which population totals were reclassified for Registra-

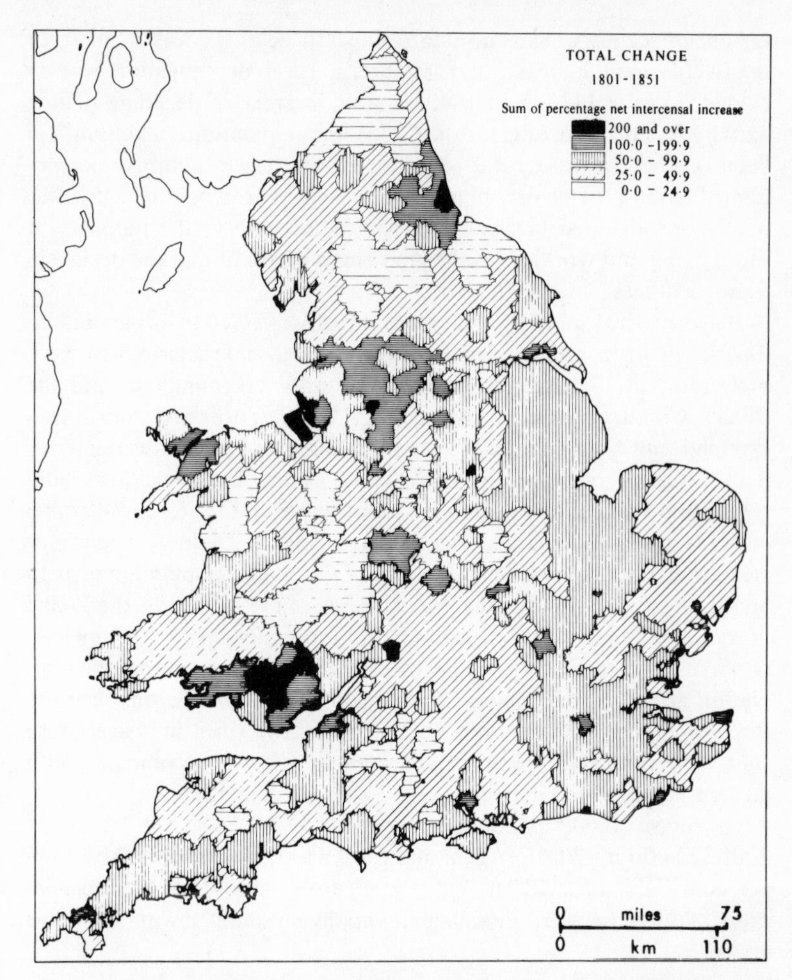

Fig. 9.2 Population change in England and Wales, 1801–51. The figures mapped for Registration Districts are the summation of the total percentage change in each census decade. Based on the Census of Great Britain, 1851

tion Districts, the amount of change due to natural and, by calculation, net migrational components are available for the period 1841–1911.

Total change

In common with national trends, the peak increase of population occurred in most rural areas between 1811 and 1821. While the early nineteenth century, like the late eighteenth century, was a phase of relatively rapid increase in rural areas, rural depopulation was in evidence in the 1830s and 1840s mainly in areas of declining mining activity in northern England. By 1851 the population maximum had been reached in most rural parishes and decline in numbers accompanied by large scale out-migration followed. The census of 1851 thus marks a watershed between a phase of increase in the numbers of those living and working on the land and a phase of marked decline in these numbers.

Between 1801 and 1851 the areas directly affected by urban and industrial growth were limited in extent, though characterised by very high rates of increase, especially in London, Birmingham and the Black Country, South Lancashire, West Yorkshire, north-east England and South Wales (figure 9.2). But there were also relatively high rates of increase in many rural areas. Late enclosure and reclamation and conversion to arable of wasteland led to considerable increases of population in the Fenland and the light soil lands of eastern and southern England. On the other hand, population growth had been slow in some of the grassy shires of the Midlands, the Welsh border and south-western England, and especially slow in the uplands of Wales and northern England which had failed to maintain the population growth and agricultural expansion of the prosperous years of the early nineteenth century. In aggregate, the rural increases were shared by both farming areas and country towns: as compared with an aggregate national increase of 74·9 per cent between 1801–51, towns over 20,000 population grew by 117·2 per cent, towns of 2000–20,000 by 70·0 per cent and rural areas of under 2000 by 52·9 per cent (Williams, 1880). But, significantly, after 1841 the decadal rates of increase were diminishing rapidly in small towns and rural areas.

Between 1851 and 1911 the sum of total decadal changes shows a loss of population in a large belt of country extending from East Anglia to south-west England, in almost the whole of Wales (outside the coalfields) and in the northern Pennines, East Yorkshire and the Vale of York (figure 9.3). These widespread losses generally began in the decade 1851–61 and continued, though intermittently in places, until 1901 (Welton, 1900; Bowley, 1914). Only around the large towns and industrial areas was the effect of rural decline offset by higher wages and better markets, especially for market garden and dairy products, factors which helped to keep labour on the land and to retain secondary population. In addition, close to the towns there were growing numbers of 'adventitious' population who commuted to work but lived in 'rural' areas. Over these areas the 'penumbra of the towns', as Bowley described it, fell more widely as time went on (figure 9.1). After 1901, though the fall of population was arrested in many rural parishes, it continued in the remote areas of Wales, the south-

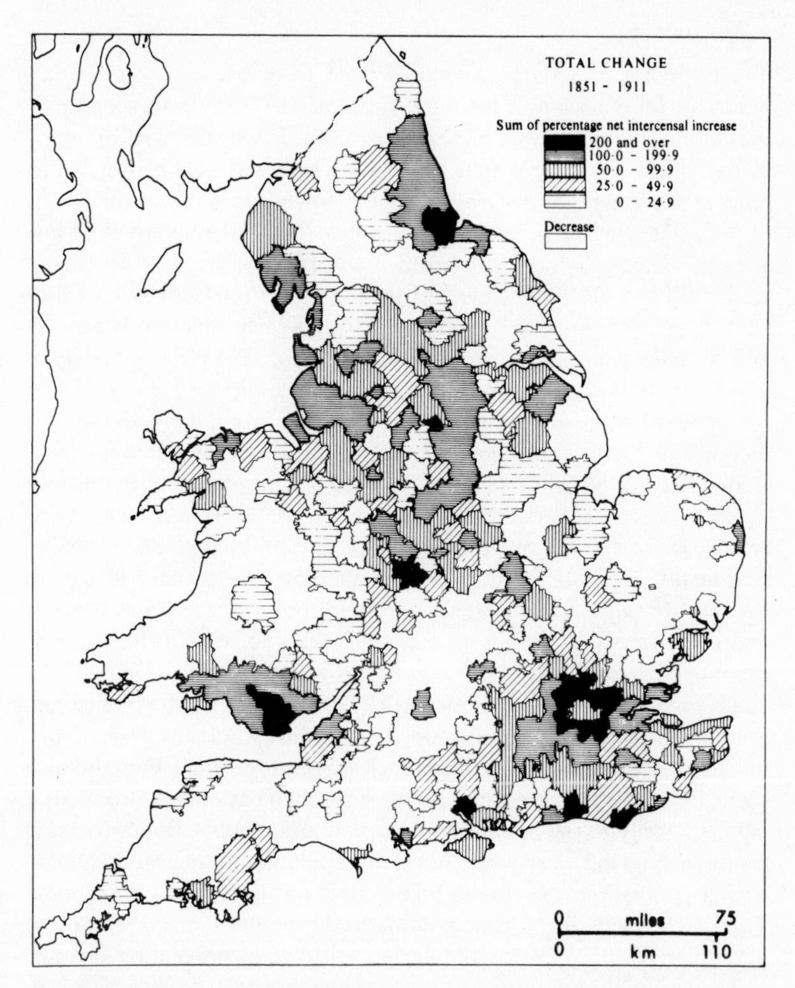

Fig. 9.3 Population change in England and Wales, 1851–1911. The figures mapped are the summation of total percentage change in each census decade. Based on the censuses of England and Wales, 1861–1911

west and the Pennines which were most dependent on primary activities. Elsewhere, partly because of the upswing in the fortunes of farming, more because of the closer linking of town and country through the growth of suburbs arising out of fuller use of tramways and railways, rural decline was arrested, though the fall in the primary population continued.

Natural change

The estimates of natural change derived from baptisms and burials made by John Rickman for the Census of 1831 are too uncertain to permit a reliable analysis of regional trends. It was believed by many in the 1820s and 1830s that the countryside was losing some of its natural increment by migration to the towns. Equally, prior to the railway age, surplus labour and a good deal of underemployment and seasonal unemployment existed in many rural areas. The settlement clauses of the old Poor Law and the system of out-door relief which became general in many rural areas in the early nineteenth century helped to keep labour in the villages (Hasbach, 1908). The diversity of employment in local craft trades and the handicraft basis of much manufacturing industry gave strength to the rural economy despite the increase in factory production powered by water and steam.

In the early years of civil registration the record of births in particular was severely defective. Cairncross (1938–9) considers it unreliable before 1841, but the figures of natural change are probably reasonably accurate from 1851. The increase due to natural growth between 1851 and 1911 was greatest in the manufacturing districts and large towns, especially in areas of rapid recent suburban growth around greater London and in fast growing industrial areas in the coalfields of South Wales and north-east England, in Merseyside and South Lancashire, on Humberside, in the East Midlands and the Birmingham area (figure 9.4). But much of rural, lowland England also had natural growth rates only a little below the national figure of 80·1 per cent. Only in the upland regions of Wales, and south-western and northern England were early losses of population by migration and an ageing population reflected in relatively low rates of natural increase. Thus, while regional variations in natural growth existed, they do not in themselves account for the variations in total population change.

The regional variations in birth and death rates in nineteenth century Britain have yet to be analysed. High natural increases in the towns were largely the result of high birth rates, in turn the outcome of a youthful age structure. However, these were offset by relatively high death rates (Farr, 1885). Francis Galton long ago pointed out that 'the population of towns decays and has to be recruited by immigrants from the country' (Galton, 1873). From a study of labouring population in urban and rural areas of Warwickshire he concluded that 'the

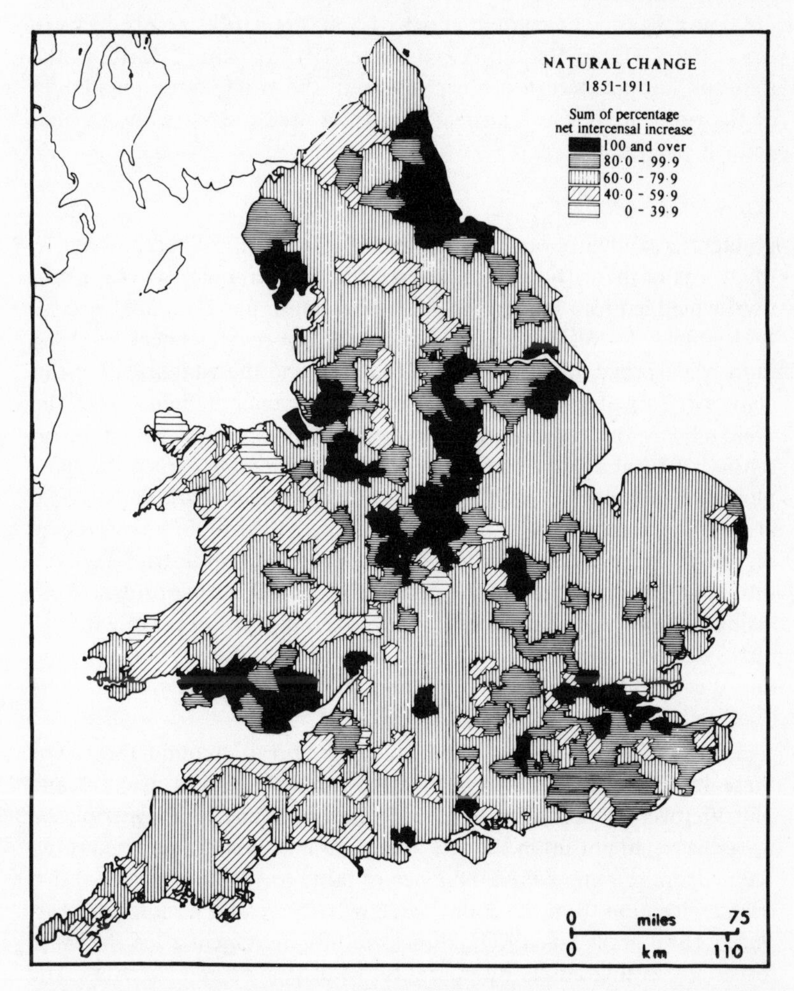

Fig. 9.4 Natural change in England and Wales, 1851–1911. The figures mapped are the summation of percentage natural change (i.e. the balance between births and deaths) in each census decade. Based on the censuses of England and Wales, 1851–1911

rate of supply in towns to the next adult generation is only 77 per cent . . . of that in the country'. The same conclusion was reached by the Land Enquiry Committee of 1913 which showed that the corrected death rate for urban counties was about 16½ per thousand as compared with 12½ in rural counties, much of which was due to higher infant and child mortality in cities where crude death rates were 4¾ per 1000 at ages 0–5, as compared with 4 and 3 per 1000, respectively, in the country (Land Enquiry Committee, 1913, p. xli). Clearly, in the mid and late nineteenth century, much of the young adult population of the rural areas was transferred to the towns, taking with it a high growth potential.

Migrational changes

Numerous contemporary writers testify to the drift of rural labour to the towns in the early nineteenth century. The 'complex wavelike motion' which led to a redistribution of population has been analysed by A. Redford (1926). But this movement did not reach its peak until the more widespread concentration of industry and the vital link of cheap transport forged by the railway permitted greater mobility from the 1840s. From this time, all observers – even those who disputed the intensity of rural depopulation in Victorian England – agreed that surplus rural labour was moving to the towns and industrial areas. The areas of aggregate gain by migration between 1851 and 1911 were few (figure 9.5), and concentrated upon urban and industrial regions, though in the latter part of the period the central areas of towns were losing population to the suburbs. Moreover, in some areas of early industrialisation, particularly in East Lancashire, West Yorkshire and the West Midlands, there were migrational losses from the 1860s (Cairncross, 1953).

The chief areas of loss were, however, rural. Around the towns these losses were small, movement towards the towns in early and mid-Victorian times being replaced later by gains as the peripheral areas were caught up in the late Victorian and Edwardian expansion. Away from the immediate influence of large towns and industrial districts, migration from the countryside was severe and prolonged. Most purely rural areas failed to hold their natural increment after 1851 and lost many young adults by migration to the towns and overseas. The enumerators' notes in the mid-nineteenth century censuses reveal the widespread incidence of this early flight from the land (Smith, 1951). Heavy losses continued until 1901, though movement to industrial areas in Britain was replaced to some degree by emigration in periods of economic depression such as 1881–91 (Cairncross, 1953). Overseas emigration was largely balanced by immigration from Ireland, Scotland and, in the later nineteenth century, from Europe. In aggregate there was a slight net migrational loss of population from

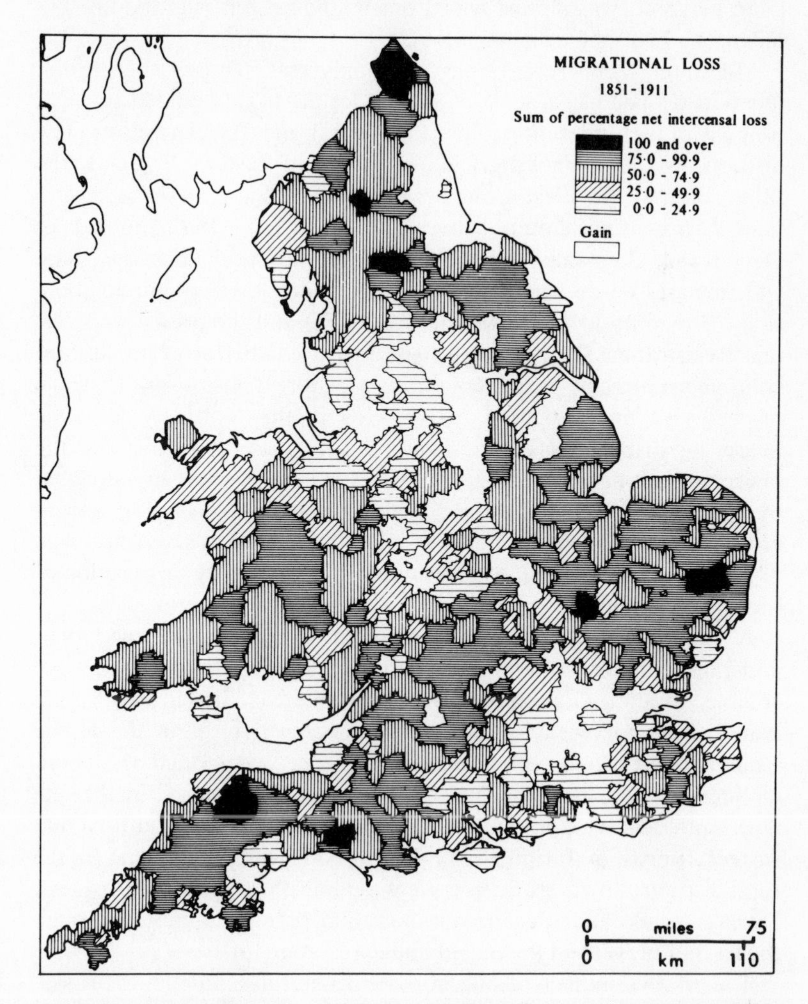

Fig. 9.5 Migrational losses in England and Wales, 1851–1911. The figures mapped are the summation of percentage net migrational change (i.e. the differences between natural and total change) in each census decade. Based on the censuses of England and Wales, 1851–1911

England and Wales of 6·6 per cent (1·21 million) between 1851 and 1911. Most immigrants, however, went to the towns while many emigrants were from the rural areas. In aggregate, total numbers of people in the rural residues defined by Welton (1911) virtually stagnated (+12·9 per cent), and a natural increment of 5·3 million (+86 per cent) was almost wiped out by the net out-migration of 4·5 million (–73·2 per cent) (table 9.2).

Migration from rural areas was universal. Those Registration Districts defined as rural by A. R. Bowley (1914) are related strongly to areas of high migrational loss (figures 9.1 and 9.5). There were few districts in the mainly agricultural areas of eastern England, the Midlands and the West Country where migrational losses were less than 1 per cent per annum between 1851 and 1911. In the uplands of Devon and Cornwall, mid-Wales and the northern Pennines, there was similarly severe depopulation, despite much lower population densities. Proximity to towns (notably London) and the presence in certain Registration Districts of urban growth points (for example, Lincoln and Grimsby in Lincoln and Caistor Registration Districts respectively) or of mining activity (as in the North Wales slate quarrying districts) offset agricultural losses and accounts for the lower migrational loss encountered in northern districts as tabulated by Cairncross (1953). But the conclusion must be that distance from growth points was more important than the quality of soil or the type of farming in accounting for variations in the intensity or duration of loss of population.

A summary of decadal trends in migration between 1851 and 1911 underlines this conclusion (figure 9.6). The areas of constant gain were confined to a few city regions and industrial areas, though trends fluctuated. Loss followed by gain was general where, as in the Home Counties and Sussex, metropolitan influences penetrated the countryside or where new industrial development took place in the late nineteenth century (for example, the East Midlands, the southern and eastern fringes of Birmingham, Humberside and Tees-side). In the rural districts, however, the picture was almost universally one of loss. During decade after decade out-migration reduced numbers, though the level of movement fluctuated and eased after 1901.

The relative impact of migration and natural components of population change may be summarised by following the method outlined by J. W. Webb (1963). Figure 9.7, on which four types of trend are shown, is based on the summation of total, natural and migrational components of population between 1851 and 1911. Areas of gain in which natural increase is combined with net in-migration (types 1 and 2) are confined to a limited number of highly urbanised and industrialised regions. In many areas natural gains were partly offset by net out-migration, particularly in the central areas of conurbations and in declining industrial areas. But in many rural districts around

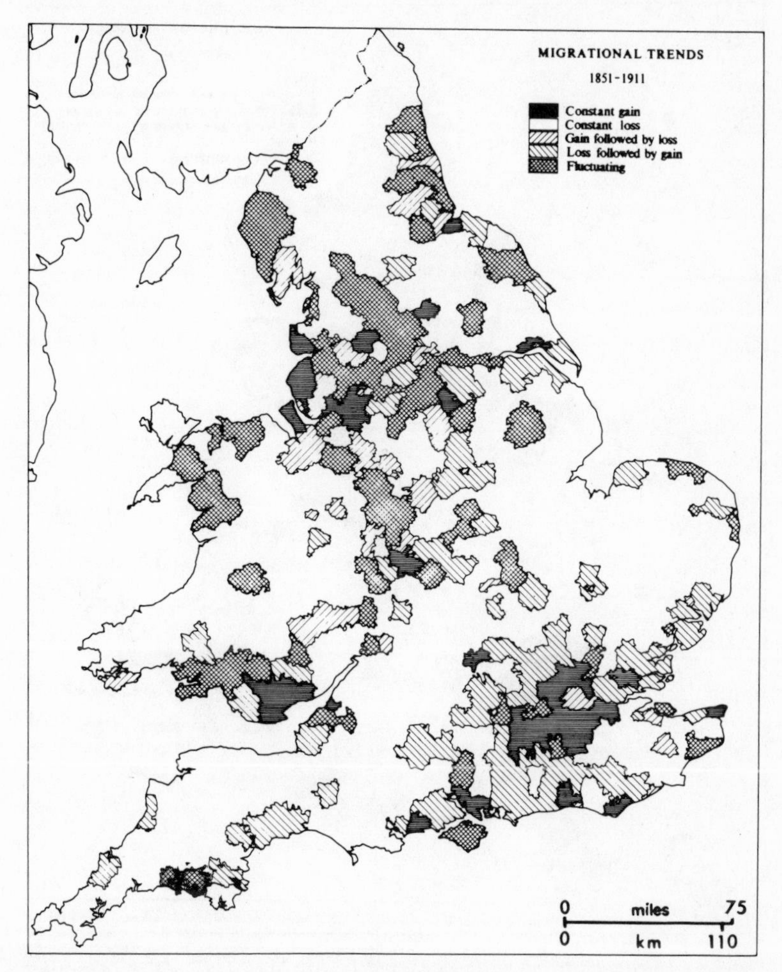

Fig. 9.6 Trends in migration in England and Wales, 1851–1911. The categories relate to the trends over the census decades 1851–1911, regardless of the amount of net migration involved. Based on the censuses of England and Wales, 1851–1911

the towns, decreases in primary population were more than offset by overspill from the towns, especially in the late nineteenth century. A few prosperous agricultural districts like the Fenland which had retained primary population also increased in population though they shared in the migration of population from the countryside. The most common trend was that of continuous population decline in the rural

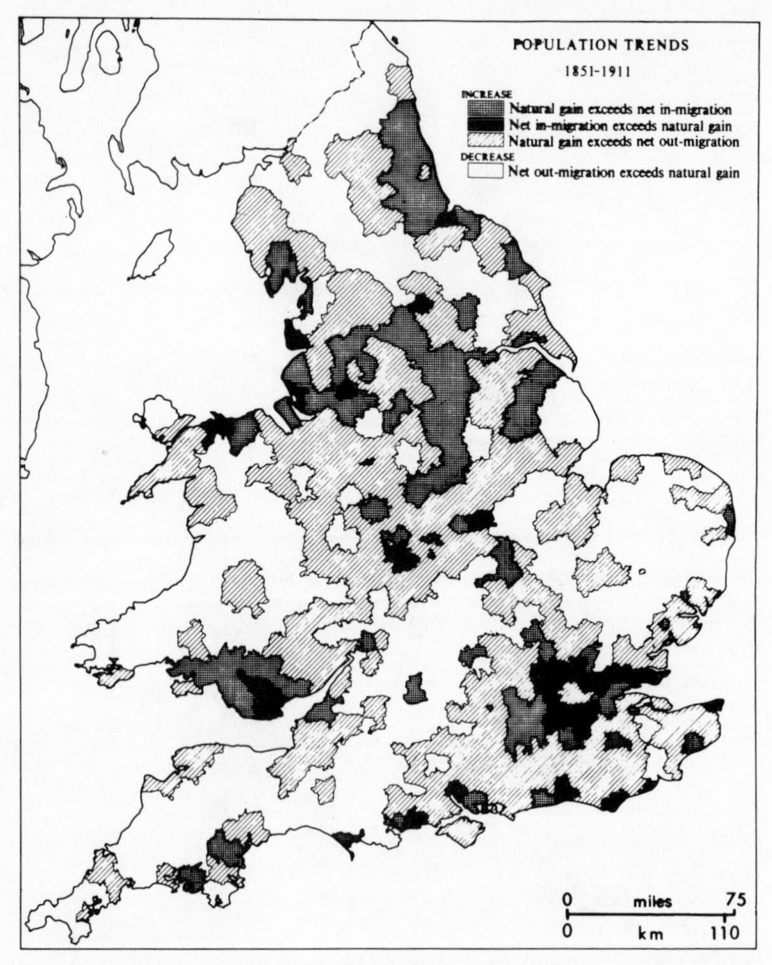

Fig. 9.7 Population trends in England and Wales, 1851–1911. Areas of increase and decrease are shown and the relationship of natural change to net migration indicated. Based on the censuses of England and Wales, 1851–1911, following a method used by Webb (1963)

areas, where a fall in total numbers between 1851 and 1911 was due almost entirely to heavy and continuous out-migration.

P. M. Roxby (1912) argued that rural depopulation, though general after 1851, was not uniform, varying in intensity from one type of farming region to another. He suggested that depopulation was heavier in clayland arable districts, lesser in lightland arable areas, and least in areas of fruit production and market gardening. But his examples were limited and, while the changes in total numbers of population in the sample areas suggested variations in the rate of decline, the figures of net migration loss for the Registration Districts in which they were located are remarkably similar for the examples he selected, being heavier only in the clayland arable area (table 9.4).

Similarly Lord Eversley (1907) showed in six groups of counties with differing proportions of arable that there was a remarkable constancy in the rate of loss of farm labour between 1861 and 1901 (table 9.5). In no group was the total reduction in farm workers less than 22 per cent, and in most counties it exceeded one-third.

More recently, S. W. E. Vince (1955) has shown that only on the best quality arable land (IA in the classification of L. D. Stamp, 1948) were losses of primary rural population between 1831 and 1931 markedly lower (–11 per cent on average) than on other types of land. On other arable land losses ranged from –42 per cent in second class land (2AG) to –56 per cent (5A); on grassland types from –43 per cent (3G) to –52 per cent (4G); and on the poorer lands from –45 per cent (6AG) to –49 per cent (8H).

THE CAUSES OF RURAL DEPOPULATION

The basic causes of rural depopulation in England summarised by G. P. Hirsch (1951) were the outcome of both a push from the countryside and a pull to the town. The reduced demand for farm labour, the loss of craft industry to factory mass production at precisely the time of agricultural decline, and the fall in demand for services leading to a proportionate fall in the secondary population all contributed to the push. But growing industrial and service employment in the towns, the wider range of social amenities and higher wages were positive pulls to rural labour.

Agricultural labour

The decline in primary rural labour was general. Bowley (1914) pointed out that where rural population had increased, or even held its

Table 9.4 Population trends in selected arable districts of England, 1851–1911

		1851	Per cent 1801–1851	1871	Per cent 1851–1871	1891	Per cent 1871–1891	1911	Per cent 1891–1911
Clayland arable									
Kimbolton (Hunts.)*	Total change	9.339	+57·5	9.126	−2·3	6.836	−25·1	6.141	−10·2
St Neots Reg. Dist.†	Total change	18.825	+64·8	18.511	−1·7	15.239	−17·7	14.402	−5·5
	Natural change	—	—	+5.359	+28·5	+4.444	+24·0	+ 12,581	+17·0
	Migrational change	—	—	−5.673	−30·2	−7.701	−41·6	−3.418	−22·4
Lightland arable									
Bungay (Suffolk)*	Total change	6.539	+44·8	6.331	−3·2	5.803	−8·3	5.436	−6·3
Wangford Reg. Dist.†	Total change	14.014	+41·5	14.037	+0·2	15.301	+9·0	15.308	+0·0
	Natural change	—	—	+3.050	+21·8	+3.894	+27·8	+3.111	+20·3
	Migrational change	—	—	−3.027	−21·6	−2.630	−18·8	−3.094	−20·7
Fruit and vegetables									
(*a*) Evesham (Worcs.)*	Total change	7.690	+52·3	8.324	+8·2	9.112	+9·5	12.307	+35·1
Evesham Reg. Dist.†	Total change	14.463	+42·5	15.623	+8·0	16.069	+2·9	20.674	+28·6
	Natural change	—	—	+4.149	+28·6	+4.282	+27·4	+5.125	+31·9
	Migrational change	—	—	−2.989	−20·7	−3.836	−24·5	−520	−3·2
(*b*) Spalding (Lincs.) Reg. Dist.*	Total change	22.388	+108·3	23.184	+3·6	21.733	−6·3	23.497	+8·1
Spalding Reg. Dist.†	Total change	22.470	+108·1	23.184	+3·2	21.733	−6·3	23.494	+8·1
	Natural change	—	—	+5.643	+25·1	+5.762	+25·9	+4.560	+21·0
	Migrational change	—	—	−4.929	−21·9	−7.213	−32·2	−2.799	−12·9

* These figures are for subdistricts selected by P. M. Roxby (1912).

† Figures for registration districts are derived from the censuses of Great Britain, 1851 and of England and Wales, 1861–1911. Per cent changes for the periods indicated are the sum of changes for each decade.

Table 9.5 Trends in adult male farm population in six groups of counties, 1861–1901

	Percentage reduction		Males per 100 acres					
			1861		1881		1901	
	All farm workers	Labourers	20 and over	Under 20	20 and over	Under 20	20 and over	Under 20
Group 1	28	47	3·3	0·7	2·4	0·5	2·1	0·5
Group 2	40	53	5·3	1·3	3·7	0·8	3·0	0·5
Group 3	34	46	3·9	1·0	3·0	0·8	2·5	0·7
Group 4	33	45	4·1	1·1	3·3	0·8	2·8	0·6
Group 5	38	46	4·3	1·5	3·6	0·9	2·7	0·6
Group 6	22	33	4·1	1·3	3·6	1·0	3·2	0·8
Wales	27	47	3·5	0·8	2·5	0·5	2·3	0·4

Based on Eversley (appendix, tables I–VII, pp. 294–300).

Group 1 (under 20 per cent of cultivated area arable) Derby. Westmorland. Monmouth.
Group 2 (20–30 per cent arable) Lancashire. Leicester. Middlesex. Somerset. Stafford.
Group 3 (30–40 per cent arable) Buckingham. Cheshire. Dorset. Durham. Gloucester. Hereford. Northampton. Northumberland. Rutland. Salop. Warwick. Worcester.
Group 4 (40–50 per cent arable) Cumberland. Devon. Kent. Surrey. Sussex. Wiltshire. North Riding of York. West Riding of York.
Group 5 (50–60 per cent arable) Bedford. Berkshire. Cornwall. Hampshire. Huntingdon. Nottingham. Oxford.
Group 6 (over 60 per cent arable) Norfolk. Suffolk. Essex. Lincoln. Cambridge. Hertford. East Riding of York.

own, it was due to growth of non-primary population, for the numbers of adult males occupied on farms fell after 1861, steeply at first then rather less steeply from 1881 to 1901, when the fall was arrested (table 9.6). Eversley (1907) had shown that the total agricultural population fell from a maximum of 1·9 million in 1861 to 988,000 in 1901. The fall was particularly marked among young people under twenty (from 428,000 to 195,000) and among women (from 436,000 to 52,000), though the inclusion of wives and female relatives in the census for 1851–71 must have inflated the latter figures.

The reduction in the numbers of farmers was slight by comparison, apart from the sharp fall in the 1870s when arable prices dropped sharply in the face of foreign competition, and in marginal arable areas farms went out of cultivation or amalgamated. The land in farms in England, estimated (Caird, 1852) at 27 million acres in 1851 (the figure given in the *Census of Great Britain*, 1851, is 24·9 million acres) fell to 24·6 million acres by 1895 (Eversley, p. 277). The number of holdings – 223,271 according to the 1851 Census – increased to 389,057 in 1870 but decreased to 342,655 by 1895. For the average countryman, one of

Table 9.6 Agricultural and horticultural labour (adult males) in England and Wales, 1851–1911

	Total numbers employed (over 20 years) in thousands						
	1851	1861	1871	1881	1891	1901	1911
Farmers	225·7	226·0	224·5	202·4	200·5	202·0	208·1
Farmers' relatives	73·6	60·0	47·9	47·1	43·4	55·7	63·3
Bailiffs and foremen	10·5	15·6	16·3	19·4	18·0	22·4	22·0
Shepherds and labourers	735·1	809·4	657·8	606·0	545·6	458·4	498·2
Gardeners	64·9*	28·2	46·7	58·9	78·9	105·4	121·5
Agricultural machine workers	—	1·4	2·0	3·9	4·3	6·1	6·9
Others (inc. woodmen)	10·3	8·4	7·9	9·7	10·3	16·4	19·7
Total	1210·1	1149·0	1003·0	947·4	901·9	866·4	939·7
Domestic gardeners	*—	50·2	61·0	62·1	68·8	75·2	100·6
Gamekeepers	7·2	9·4	11·8	11·3	12·7	15·1	15·5
Grand total	1217·3	1208·6	1075·8	1020·8	983·4	956·7	1055·8

Based on Census (1851) Eversley (1907) and Bowley (1914).
In the censuses prior to 1901 domestic gardeners were not adequately separated from other gardeners.
The steep fall in labourers between 1861–71 may be due in part to errors in classification up to 1861.
* In 1851 gardeners and machinery workers were not separately distinguished.

the ways of staying on the land was to get a small farm. The questions of tenure, smallholdings and allotments were burning issues in the 'agricultural question', itself a great issue in late nineteenth century politics (for a useful summary see Land Enquiry Committee, 1913, vol. I).

Clearly, high loss of farm labour was largely due to the decline of numbers employed per acre. In the early and mid-nineteenth century the increased demand for labour on arable land absorbed a considerable part of the rural increase of population. Much farm work was seasonal in nature and farm gangs, employing large numbers of women and children, met this need. Developed initially to employ the parish poor (Hasbach, 1908), they included also Irish harvest gangs as seasonal migrants in hay making and at harvest time. By the 1840s private gang-masters had organised a system which persisted in the eastern arable counties into the 1860s when it was brought under control by the Gangs Act of 1867 (30 and 31 Vict., c. 130) and, in the case of child labour, by the Education Act of 1870. Moreover, by this date economy in the use of labour was being enforced by the drift of population to the towns and the consequent increase in wages, while the use of machinery permitted economies in labour in many farm operations. Ironically, at a time of agricultural depression in the 1870s to the 1890s the migration of labour from the countryside was leading to shortages of skilled labour.

Decline of industry

The decline of farming population, though heavy, could not in itself account for an estimated migrational loss of over $4\frac{1}{2}$ million from the rural residues between 1841 and 1911 (Cairncross, 1953) (table 9.2). Even if one accepts the dubious figures of female farm labour in 1851, the decline of the farm population, 1851–1911, was about 900,000, and the loss was heaviest among the younger, often unmarried workers.

Loss of rural industry accounted for much of the rural exodus. Much of it was due to the decline of rural crafts in the face of mechanisation in industries such as hosiery and knitwear, lace manufacture and shoe making. The processing of many raw materials and foodstuffs – such as leather and grain – once largely rurally located, had shifted to the ports where imported supplies were processed (W. Smith, 1949). Secondary population, estimated by Vince (1952) as generally about half the primary population which it served, declined also, leading to a fall in the numbers of craftsmen (smiths, tailors, shoemakers and the like), shopkeepers and professional people. Indeed, Graham considered that '... the shopkeepers and artisans of the village have been compelled to leave in greater numbers than the labourers' affecting not only villages but small towns which, as Welton showed (1900), declined in many primarily agricultural areas after 1861.

What detailed studies have been made show that the proportion of craftsmen in the rural areas has fallen markedly since the mid-nineteenth century (W. M. Williams, 1955; Saville, 1957). (For specific examples, see Chapter 10.) The well-balanced communities of the early nineteenth century (Lawton, 1954) had largely vanished by the 1900s.

Wages

Loss of employment and a decreasing range of jobs were but two aspects of the problem: the countryman was also more poorly paid. Agricultural workers were among the lowest paid workers, and farm wages were lower in the remote farming areas as the county averages quoted by Hasbach (1908) and Bowley (1914) show. Figure 9.8

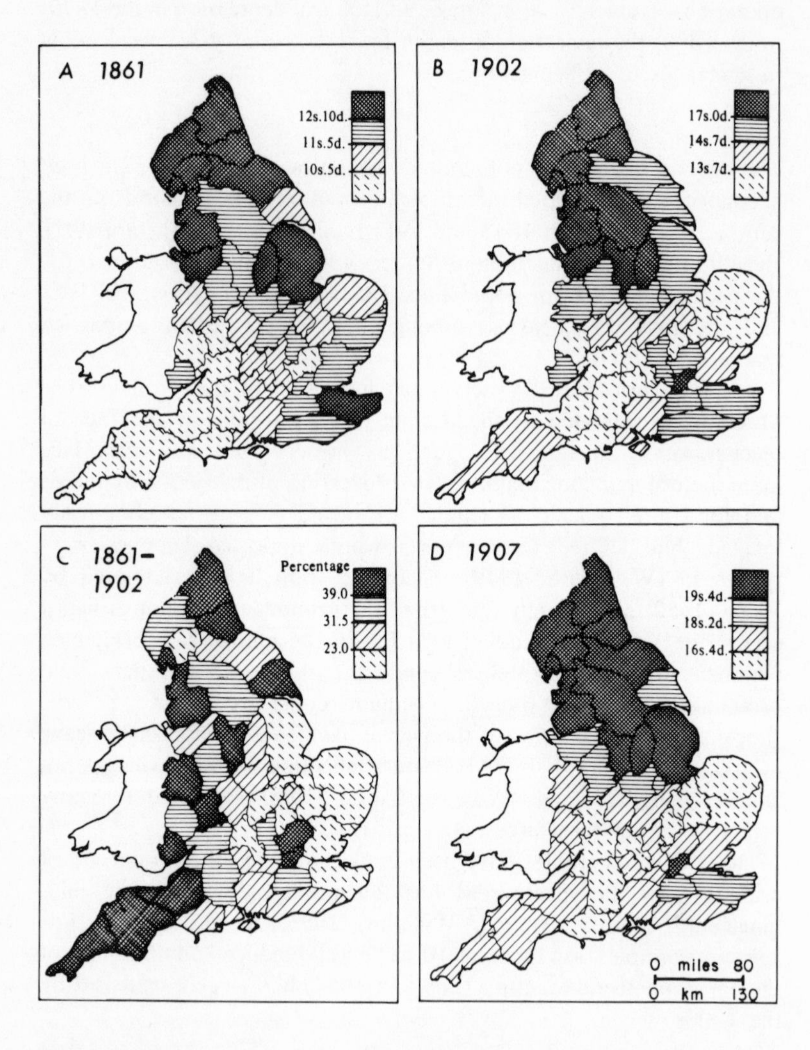

Fig. 9.8 Average weekly wages and earnings of agricultural labour in England, 1861–1907. The values are mapped by counties and grouped in quartiles. Based on Bowley (1914), Appendix III.

A. Average weekly wages 1861
B. Average weekly wages 1902
C. Wage changes 1861–1902
D. Average weekly earnings 1907

shows that during the late nineteenth century wages were higher in the northern counties of England than in the southern, and were better in industrial regions and near to the cities than in more remote areas. Both in 1861 and 1902, a belt of counties from East Anglia to the south-west were below the median while in the north and the Midlands and around London they were above the median. Some of the lowest wages were to be found on the productive arable counties of East Anglia, where, as we have seen, farm labour was abundant. Despite the lowness of wages in mid-century the southern and eastern counties showed some of the lowest rates of increase between 1861 and 1902 except in some counties adjacent to London. The same conclusions are also apparent from the estimates of the real earnings of farm labour in England in the early twentieth century. Even in a centrally located county such as Warwickshire, farm wages were higher in the vicinity of Birmingham, and this seems to have been a factor in directing rural migration not only towards the city but to rural areas adjacent to it (Lawton, 1958).

Social conditions

The countryside progressively lagged behind the town in amenity. Neither the quality nor the quantity of rural housing matched that in the towns. Although urban slums possessed an unrivalled squalor, legislation to improve urban housing conditions was generally in advance of that for rural areas and could usually be implemented more effectively. Thus poor rural housing conditions contributed to migration (Board of Agriculture, 1906, Cd. 3273). The Land Enquiry Committee (1913) reported a shortage of cottages in over one-half (1396) of the 2759 parishes investigated. Everywhere there was a tremendous backlog of rebuilding and modernisation, though on a number of large estates there was a good deal of new building from the 1850s and 1860s. Thus, despite prolonged depopulation, there was a general shortage of rural housing (H. of C. 376, 1906); newly married couples often had to share accommodation or leave the village. Condemned cottages were demolished faster than new ones were built, leading to shortage despite a falling population. Many labourers had to undertake a long daily walk to work because they were unable to get a house nearby, a problem which in part harked back to the system of 'closed' parishes of the early nineteenth century (Mills, 1959; Sheppard, 1961). In many counties, the investigation of the Land Enquiry Committee (1913) showed that over half the villages had built no cottages at all in the previous ten years. Estimates of the additional accommodation needed varied between 6 and 15 per cent with an estimated additional need for England and Wales of 10 per cent (rather under half to replace unfit cottages, the rest for additional dwellings). Tied cottages, often quoted as a side benefit increasing the real value of earnings, were generally condemned as unsatisfactory in the late nineteenth century, and by impeding mobility may have contributed to decreasing the labour supply.

There is no doubt that the social amenities of the city and the dullness of country life were important factors in the migration of young people of both sexes. Better educational opportunities, more varied entertainments and shopping – as well as wider job opportunities – all drew the young and enterprising to a new environment. These factors are not measurable and can be assessed only from the evidence gathered by Parliamentary enquiries and other contemporary investigations. G. B. Longstaff (1893), who showed that the causes as well as the incidence of rural depopulation were universal, attributed many of these causes to what he described as 'sentimental' reasons. But the basic factors were economic. The decline of employment in the countryside and its increase in towns were general; and countrymen were able to seize these opportunities after the development of railways.

SOURCE: from R. W. Steel and R. Lawton (eds.), *Liverpool Essays in Geography: A Jubilee Collection,* 1967.

REFERENCES

Board of Agriculture (1906) *The land and decline in the agricultural population 1881–1906*, Report of the Land Enquiry Committee, 1906, Cd. 3273.

Bowley, A. L. (1914) 'Rural population in England and Wales. A study of the changes of density, occupations and ages', *J. Roy. Stat. Soc.*, LXXVII, 597–652.

Caird, J. (1852) *English Agriculture in 1850–1.*

Cairncross, A. K. (1938–9) 'Trends in internal migration, 1841–1911', *Trans. Manchester Stat. Soc.* (Group Meetings), 21–9.

Cairncross, A. K. (1949) 'Internal migration in Victorian England', *The Manchester School,* XVII, 67–87.

Cairncross, A. K. (1953) *Home and foreign investment, 1870–1913.*

Clapham, J. H. (1939) *An economic history of modern Britain.*

Eversley, Lord (1907) 'The decline of the numbers of agricultural labourers in Great Britain', *J. Roy. Stat. Soc.*, LXX, 267–319.

Farr, W. (1885) *Vital statistics.*

Galton, F. (1873) 'The relative supplies from town and country families to the population of future generations', *Journ. Stat. Soc. of London,* XXXVI.19–26.

Graham, P. A. (1892) *The rural exodus.*

Hasbach, W. (1908) *A history of the English agricultural labourer* (trans. by Ruth Kenyon).

Hirsch, G. P. (1951) 'Migration from the land in England and Wales', *The Farm Economist,* VI.no. 9, 270–80.

House of Commons 376 (1906) *Select Committee on the Housing of the Working Classes Acts Amendment Bill,* 1906.

Johnson, A. H. (1909) *The disappearance of the small landowner.*

Land Enquiry Committee (1913) *Report,* 3rd edn.

Lawton, R. (1954) 'The economic geography of Craven in the early nineteenth century', *Trans. Inst. Brit. Geogr.,* XX,93–111. (See Chapter 7 of this volume.)

Lawton, R. (1958) 'Population movements in the West Midlands, 1841–1861', *Geography,* XLIII.164–77.

Lipman, V. D. (1949) *Administrative areas in England and Wales,* 1834–1945.

Longstaff, G. B. (1893) 'Rural depopulation', *J. Roy. Stat. Soc.,* LVI, 380–442.

Mills, D. R. (1959) 'The poor laws and the distribution of population *c.* 1600–1860, with special reference to Lincolnshire', *Trans. Inst. Brit. Geogr.,* XXVI, 185–95.

Ogle, W. (1889) 'The alleged depopulation of the rural districts of England', *J. Roy. Stat. Soc.,* LII.205–40.

Redford, A. (1926) *Labour migration in England,* 1800–1850.

Robertson, Isobel, M. L. (1961) 'The occupational structure and distribution of rural population in England and Wales', *Scot. Geogr. Mag.,* LXXVII.165–79.

Roxby, P. M. (1912) 'Rural depopulation in England during the nineteenth century', *Nineteenth Century and after,* LXXI.174–90.

Saville, J. (1957) *Rural depopulation in England and Wales,* 1851–1951.

Sheppard, J. (1961) 'East Yorkshire's agricultural labour force in the mid-nineteenth century', *Ag. Hist. Rev.,* IX, 43–54.

Smith, C. T. (1951) 'The movement of population in England and Wales in 1851 and 1861', *Geogr. Journ.,* CXVII, 200–10.

Smith, W. (1949) *An economic geography of Great Britain.*

Stamp, Sir L. D. (1948) *The land of Britain: its use and mis-use.*

Stevens, A. (1946) 'The distribution of rural population in Great Britain', *Trans. Inst. Brit. Geogr.,* XI, 23–53.

Vince, S. W. E. (1952) 'Reflections on the structure and distribution of rural population in England and Wales, 1921–1931', *Trans. Inst. Brit. Geogr.,* XVIII, 33–76.

Vince, S. W. E. (1955) 'The rural population of England and Wales, 1801–1951', Ph.D. thesis, University of London.

Webb, J. W. (1963) 'The natural and migrational components of population changes in England and Wales, 1921–31', *Econ. Geog.,* XXXIX, 130–48.

Welton, T. A. (1900) 'On the distribution of population in England and Wales, and its progress in the period of ninety years from 1801–1891', *J. Roy. Stat. Soc.,* LXXVI, 304–17.

Welton, T. A. (1911) *England's recent progress.*

Welton, T. A. (1913) 'Urban and rural variations according to the English Census of 1911', *J. Roy. Stat. Soc., LXXVI,304–17.*

Williams, R. P. (1880) 'On the increase of population in England and Wales', *J. Roy. Stat. Soc.,* XLIII, 462–96.

Williams, W. M. (1958) *The country craftsman.*

10 Rural Population Changes Since 1851: Three Sample Studies

JUNE A. SHEPPARD

THE broad pattern of population change in the rural parts of England during the past century is well known, thanks to several recent studies.[1] The details have been less fully analysed,[2] and we rarely know the exact process by which change has been brought about in individual parishes and why trends should vary from parish to parish. For instance, how close is the relationship between the decline in population numbers and the decreased labour requirements on the land? Do variations in type of farming help to explain the differences in extent of decline? Is there any significant relationship between the size of villages and population loss? And within individual parishes, has the loss of population been principally from the villages or from the scattered dwellings? Answers to such questions can only be obtained by detailed studies of small areas and the purpose of this study is to elucidate the population trends of three parishes in the East Riding of Yorkshire.

The three parishes are Wheldrake, Kilham and Humbleton, and their locations are shown in figure 10.1. They were chosen to represent the range of village and farm sizes present in the county. Wheldrake has a medium-sized village (population 327 in 1959) and relatively small farms (50–200 acres) and is typical of many parishes in the Vale of York. Kilham has a large village (population 591 in 1960) and many large farms (over 300 acres), and is characteristic of many parishes in the Yorkshire Wolds. Humbleton is like many Holderness parishes in having a small village (95 inhabitants in 1961) and medium-sized farms (150–300 acres). Figure 10.2 shows the population trends in these parishes since 1801. A loss has occurred in all three since the middle years of the nineteenth century, although in Humbleton this takes the form of fluctuations rather than a clearly defined trend.

Many details of the populations of the three parishes at about the time when numbers were at their maximum may be extracted from the 1851 Census Enumerators' manuscript schedules in the Public Record

For references to this chapter, see p. 233.

Office.[3] These tell us the number of people in each household, and the age, sex, relationship to head of household, occupation and place of birth of each individual. The households can be divided between those in the villages and those outside. In Wheldrake this distinction is very clearly drawn, for the enumerator headed one section of his return 'Wheldrake lone houses' and the remainder 'Wheldrake village'. The Kilham enumerators showed the difference by naming all the outlying dwellings, but in the village giving only the street names. The Humbleton enumerator was less conscientious and gave no names or indication of location for any house. It is possible to separate the outlying dwellings from the rest, however, because the Ordnance Survey First Edition Six-inch map (1854) shows only five farms outside the village, and it is presumed that these must have been occupied by the five large farmers enumerated.

Comparable information about the present rural population was obtained by house-to-house visits in the summers of 1959 (Wheldrake), 1960 (Kilham), and 1961 (Humbleton). The

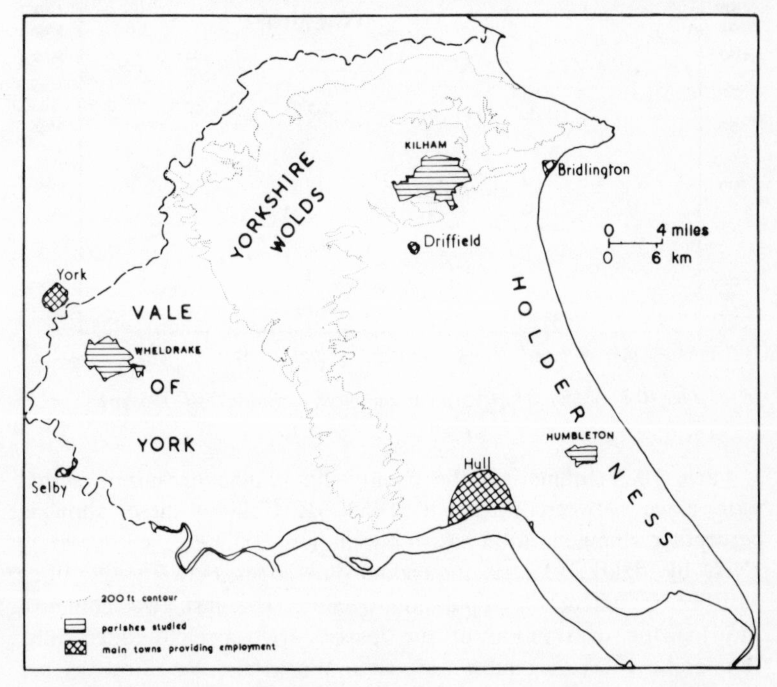

Fig. 10.1 The East Riding of Yorkshire: location of parishes studied

cooperativeness of the inhabitants resulted in a 100 per cent enumeration, but where people were away on holiday or out at work all day there are a few gaps in the data concerning occupations. The information is not so full as that available for 1851 for obvious reasons; for example, no questions were asked about ages. But sufficient data were collected to make possible a comparison for the two dates of such significant aspects of population as total numbers, household sizes and composition, and male occupations.[4]

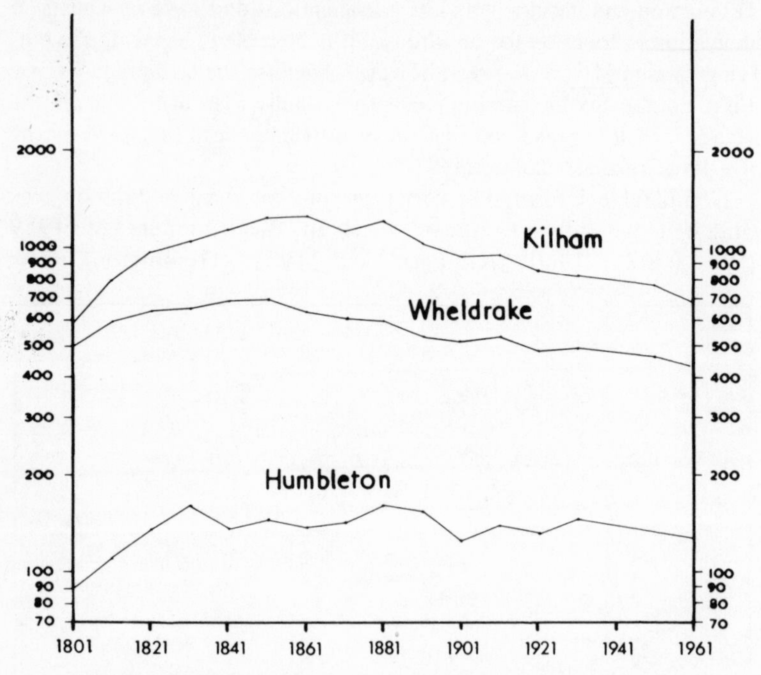

Fig. 10.2 Population changes in the three parishes, 1801–1959/61

Table 10.1 summarises the changes in population numbers that took place between 1851 and 1959–61. Column three, showing percentage change in total parish population, confirms the impression given by figure 10.2 of important differences between the three parishes in extent of population decline. The last two columns, showing the distribution of the losses, are especially interesting. Wheldrake village declined more than Wheldrake 'lone houses', but the difference was relatively small; the contrast was greater in Kilham, where the loss from the outlying dwellings was the same as in Wheldrake but the loss from the village was greater than that from Wheldrake village. Humbleton shows a completely different pattern, having lost nearly half of its outlying population, while the village population has actually increased. The reasons for these differences in trend may be understood when other aspects of population change are considered.

Table 10.1 Changes in population numbers

	Total population 1851	Total population 1959/61	% change 1851–1959/61
Wheldrake	689	434	−37
Kilham	1247	682	−45
Humbleton	142	127	−10

	Population in village 1851	Population in village 1959–61	% change in village population	% change in dispersed population
Wheldrake	536	327	−39	−30
Kilham	1118	591	−47	−30
Humbleton	85	95	+11	−48

Certain distinctive types of household can be readily identified in the 1851 Enumerators' schedules. The simplest means of classification is by the occupation of the head of the household. The main types were:

(1) Agricultural labourer households. These usually consisted of parents and children under 15 years of age, with occasionally an older child, a grandparent, or an unmarried brother or sister. The size of the household varied with the age of the parents, but there would often be six or more children at home. The outstanding feature was the virtual absence of young people between about fifteen and twenty-five, for children normally left home when they reached their early teens, the boys to work as apprentices to craftsmen or as farm servants,[5] the girls to become domestic servants on farms or in town households, in all cases living in their master's house.

(2) Service households. These were of two types. In about a third of the total, where the head was a journeyman craftsman or a small shopkeeper, or had some menial occupation like rat catching, the household was identical with those in type (1). The remainder, where the head was a master craftsman, a larger shopkeeper or a professional man like a doctor or clergyman, consisted of parents, unmarried children of all ages, and often one or two young male apprentices and one or two female domestic servants. There were usually fewer children than in agricultural labourer households and the age structure was more balanced.

(3) Farmer households. Some of these were similar to the larger service households, but others employed and housed more young men as farm servants, so that the total size was considerable, there often being as many as fifteen persons. Such households had a peculiar age and sex structure resulting from the preponderance of young men.

(4) Those comprising one person living alone or an elderly couple.

The number of households that cannot be included in any one of these groups is small.

These household types were not evenly distributed, as table 10.2 indicates. In the villages all four were represented, but in each case agricultural labourer households were most numerous, followed by service households. The village farmer households were almost all small ones containing relatively few farm servants. The differences between the three villages were fairly small, although the relatively higher proportion of service and farmer households in Wheldrake is worth noting. Outside the villages, farmer households predominated, and in Kilham and Humbleton these were principally of the larger type with many farm servants. (See Chapter 3, pp. 105–7 and 111 for other East Riding evidence.)

Table 10.2 Classification of households, 1851

	Agricultural labourer	Service	Farmer	Elderly	Others
Wheldrake village	35	32	21	15	12
Wheldrake outlying	5	0	18	0	0
Kilham village	101	77	18	25	18
Kilham outlying	3	1	13	0	0
Humbleton village	9	6	1	4	0
Humbleton outlying	0	0	5	0	0

One result of this distribution was that the average outlying household in each parish was larger than the average village household. In Wheldrake the average village household comprised 4·6 persons, the average outlying household 6·6; in Kilham the comparable figures were 4·6 and 7·6, and in Humbleton 3·2 and 11·4. A second result was that the age and sex composition of the village populations differed from that of the 'lone houses'. Figure 10.3 shows the age and sex pyramids for the six units in 1851, in each case superimposed on the pyramid for all England and Wales. The villages have

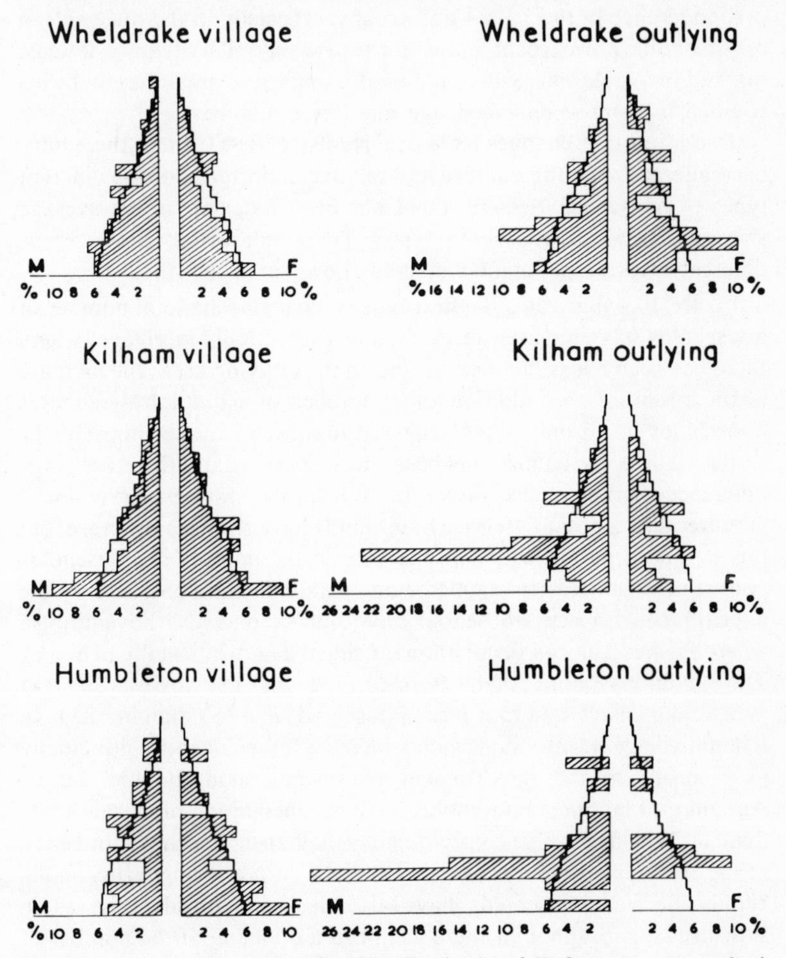

Fig. 10.3 Age and sex pyramids, 1851 (England and Wales average in outline)

pyramids that taper irregularly towards the higher age groups, with the sexes approximately equally represented. The irregularities that occur in each pyramid must to some extent be the chance results of the small size of the populations (especially in Humbleton), but it is probable that the marked indentations on the male sides of the Humbleton and Kilham pyramids in the 15–19 and 20–24 age groups are the result of the absent sons of agricultural labourer and similar households. The pyramids for the outlying parts of the parishes depart much farther from the England and Wales average, each showing a preponderance in the 15–24 age groups, especially in the male side, a result of the presence of many farm servants. This feature is least marked in Wheldrake, where the predominance of small family farms resulted in a more balanced age and sex structure.

Two important changes have occurred since 1851. First, there have been alterations in the number and relative importance of the different types of household. Second, there has been a decline in the average size of almost all household types. These interact to produce the different rates of population change shown in table 10.1.

Figure 10.4 illustrates the first type of change. The total number of households has increased in every unit except Kilham village, where there has been a loss of twenty-eight. In the outlying areas the increase is the result of the addition of a number of agricultural labourer households to an only slightly altered number of farmer households. In the villages the change has been more complex and there are some differences between the three. In Wheldrake, farmer, agricultural labourer and especially service households have shown a decrease, but this has been paralleled by an increase in the number of households consisting of an elderly couple or one person living alone, and by the appearance of a new household type that we may call adventitious, where the head has an occupation outside the parish (usually in York). The additions more than compensated for the losses, so that Wheldrake village had four more households in 1959 than in 1851. In Kilham village, farmer households have increased slightly, principally as a result of the development of several small poultry farms. Agricultural labourer households have declined much more markedly than in Wheldrake,[6] to approximately half their original number, a result of the extensive mechanisation of the corn growing farms on the Wolds. Service households have also declined considerably, as in Wheldrake, and although there has been a doubling of the number of elderly households and the addition of a large group of adventitious households, these have not been able to compensate completely for the losses, hence the decline in total number of households. The most striking feature in Humbleton village is the increase in number of agricultural labourer households, and it is this, together with the small but proportionately significant increase in number of adventitious households, that explains Humbleton's growth from twenty to thirty-one households.[7]

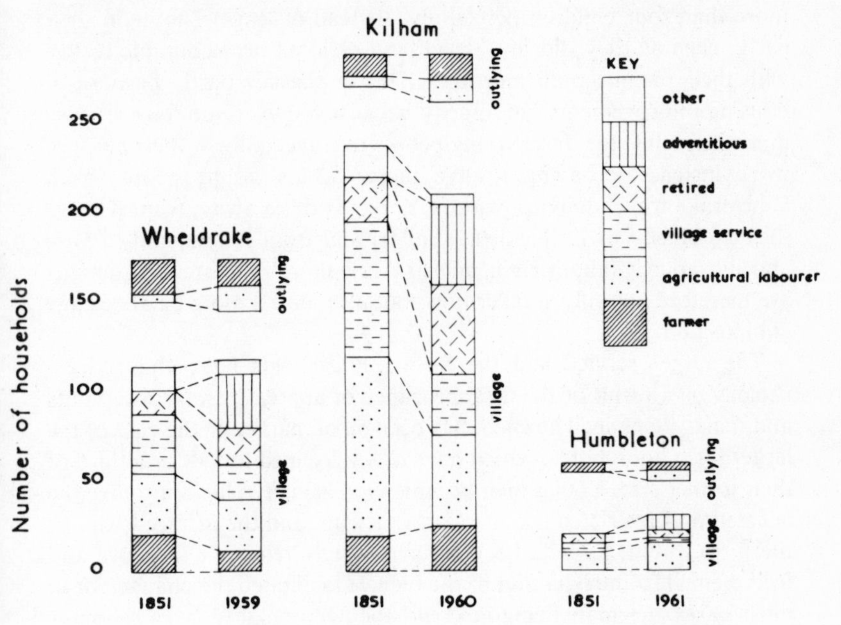

Fig. 10.4 Changes in number and type of households, 1851–1959/61

The decline in number of service households and the increase in elderly (except in Humbleton) and adventitious households have been common to all three villages. The variation between them has been chiefly in the agricultural labourer households. Thus in Wheldrake, where the decline in the number of these was small, there has been little change in the total number of households. In Kilham, where the decline was large, the net result was a loss; and in Humbleton where they increased, the total number of households also increased. Only in Kilham village has population decrease been associated with a decline in number of households, and even there the disparity between the small percentage loss of households and the large percentage loss of population shows that the decrease cannot be wholly accounted for in this way. The decline in population must therefore be associated rather with the second element of change, i.e., the reduction in average household size.

Each household type except the elderly has changed in size and character since 1851. A reduction in family size is especially apparent among agricultural labourer households, where there are now rarely more than four children per family. Instead of leaving home in their early teens as they did in 1851, many children now continue to live with their parents until marriage. This is possible partly because of housing improvements, and partly because bicycles and 'bus services make it feasible for these young people to travel daily to their place of work instead of having to live there.[8] Many young people from Wheldrake travel daily to work in York, six miles away; from Kilham they go chiefly to Driffield (five miles) and from Humbleton to Hull and its suburbs (about eight miles). Agricultural labourer households are therefore not only smaller now, but also have a more balanced age composition.

The larger service and the farmer households have changed especially as a result of the disappearance of apprentices, farm servants and maids living in. The effect has been most marked in the case of the larger farm households, which have often declined to half or a third of their former size. Young men became increasingly reluctant to live the isolated and restricted life of a farm servant, and the farmer's wife or the farm foreman's wife became increasingly reluctant to house and feed them. The introduction of the bicycle facilitated the change, for in most cases the man living-in could then be replaced by a labourer living in the village. In the same way, living-in maids could be replaced by a 'daily' who cycled out from the village. Where the farmer felt a need for immediately accessible workers, he either subdivided his now excessively large farmhouse or built a foreman's house or a row of cottages nearby. These formed the additional agricultural labourer households in the outlying parts of the parishes shown in figure 10.4.

A further significant element is the increased proportion of households consisting of an elderly couple or single person only. This has had the effect of depressing the average household size, especially of the villages.

Figure 10.5 summarises the changes in average household size since 1851. Wheldrake and Kilham villages show exactly the same decline, i.e., from 4·6 persons in 1851 to 2·8 persons in 1959/60. In

Humbleton village there has been less change, for households were already smaller there than in the other two villages in 1851. The present average size of outlying households is slightly larger than that of village households, because of the absence of 'elderly' households. On the other hand, the decline since 1851 has been greater than in the villages, especially in Humbleton where farm servants were very numerous in the nineteenth century. These outlying areas now have a much more normal age and sex structure than they had in 1851.

Wheldrake village — Wheldrake outlying
1851 — 1851
1959 — 1959

Kilham village — Kilham outlying
1851 — 1851
1960 — 1960

Humbleton village — Humbleton outlying
1851 — 1851
1961 — 1961

Fig. 10.5 Changes in average household size since 1851

The relative influence of each of the two sets of changes has varied. In the outlying areas there has been a big decline in household size, only partially balanced by an increase in the number of households. Outlying Humbleton lost more than the other two outlying areas principally because households there were so large in 1851. Among the villages, Wheldrake's loss of population is associated with a decline in number of households as well. Humbleton not only experienced little change in average household size during the period, but also had a significant increase in number of households. Its unique character as the one unit where population increased can therefore be readily understood.

Table 10.3 Male occupations

	Farmers and male relatives working on the farm		Farm servants		Agricultural labourers		Service occupations in the parish		Working outside parish		Total employed males		Retired or not working	
	1851	1959/61	1851	1959/61	1851	1959/61	1851	1959/61	1851	1959/61	1851	1959/61	1851	1959/61
Wheldrake														
Village	32	17	21	0	57	41	48	19	3	33	161	112	20	24
Outlying	29	25	19	1	5	17	0	0	0	0	53	43	3	3
Total	61	42	40	1	62	58	48	19	3	33	214	155	23	27
Kilham														
Village	21	30	28	0	143	68	108	38	1	68	301	204	31	42
Outlying	15	16	53	4	1	15	3	0	0	0	72	35	1	1
Total	36	46	81	4	144	83	111	38	1	68	373	239	32	43
Humbleton														
Village	1	0	1	0	12	23	11	2	0	9	25	34	0	2
Outlying	8	4	27	0	0	6	0	0	0	0	35	10	0	0
Total	9	4	28	0	12	29	11	2	0	9	60	44	0	2

The same two sets of changes are reflected in male occupations (table 10.3). The decline in number of occupied males is proportionately greatest in the outlying areas of Kilham and Humbleton, because of the replacement there of the former unbalanced households by more normal ones. The smaller proportionate decline in the villages of Wheldrake and Kilham may be associated partly with the reduction of average household size and partly with the decrease in number of households with occupied heads, while the increase in Humbleton may be linked with the large proportionate increase in number of village households. In each parish taken as a whole the numbers in agricultural and parish service occupations have declined, while the numbers of retired men and men working outside the parish have increased.

It is difficult to know how typical these three parishes are and how far it is legitimate to base general inferences on this analysis. It seems worthwhile, however, to suggest certain conclusions, the general validity of which might be tested by work in other areas.

Household size

For the most part the loss of population has operated through a marked reduction of average household size, and only in Kilham village has there been a decrease in number of households. Thus there is little in the appearance of the villages and outlying dwellings to suggest the significant changes in population numbers and composition that have taken place.

Occupations

Among the occupational groups represented in table 10.3, there has been a large decline in the number of men engaged in local service occupations in all three parishes (60 per cent in Wheldrake, 64 per cent in Kilham and 82 per cent in Humbleton), and in each the decline is proportionately greater than the decline in total population. This confirms the trend noted by W. M. Williams for services to become more concentrated in towns, now that improved transport has made them accessible to most country dwellers.[9]

There has been an increase in all three parishes in the number of adventitious workers, who now form 21 per cent of the total male labour force in Wheldrake, 28 per cent in Kilham and 20 per cent in Humbleton. The similarity of the figures for the three parishes is probably the result of the comparable distances of each from urban centres providing employment; if parishes with varying ease of access to towns were studied the proportion of adventitious workers would no doubt be much more variable. Retired males have also shown a fairly similar increase in each of the three parishes.

Greater differences exist between the three parishes in the extent of change among agricultural workers (using this term to include farmers, farm servants and agricultural labourers). These declined by 38 per cent in Wheldrake, 49 per cent in Kilham and 32 per cent in Humbleton, figures that show some correlation with types of farming. Kilham's big loss may be linked with the prevalence of large, highly mechanised, corn growing farms, and Humbleton's smaller loss with the importance of pig keeping and potato growing enterprises with higher labour requirements.

The agricultural worker group is the largest of the three occupational groups considered, and it is also the one in which the extent of change has varied most from parish to parish. Whereas the interaction of the other changes considered tended to produce similar population trends in each parish, the operation of the variable changes in this group has been sufficiently influential to give rise to different total population trends. Changes in population numbers in the three parishes can thus be correlated broadly with changes in the number of agricultural workers; in both cases Kilham had the largest, Wheldrake the middle and Humbleton the smallest percentage loss.

This relationship between change in number of agricultural workers and change in total population numbers has been simplified by the limitation of the study to these three parishes. If a larger number of parishes were to be considered, there is little doubt that there would be two variables operating, the decline of agricultural workers and the increase of adventitious workers. Similar population changes could therefore result from different combinations of these two variables. For example, a small population decline could be the result of a small loss of agricultural workers and no addition of adventitious workers, but it could equally be the result of a large loss of agricultural workers and a large gain of adventitious workers. In each parish the combination is likely to be different, thus analysis of occupational changes is vital for a complete understanding of varying population trends.

Settlement

The large village of Kilham lost appreciably more population than the isolated dwellings of the parish, the medium-sized village of Wheldrake lost slightly more than Wheldrake 'lone houses', whilst in Humbleton parish the isolated dwellings lost heavily and the small village has grown. In this considerable diversity of locational changes, the recognition of general trends is difficult. A clue to these changes, however, lies in the relative proportions of agricultural labourers and farm servants in the nineteenth century agricultural labour force. In Humbleton, where farm servants were the most numerous group, their disappearance has affected especially the isolated dwellings, while many of the labourers who have partly replaced them have been added to the village population. Other parishes with the same heavy dependence on farm servants in the nineteenth century might be expected to show a similar increased clustering in the population, with either a growth or only a relatively small decline of the village. In Kilham, where labourers formed the largest proportion of the agricultural workers in the nineteenth century, much of the loss has been from this group and therefore from the village. Other parishes with a similar high proportion of agricultural labourers might be expected to show a similar trend towards greater dispersion of population. Where the different components of the nineteenth century agricultural labour force were more evenly balanced, as in Wheldrake, significant changes in population distribution are less likely to have taken place.

These detailed studies thus illustrate the intricate nature of the changes that have occurred during the past century in the structure and location of population in rural areas. Trends in total numbers form merely the most readily measurable facet of this complex of changes.

SOURCE: *Sociological Review,* vol. 10, 1962.

REFERENCES

The author is grateful for the co-operation and assistance of many persons in the three villages, especially Mr H. Cutler, head teacher of Wheldrake School, and Mr Stone, head teacher of Kilham School. Mr D. Baldock, then a student in the Department of Geography, Queen Mary College, gave valuable help in visiting Kilham households in August–September 1960. The cost of travel to and around Kilham was met by a grant from the University of London Central Research Fund.

1. Especially S. W. E. Vince, 'Reflections on the structure and distribution of rural population in England and Wales, 1921–31', *Institute of British Geographers Transactions and Papers* (1952), and John Saville, *Rural depopulation in England and Wales 1851–1951* (London, 1957). See also the previous chapter.

2. The principal contributions are: H. E. Bracey, 'A note on rural depopulation and social provision', *Sociological Review*, VI, no. 1 (1958) 67–74; G. D. Mitchell, 'Depopulation and rural social structure', *Sociological Review*, XLII, (old series) (1950) 69–85.
3. H.O. 107.
4. Female occupations are not included in this study principally because their significance was not appreciated when the work was started.
5. The term applied to men engaged by the year and living as members of the farmer's household.
6. The relatively small decrease in Wheldrake may be attributed partly to afforestation in the northern part of the parish and to an increase in the number of forestry workers, who have been included with the agricultural labourers.
7. The growth of Humbleton village is fairly recent. In 1954 the Holderness Rural District Council pulled down five old cottages and erected twelve houses in their place, in order to meet the needs of local farmers for more dwellings for agricultural labourers. (Since this time there have been heavy general losses of farm labour – ed.)
8. Wheldrake and Kilham each have several buses a day, to York and Driffield respectively. Humbleton has only one bus a day, but buses from Aldbrough to Hull pass along the boundary of the parish, about a mile from the village.
9. W. M. Williams, *The Country Craftsman* (London, 1958).

11 The Metropolitan Village

F. I. MASSER and D. C. STROUD

ON the outskirts of all large conurbations pressures of residential development are mounting rapidly as people move out from the older built-up areas to new and improved surroundings. This large scale movement, either publicly controlled overspill or voluntary migration, is generally to existing towns or new townships lying within or near the periphery of the conurbation. A growing proportion of this movement is to smaller settlements lying within the green belt or near the edges of existing development. These settlements are often old villages which have a pleasant rural character. The movement of population into them presents, on a small scale, some planning problems which, it is felt, deserve more consideration than they are given today. Many villages possess an environmental quality that is worth keeping and which is one of the main forces attracting people to live in them. The questions of how big they can grow and what forms of new development should be permitted are closely bound up with the problem of how to preserve their special character. There is here an opportunity for sensitive and imaginative design; and also for an exercise in quantitive assessment to determine how large a village can grow before it becomes a town. This study is largely concerned with the second of these problems.

The questions raised by growth in small villages on the edges of large urban areas have social and physical implications. The more people move into the villages the sooner the rural character disappears. New residential development breaks up farm units and the agricultural population gradually dwindles in size. It is not long before the village is really a suburban growth point with rural overtones giving only a slightly better environment than that which is found in the town.

To the outsider these villages appear to preserve their physical identity. Newcomers are absorbed into the local scene and are frequently the most vociferous in wishing to protect whatever is left of the rural atmosphere. The need to preserve and protect, the desire to live in a village with its neighbourliness and special feeling of identity of the residents with a small community; these are still features of villages

For references to this chapter, see p. 248.

within conurbations and are particularly noticeable where there is a real danger that peripheral expansion may envelop and destroy. Unfortunately isolation has its drawbacks, since the very smallness of the villages sometimes leads to poor facilities in terms of drainage, street lighting, shops, public transport and local entertainment of sufficient variety to suit people of all ages and varied incomes. Isolation also brings the feeling that insufficient attention is being given at centres of local government or administration. But, again, the strength of a minority group of a village may be sufficient to enable something to be done to preserve all that is best in the village and to provide sufficient services and reasonable town comforts without destroying the rural character.

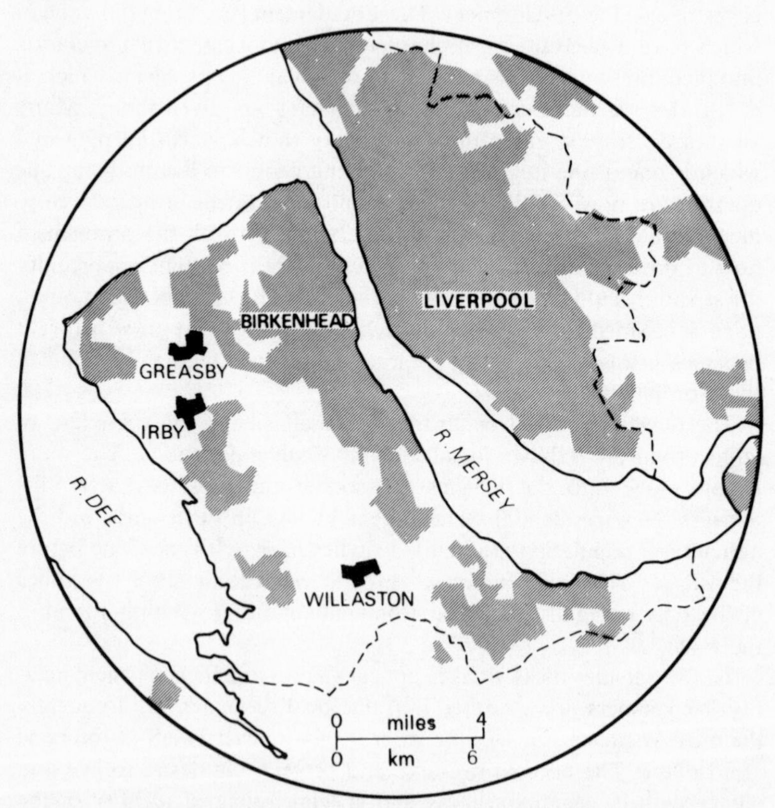

Fig. 11.1 Map of the Merseyside conurbation showing the location of the three villages on the Wirral Peninsula. The dotted line shows the conurbation boundary as defined in the Census; hatching indicates the built up area

Three recent studies[1] suggest some broad pointers which might well be considered in the formulation of planning policies designed to deal with the problems noted above. These studies were initiated by a group of preservationists in the Wirral village of Irby. In 1962 this group approached the Department of Civic Design for help in 'protecting' their village because it was felt that insufficient attention was being paid to the detailed planning and control of its development. They were particularly concerned about the village centre, which, while not being of great architectural merit, contained some pleasant buildings in the local tradition of red sandstone and typical Cheshire black and white half-timbering. A survey and sketch plans for the village was placed on exhibition in the centre of Irby and, unexpectedly, provoked great interest not only among Irby residents but also in villages in similar circumstances in other parts of Wirral. As a result, two other studies of Wirral villages were made and similar exhibitions were held at Willaston in 1963 and Greasby in 1965.

The three studies were not part of a research project. They were treated wholly as student exercises. Because the villages are small, it was possible to conduct house-to-house sample surveys, carry out physical surveys and provide a policy and plans for the development of the villages, including sketch designs for the village centre, and at Greasby, for a housing layout (see figures 11.2, 11.3 and 11.4). Conceived as teaching exercises the results of the surveys have had their limitations and not all the information is on a comparative basis. But the plans suggested that, provided the best of the villages were preserved, major changes were acceptable and some of the ideas were discussed at great length and with much interest at the exhibitions that were held in each of the three villages. It was also clear that the plans were considered as reinforcing the desire of certain groups of residents to achieve more recognition and notice in local government circles and in demonstrating to the residents as a whole that there were, in fact, people in each village who cared for its future, who wished to preserve all that was best in it, while at the same time seeing that the best services were available, including the preparation of interesting and well designed plans.

THE THREE VILLAGES

Irby, Willaston and Greasby all lie within the Merseyside conurbation as defined for Census purposes (see figure 11.1). As their names imply, they are all old settlements. They have grown in size during the last fifty years when voluntary migration has taken place, particularly during the period after World War I. While Willaston is still partly rural (as denoted by the number of agricultural workers and presence of farm buildings), generally speaking, in each village people work in business and industry in Liverpool and Birkenhead, and by this definition they are socially and economically no longer rural. Each has a village centre which contains a few old buildings worthy of protection and some other features such as the stone monument in Irby. The character of the village centre is typically made up of a variety of buildings lining a picturesque winding street that is no longer suitable for motor traffic. There is considerable congestion in all three places on Saturday, which is the local shopping day, since in all three cases about 80 per cent of convenience shopping is undertaken locally, even though more than half the households have cars.

Each of the three villages is isolated from its parent centre which contains the seat of local government. Irby is approximately two miles from Heswall (Wirral Urban District), Willaston three miles from Neston (Neston Urban District) and Greasby, which lies on the fringe of Birkenhead, is about three miles from Hoylake, where the council

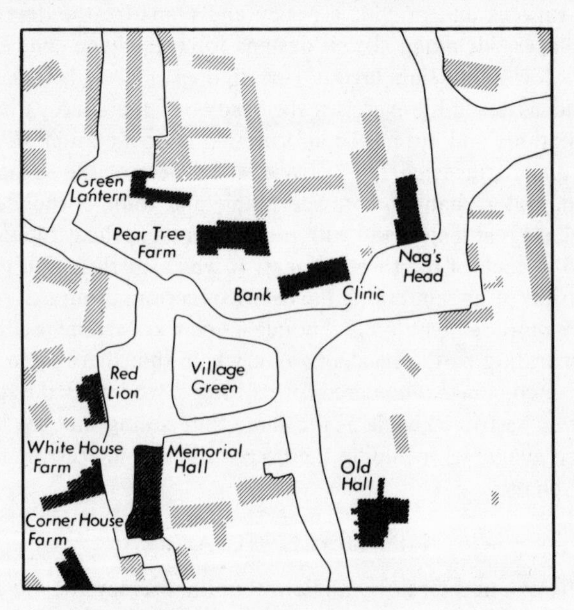

Fig. 11.2 Willaston Village centre showing the village green and the old buildings surrounding it

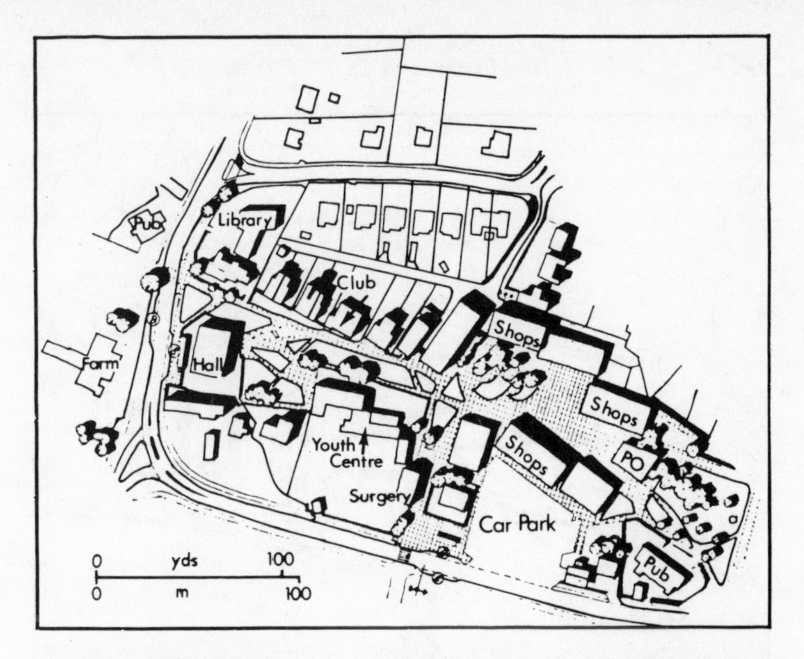

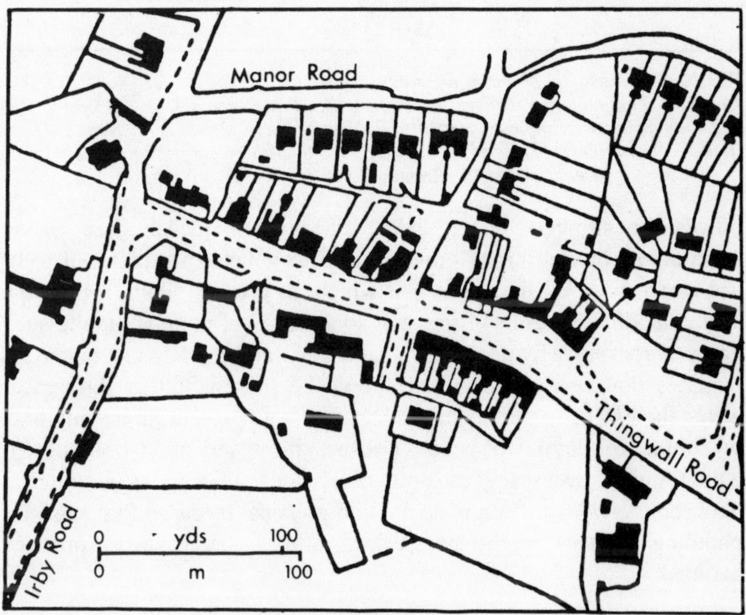

Fig. 11.3 Irby: below, the existing village centre; above, a proposal for by-passing the village, using the existing village street as a pedestrian way, car parking being provided behind the new shops

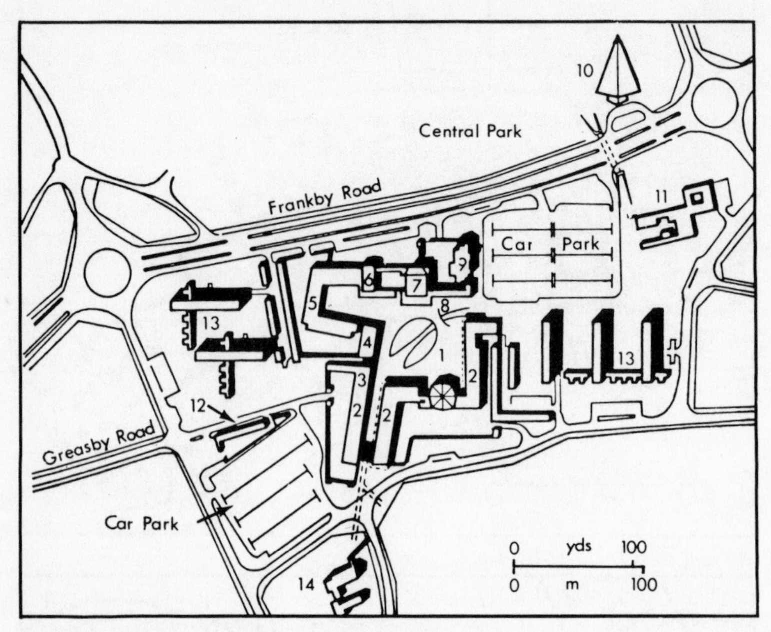

Fig. 11.4 Greasby: a proposal for a new centre. Key: 1. Piazza; 2. Shops; 3. Public House; 4. Post Office; 5. Offices; 6. Library; 7. Multi-purpose hall; 8. Cafe; 9. Red Cat Public House (newly constructed); 10. New Anglican Church; 11. Health Centre (under construction); 12. Service industry; 13. Flats above old persons' dwellings on ground floor; 14. Roman Catholic Church (existing)

offices are situated for Hoylake Urban District. All three Urban Districts lie in Cheshire County. All three villages are adjacent to or are surrounded by the green belt which, at present, limits expansion. The chief differences lie in size and social class of population and such items as reasons why people moved to them and the absence of certain facilities that residents thought should be present. Other differences were: the extent to which rural character was present physically and, of course, the layout of roads, houses, shops and other buildings. It was thought necessary to note differences as well as similarities between the villages both in social and physical terms so that sensitive planning policies might be derived and a stereotyped approach avoided.

General character

Existing gross densities in the built-up areas of three villages give some idea of the environment that is to be found. Excluding major open spaces in Irby, it is 14·5 persons per acre, in Willaston, 12 persons per acre, while in Greasby it is 19 persons per acre. A large proportion of the houses in Irby and Greasby are three-bedroomed semi-detached houses. In Willaston, where there is a greater proportion of detached family houses and groups of farm cottages, the number of such houses is smaller. The lower density in Willaston reflects both the openness and rural quality of the area, but even Greasby, with its higher density, still retains the open character attractive to new migrants. The proximity of the green belt and the smallness of the villages promotes, of course, an awareness of and a desire to protect this openness.

Population characteristics

The survey showed that in 1961, Greasby, with a population of 7000, was much larger than the other two villages. Willaston was the smallest with 1600 while Irby had an estimated population of 3000. The analysis of population change showed that all three villages had grown substantially since the turn of the century and especially since the end of World War I. Greasby and Irby had expanded rapidly in the last 30 years and both had virtually doubled their population between 1951 and 1961. Willaston's growth on the other hand was much less spectacular as an increase of only 31 was recorded between 1951 and 1961 (table 11.1).

Table 11.1 Population change 1901–61

Village	Area in acres		Population					
			1901	1911	1921	1931	1951	1961
Greasby (parish/ward)	Areas at all censuses	Slightly over 800	290	476	585	747	4367	6978
Irby (parish/wards)	Area at 1901–31 censuses	842	146	161	233	1062	—	—
	Area at 1951 census	1109	—	—	—	1082	4032	—
	Area at 1961 census	2182	—	—	—	—	4925	7420*
Willaston (parish/ward)	Area at 1901–31 census	1994	597	806	997	1296	—	—
	Area at 1951 census	1764	—	—	—	1260	1458	—
	Area at 1961 census	2069	—	—	—	—	1552	1583

* The survey area in the Irby study, within the limits of the green belt, contained about 3000 people.

Migration

Surveys on length of residence and reasons for moving in the villages were only taken at Greasby and Willaston. Analysis of the birthplace of the head of household showed that only 28 per cent had been born in Willaston and that about 35 per cent of all the households interviewed had come to Willaston in the last 10 years. The amount of immigration was even more marked in Greasby. Only 2 per cent of the heads of household were born in the village and over 50 per cent of the entire population had lived there for less than 10 years. Nearly half the heads of household interviewed in Greasby were born in either Liverpool or Birkenhead.

Two main reasons were given for movement to Greasby and Willaston; the desire to live in a better environment and the desire for a house of a preferred type. The desire to be near employment featured largely in Willaston (because of proximity to the growing industrial area centred on Ellesmere Port), and moves as part of retirement or in order to be near friends or relatives were important subsidiary reasons in both Willaston and Greasby.

Occupations and social class

All three villages had a relatively high proportion of heads of households in professional and managerial occupations in comparison with the rest of Merseyside. Irby and Greasby are predominately middle class with very few in semi-skilled and unskilled occupations. On the other hand, reflecting the rural character of Willaston, there is a relatively high proportion working in semi-skilled agricultural occupations (table 11.2).

Table 11.2 Social class of head of household*

	Occupation	Greasby %	Irby %	Willaston %
1	Professional etc.	13	8	22
2	Intermediate	31	37	11
3	Skilled	49	50	32
4	Partly skilled	4	2	32
5	Unskilled	3	2	3
6	Unspecified	0	1	0
	Total	100%	100%	100%

* Source: Surveys of Irby, Willaston and Greasby.
Classification according to General Register Office, Census 1951, *Classification of Occupations*, London H.M.S.O. 1956, p. vii.

Car ownership

The comparatively large number of middle class households in the three villages is reflected in their levels of car ownership. In all three villages at least half the households had the use of a car and 11 per cent of the households interviewed in Willaston had two cars or more. Despite the relatively high car ownership only 35 per cent of the employed population in Willaston and only 31 per cent of the employed population in Greasby went to work by car. In Greasby only 38 per cent of wives in car-owning households used the car for shopping.

Place of work

In all three villages the majority of the employed population worked outside the village itself. Nearly two-thirds of the employed population in Irby and Greasby and one-third in Willaston travelled daily to the centre of the conurbation in Liverpool or Birkenhead. Only 9 per cent in Irby and 15 per cent in Greasby worked within the village. Most of these performed various services for the residents, but in Willaston, with its agricultural element, 30 per cent of the employed population worked in the village.

Shopping

Existing facilities in both Irby and Willaston consisted largely of food and general shops along the main street. Willaston, with a population of 1600 possessed 12 shops whereas Irby with a population of about 3000 had 28 shops. Shopping facilities in Greasby were more highly developed than in the other two villages. There were four shopping parades and only 40 per cent of the households interviewed used the central area more frequently than the others.

Between 80 and 85 per cent of the households interviewed did their daily shopping in the village and between 60 and 70 per cent also used the village facilities for their weekly needs, but virtually everyone went to one of the larger centres outside the village to buy specialist or luxury goods. The central area of Liverpool was the most favoured of the larger centres for all three villages but Birkenhead also attracted a considerable number of people from Greasby and Irby, while Chester had a similar secondary attraction for people from Willaston.

In all three villages there was considerable dissatisfaction with existing shopping facilities, especially in the two larger villages. The provision of better and/or more shops ranked first in Greasby, second in Irby and third in Willaston, in the order of planning priorities listed by respondents. In Greasby criticism centred on the inadequacies of the existing central area facilities and the provision of a new and enlarged centre ranked as by far the most urgently desired planning objective. In Irby there was criticism of high prices, the lack of certain types of shopping facilities, and general dissatisfaction with existing facilities from 48 per cent of the households interviewed. In spite of the more limited range available in Willaston there were few criticisms of existing shopping facilities. Although there were criticisms of high prices and lack of competition, only 21 per cent of the households interviewed considered themselves dissatisfied.

Community facilities

The range of community facilities in the three villages was related to the size of each village – Greasby, with its larger population, possessed the greatest range of facilities including two churches, a community centre as well as a library and clinic. Irby had a village hall, small church and a club. The range of facilities in Willaston was more limited but the village contained a church and two halls.

In all three villages there was a relatively large number of associations covering a wide range of activities. The survey showed that 51 per cent of the households interviewed in Greasby and 57 per cent of those interviewed in Willaston participated in one or more of these village activities. There was also a considerable amount of overlapping in membership between different places. Some 18 per cent of the households interviewed in Greasby belonged to associations outside the village, but in Willaston it was estimated that a quarter of the membership of associations came from outside the village, from as far away as Birkenhead.

In spite of the large number of associations and the high degree of local participation in them, many of the households interviewed were not satisfied with existing conditions. Demands for a new community centre and a new library ranked second and third in order of the most important priorities of the households interviewed in Greasby. A wide range of community facilities was specified in Irby where at least 5 per cent of those questioned wanted each of the following items: a non-denominational youth club, a better library, public conveniences, a community centre and a Church of England church.

In all three villages there was a lack of facilities for particular sections of the population, for old people and teenagers. In Irby the most urgent need was for a non-denominational youth club. Some 52 per cent of all households wanted improved facilities for teenagers and 71 per cent of the households in the sample with teenagers in the family had this desire. Nearly a quarter of the households containing people over 60 in the sample thought that something more could be done for the over 60s by providing them with better facilities for meetings and also by building special houses for them.

Transport

There were complaints in all three villages about the inadequacy of public transport services, and households in Willaston in particular found a high degree of isolation from central Merseyside. The survey here showed that 51 per cent of the persons interviewed were dissatisfied with public transport services and the need to improve bus transport ranked first in the list of planning priorities given by interviewees. Nearly half the suggestions made by those interviewed in Willaston about improvements concerned better road or rail links to the rest of the metropolitan area.

Many households in Greasby and Irby were also dissatisfied with aspects of public transport facilities generally. In both villages there were complaints about infrequency and the lack of late evening services which often made it necessary to cut short an evening out in Liverpool.

THE METROPOLITAN VILLAGE

The results of the surveys suggest that a distinction may be drawn between villages that are close enough to large urban areas, or motorways, to attract commuters, and villages virtually depending on agriculture that are beyond the reach of daily commuters. The distinction is broad for there are villages which are not dormitories but which nevertheless perform what might be styled urban functions. Moreover, there is little apparent correlation between distance from urban area and the extent to which villages satisfy concepts of rural character and communal identity. Indeed, some would dispense with the term 'village' for the settlements studied in the Wirral – all are towns by the standard suggested by the Scott Committee and adopted by Sharp. None of the settlements can be properly termed towns, however, and they might be more accurately described as varying from inflated villages to embryo suburbs.[2] These 'in-between' conditions arise because of proximity to dynamic urban areas, and the problems highlighted by Greasby, Irby and Willaston are essentially those of growth and pressure for growth. This dominant feature, growth, distinguishes the metropolitan village from the village beyond commuter range which usually has the opposite problem – decline.

Growth has occurred for two main reasons. Firstly, people have moved to villages as a preferred environment and, perhaps, to fulfil dreams of a life in the country. Secondly, people have moved to villages as alternative suburban locations have become more difficult to find. This second wave of movement to villages has gathered extra impetus from the imposition of green belts which have diverted the growing housing demands arising from household formation and redevelopment. The impact is most marked within and on the immediate fringes of metropolitan areas although movement to accessible village locations well outside metropolitan areas is gaining significance. Problems ensuing from growth, deficiencies in public services (sewers, roads, transport, education) and in commercial services, particularly shops, suggest the formation of pieces of suburbia in a rural setting and seem to justify fears that the 'village community' is an irrelevant concept for a metropolitan area.

The Wirral surveys largely reveal the expected symptoms of rapid suburban accretion, but there are significant differences between the three settlements and there are other, less obvious problems. In all three villages the shortcomings of public transport which made utilisation of both local facilities and the metropolitan facilities of Liverpool difficult were a recurrent source of dissatisfaction. The necessity to travel for certain education facilities and the high prices charged by local shops also gave rise to discontent in all three settlements. Greasby, by far the largest of the trio, which has developed rather haphazardly with a number of separate shopping parades, exhibited clear evidence of a lack of social focus. Demands for extra shops and community facilities were here most urgent. As Greasby has experienced the greatest suburban type growth the preponderance of housing stock consists of three-bedroomed dwellings so that changes in family size may sometimes promote outward movement to more suitable accommodation. The demand for aged persons' accommodation was common to all three settlements. In Willaston and Irby there was less general dissatisfaction with facilities but desires for change were more specific – for a particular type of shop, for example. The Willaston survey showed that in this small settlement the emphasis was on preserving what exists rather than seeking changes but a restrictionist outlook means that the second generation of migrant families is unlikely to find local accommodation easily.

What part villages in close proximity to large cities, such as those in the Wirral, may play in overall strategy for metropolitan areas is as yet far from clear. To a greater or lesser extent local planning authorities and central government have viewed village expansion as a welcome outlet for the population of county boroughs 'bottled up' by green belts. Expansion of villages in preference to the further sprawl of large towns has satisfied the canons of both traditional planning theory and political expediency. In some areas the controlling factor would appear to be the capacity of sewerage systems. But the ready relief of urban housing pressure has brought problems in its train. In parts of Britain the difficulties are severe; chronic shortage of school places being, perhaps, the worst. Moreover the ground is not always won easily and opposition to growth is voiced powerfully, although often by the most recently established residents.

What criteria might planning authorities adopt in selecting villages for expansion and in determining their future size? Does a settlement relinquish the qualities of village life once it has exceeded 1600, the population of Willaston? And is it appropriate to expand a settlement such as Greasby (7000) so that it becomes a fully fledged small town rather than a nondescript in-between? Is it more realistic to regard all these settlements as eventually becoming variations on the suburban theme, losing their visual character and communal life?

The Wirral studies provide but a small part of the answer to such questions. Certain common features, all stemming from accessibility to urban areas, distinguish what is termed the 'metropolitan village'. There is strong economic dependence on the metropolitan area itself, a dependence which is likely to grow even when new building is prevented. Absorption into village life is not as painful as might be supposed but a wider pattern of social associations within the metropolitan area is emerging in all three settlements. As the strength of both economic and social links is likely to grow there is a case for facilitating contact rather than attempting to preserve isolation. On the other hand many desired improvements to transport and other facilities would be quite uneconomic to provide and this suggests the need for an overall policy for groups of villages. In social terms, the differences between the villages are slight. There is a greater degree of participation in the smallest settlement, Willaston, and apparently less dissatisfaction with local amenities. On the other hand, where complaints are made they are more specific and it may be that dissatisfaction will grow as more people move to Willaston for housing accommodation rather than to live in a village. In Greasby there is a clear inference that having reached a population of 7000 there are strong arguments for further increase, but the level of participation in Greasby is only slightly less than that in Willaston and the need for growth stems mainly from demands which a larger population may reasonably make for more sophisticated services.

Of perhaps equal significance to social factors are design criteria. In particular, thought must be given to the probable effects of expansion of village centres. If there is a paramount need to preserve the essential features of the village then any expansion may be detrimental, but in other cases minor but careful changes to existing structure will permit some growth. Where there is little worthy of preservation in the existing centre, redevelopment may permit the wholesale reorganisation of unsatisfactory facilities. When villages on major traffic routes are by-passed expansion may occur which otherwise might have been unacceptable. Metropolitan villages have many advantages – immediate accessibility to the countryside, local and metropolitan social associations and the pleasure of the village scene. The attempt to enhance these qualities is an exacting but necessary task if the metropolitan village is not to be drawn into the anonymous web of suburbia.

As the number of villages surveyed in the Wirral is small and the observed differences unspectacular any generalisations must be qualified. Clearly there is much room for further investigation of both existing conditions in metropolitan villages and possible future patterns. It is hoped that the Wirral studies may provoke further work which will help to inform us on what is, as yet, a little chartered area.[3]

SOURCE: *Town Planning Review,* vol. 36, 1965–6.

REFERENCES

1. This paper is based on the studies of three villages lying in the Wirral Peninsula on the south side of the River Mersey. The studies were carried out in the Department of Civic Design, University of Liverpool by postgraduate students.
2. For a further discussion of definitions see above in the Introduction (ed).
3. Since the original publication of this article there has appeared R. Lawton and C. M. Cunningham (eds), *Merseyside: social and economic studies* (Longman, 1970), which includes chapters on the population and social structure of the conurbation; and on migration, with special emphasis on the spiralist community of Formby.

Selected Bibliography

AGGLOMERATION AND DISPERSAL

Beresford, M. W. (1964) 'Dispersed and grouped settlement in medieval Cornwall', *Agric. Hist. Rev.,* XII, 13–27.

Jones, G. R. J. (1961) 'Basic patterns of settlement distribution in northern England', *Advancement of Science,* XVII, 192–200. Ibid., (1961) 'Settlement patterns in Anglo-Saxon England', *Antiquity,* XXXV, 221–32. A new view of British and Anglo-Saxon settlements and the relationships between them.

Sharp, T. (1946) *The anatomy of the village,* London.

Sharp, T. (1955–6) 'Forest villages in Northumberland' *Town Planning Rev.,* XXVI, 6, 165–70. Describes the twentieth century villages established in an area of re-afforestation.

Swainson, B. (1944) 'Dispersion and agglomeration of rural settlement in Somerset', *Geog.,* XXIX, 1–8.

Tucker, D. N. (1972) 'Linear parishes and farm structures in the Vale of Pickering', *Geog.,* LVII, 120–6.

Yates, E. M. (1960) 'History in a map', *Geog. Jnl.,* CXXVI, 32–51. Describes the changes in settlement patterns in two Wealden parishes over the medieval and modern periods, up to 1948.

Yates, E. M. (1961) *A study of settlement patterns,* reprint by Field Studies Council available from E. W. Classey Ltd., 353 Hanworth Road, Hampton, Middlesex. This is a methodological study illustrated in an area situated between Reigate and Guildford. As with Yates (1960) the approach is longitudinal.

DESERTED VILLAGES

Allison, K. J. (1965) *The deserted villages of Oxfordshire,* Leicester Univ. Occ. Papers in local history, XVII.

Allison, K. J. (1970) *Deserted villages,* London. A most useful introduction to the subject.

Allison, K. J., Beresford, M. W. and Hurst, J. G. (1966) *The deserted villages of Northamptonshire,* Leicester Univ. Occ. Papers in local history, XVIII.

Beresford, M. W. and Hurst, J. G. (1971) *Deserted medieval villages: Studies,* London. The standard work on this subject.

MOBILITY

Constant, A. (1948) 'The geographical background of inter-village population movements in Northants and Hunts., 1754–1943', *Geog.*, XXXIII, 78–88.

Holderness, B. A. (1971) 'Personal mobility in some rural parishes of Yorkshire 1771–1822', *Yorkshire Archaeological Journal,* XLII, 444–54. Farmers were less mobile than tradesmen, and tradesmen less mobile than labourers; but the mobile farmers and tradesmen included more long distance migrants.

Lawton, R. (1958) 'Population movements in the West Midlands, 1841–61', *Geog.*, XLIII, 164–77. Refers to the counties of Stafford, Warwick and Worcester.

Peel, R. F. (1942) 'Local intermarriage and the stability of the rural population in the English Midlands', *Geog.*, XXVII, 22–30.

Perry, P. J. (1969) 'Working class isolation and mobility in rural Dorset, 1837–1936: a study of marriage distances', *Trans. Inst. Brit. Geogrs.*, XLVI, 121–41.

Sheppard, J. A. (1961) 'East Yorkshire's agricultural labour force in the mid-nineteenth century', *Agr. Hist. Rev.*, IX, 43–54. This article describes the imbalance of supply and demand in labour and the commuting patterns between surplus and deficit areas.

Smith, C. T. (1951) 'The movement of population in England and Wales in 1851 and 1861', *Geog. Jnl.*, CXVII, 200–10.

Webb, J. W. (1963) 'The natural and migrational components of population changes in England and Wales, 1921–1931', *Econ. Geog.*, XXXIX, 130–48.

OPEN AND CLOSED VILLAGES

A variety of terms has been used to describe the social, economic and landscape differences between villages with concentrated landownership (closed) and fragmented ownership (open). Closed villages are often described as estate villages, but a clear difference can be seen between those with and without a resident landlord. The open villages are often called freehold villages but as the number of freeholders could vary considerably it is useful to distinguish between villages with many (which I have called peasant villages in my papers of 1965–6 and 1972) and villages with a smaller number of freeholders (divided villages).

Ashby, M. K. (1961) *Joseph Ashby of Tysoe,* London. An important study of a peasant village.

Havinden, M. A. (1966) *Estate villages,* London. A case study of two villages in Berkshire with resident gentry.

Hoskins, W. G. (1957) *The Midland peasant: the economic and social history of a Leicestershire village,* London. A classic study of the longitudinal history of a large open village, Wigston Magna.

Mills, D. R. (1965–6) 'English villages in the eighteenth and nineteenth centuries: a sociological approach', *Amateur* (now *Local*) *Historian,* VI, 271–8 and VII, 7–13. Describes a four-fold classification based on landownership: two kinds of open village; and two kinds of closed village.

Mills, D. R. (1972) 'Has historical geography changed?' in Open University, *New Trends in Geography, Block IV: Political, Historical and Regional Geography,* pp. 58–75. Presents a model of nineteenth century villages.

Mortimore, M. J. (1969) 'Landownership and urban growth in Bradford and its environs 1850–1950', *Trans. Inst. of Brit. Geogrs.,* XLVI, 105–19.

Rogers, A. (ed) (1969) *Stability and change: some aspects of North and South Rauceby, Lincolnshire, in the nineteenth century,* University of Nottingham, Department of Adult Education.

Springall, L. M. (1936 *Labouring life in Norfolk villages, 1834–1914,* London.

Spufford, Margaret (1965) *A Cambridgeshire community: Chippenham from settlement to enclosure,* Leicester University, Occ. Papers in local history, XX. Another longitudinal study, but of a closed village.

PLANNING

Bracey, H. E. (1952) *Social provision in rural Wiltshire,* London. A pioneer study in post-war planning of rural communities.

Clout, H. D. (1969) 'Planning studies in rural areas', in Cooke, R. U. and Johnson, J. H., *Trends in geography,* London, pp. 222–32.

Drudy, P. J. and Wallace, D. B. (1971) 'Towards a development programme for remote rural areas: a case study in north Norfolk', *Regional Studies,* V, 281–8.

Green, R. J. (1966) 'The remote countryside – a plan for contraction', *Planning Outlook*, I, 17–37.

Green, R. J. (1971) *Country planning: the future of the rural regions*, Manchester.

Hampshire CC and Mass Observation Ltd. (1966) *Village life in Hampshire*, Winchester, Hants CC.

Thorburn, A. (1971) *Planning Villages*, Estates Gazette Ltd., 151, Wardour St., London, W.1.

Wibberley, G. P. (1954) 'Some aspects of problem rural areas in Great Britain', *Geog. Jnl.*, CXX, 43–61.

POPULATION CHANGES

Dickinson, G. C. (1958) 'The nature of rural population – an analysis of seven Yorkshire parishes based on electoral returns from 1931–54', *Yorks. Bull. Econ. Soc. Res.*, X, 95–108.

Dunn, M. C. and Swindell, K. (1972) 'Electoral registers and rural migration: a case study from Herefordshire', *Area*, IV, 39–41. Draws attention to the limitations of the data.

House, J. W. (1965) *Rural North-East England, 1951–1961*, Department of Geography, University of Newcastle.

Johnston, R. J. (1965–6) 'Components of rural population change', *Town Planning Rev.*, XXXVI, 279–93. An account of post-war changes in the area between Hawes and York.

Johnston, R. J. (1967) 'A reconnaissance study of population change in Nidderdale, 1951–61', *Trans. Inst. Brit. Geogrs.*, XLI, 113–23.

Kirby, D. A. (1972) 'Population density and land values in County Durham during the mid-seventeenth century', *Trans. Inst. Brit. Geogrs.*, LVII, 83–98.

Lawton, R. (1968) 'Population changes in England and Wales in the later nineteenth century: an analysis of trends by registration districts', *Trans. Inst. Brit. Geogrs.*, XLIV, 55–74.

Redmill, C. E. (1931) 'The growth of population in the East Warwickshire coalfield', *Geog.*, XVI, 125–140. A useful article, especially for the insight it gives to earlier methodology.

Saville, J. (1957) *Rural depopulation in England and Wales: 1851–1951*, London.

Smailes, A. E. (1938) 'Population changes in the colliery districts of Northumberland and Durham', *Geog. Jnl.*, XCI, 220–32.

Smailes, A. E. (1950) 'Early industrial settlement in northeast England', *Advancement of Science,* VI, 325–31.

Willatts, E. J. and Newson, M. G. (1953) 'The geographical pattern of population changes in England and Wales, 1921–51, *Geog. Jnl.,* CXIX, 431–55.

RURAL INDUSTRIES

Birrell, J. (1969) 'Peasant craftsmen in the medieval forest', *Agr. Hist. Rev.,* XVII, 91–107. Shows that certain industries were located near the source(s) of raw material in a rural setting.

Blowers, A. (1972) 'The declining villages of County Durham', in Open University, *New Trends in Geography, Block III: Social Geography.*

Dewhirst, R. K. (1960–1) 'Saltaire', *Town Planning Rev.,* XXXI, 135–44. Sir Titus Salt's model village near Bradford.

Heaton, H. (1965) *The Yorkshire woollen and worsted industries,* London, 2nd ed. On pp. 290–2 gives information about weavers' smallholdings.

Hey, D. G. (1969) 'A dual economy in south Yorkshire', *Agr. Hist. Rev.,* XVII, 108–19.

Hunt, C. J. (1970) *The lead miners of the Northern Pennines in the eighteenth and nineteenth centuries,* Manchester. Chapter VII, pp. 138–68, describes the pattern of settlement, including the miners' smallholdings.

Jones, E. L. (1968) 'Agricultural orgins of industry', *Past and Present,* XL, 58–71.

Joy, D. (1966) 'The town that Titus built', *The Dalesman,* XXVII, 861–6. A popular but accurate account of Sir Titus Salt's factory village at Saltaire, near Bradford.

Patten, J. (1972) 'Village and town: an occupational study', *Agric. Hist. Rev.,* XX, 1–16. Based on a study of early sixteenth century Suffolk, this article discusses the occupational overlap between town and country.

Pollard, S. (1964) 'The factory village in the industrial revolution', *Eng. Hist. Rev.,* LXXIX, 513–31.

Smith, D. M. (1966) 'The hatting industry in Denton, Lancs.', *Ind. Arch.,* III, 1–7. An account of a dual occupation with farming and the relicts it has left behind from *circa* 1800.

Smith, W. (1954–5) 'Industry and the countryside', *Town Planning Rev.*, XXV, 207–15.

Thirsk, J. (1961) 'Industries in the countryside', in Fisher, F. J. (ed.), *Essays in the economic and social history of Tudor and Stuart England,* London, pp. 70–88.

Weaver, M. E. (1966) 'Industrial housing in west Cornwall', *Ind. Arch.*, III, 23–45.

Woods, K. S. (1968–9) 'Small scale industries in the rural and regional economy to-day', *Town Planning Rev.*, XXXIX, 251–61.

SOCIOLOGICAL STUDIES

Frankenberg, R. (1966) *Communities in Britain: social life in town and country,* London. An outstanding contribution to the sociology of British Communities, synthesising work of many other authors. Has a chapter on 'Truly Rural England'.

Hobsbawm, E. J. and Rude, G. (1970) *Captain Swing,* London. A discussion of the farm labourers' riots of the early 1830s and the causes of village discontent.

Littlejohn, J. (1963) *Westrigg: the sociology of a Cheviot parish,* London.

Moreau, R. E. (1968) *The departed village,* Oxford. Describes life in Berrick Salome, an Oxfordshire village, at the turn of the century.

Reade, E. (1968) 'Community and the rural-urban continuum – are the concepts outdated', *Jnl. Town Planning Inst.*, LIV, 426–9.

Williams, W. M. (1957) *Gosforth: the sociology of an English village,* London.

Williams, W. M. (1963) *A West Country village: Ashworthy,* London.

SUBURBANISATION OF THE COUNTRYSIDE

Coppock, J. T. and Prince, H. C. (1964) *Greater London,* London. For a chapter on dormitory settlements around London.

Crichton, R. (1964) *Commuters' village,* Newton Abbot. Describes the Berkshire village of Stratfield Mortimer.

Gasson, R. (1966) *The influence of urbanization on farm ownership and practice,* Dept. Agr. Econ., Wye College, Kent.

Giggs, J. A. (1970) 'Fringe expansion and suburbanization around Nottingham: a metropolitan area approach', *East Mid. Geogr.*, V, 9–18.

Martin, I. (1972) *Second homes in Denbighshire,* County of Denbigh, Tourism and Recreation Report, III.

Pahl, R. E. (1965) *Urbs in rure: the metropolitan fringe in Hertfordshire,* London School of Economics Geog. Papers, II.

Pahl, R. E. (1966) 'The rural-urban continuum', *Sociologia Ruralis,* VI, reprinted in Pahl, R. E. (ed) (1968), *Readings in urban sociology,* London, pp. 263–300. Pahl argues against *both* the dichotomy of rural and urban and a continuum. He urges instead that attention be focused on the local mix of national classes and stresses the importance of scale.

Radford, E. (1970) *The New Villagers: urban pressure on rural areas in Worcestershire,* London.

GENERAL

Baker, A. R. H. (1969) 'The geography of rural settlements', in Cooke, R. U. and Johnson, J. H., *Trends in geography,* London, pp. 123–32.

Chisholm, M. (1968) *Rural settlement and Land use,* 2nd ed., London.

Clout, H. D. (1972) *Rural geography: an introductory survey,* London.

Everson, J. A. and Fitzgerald, B. (1969) *Settlement patterns,* London.

Harris, A. (1961) *The rural landscape of the East Riding of Yorkshire 1700–1850,* London. Reprinted SR Publications, Wakefield 1970.

Harvey, N. (1970) *A history of farm buildings in England and Wales,* Newton Abbot.

Holderness, B. A. (1972) ' "Open" and "close" parishes in England in the eighteenth and nineteenth centuries', *Agr. Hist. Rev.*, XX, 126–139. An extremely useful summary article, especially from the point of view of labour supply.

Laslett, P. (1965) *The world we have lost,* London. A comparison of the traditional society with present day society.

Martin, E. W. (1954) *The secret people: English village life after 1750,* London.

Martin, E. W. (1965) *The shearers and the shorn,* London. Deals with the class struggle in rural S.W. England.

Mingay, G. E. (1963) *English landed society in the eighteenth century,* London.

Open University (1973) *The spread of cities,* Units 23–5, Course DT201, *Urban Development.* Unit 24 deals with *Suburban and ex-urban growth* and is a useful follow-up to Chapter 11.

Robertson, I. M. L. (1961) 'The occupational structure and distribution of rural population in England and Wales', *Scot. Geog. Mag.,* LXXVII, 165–79. Delineates three distinct types: agricultural-rural, rural and rural-urban.

Tarn, J. N. (1971) *Working class housing in nineteenth century Britain,* Architectural Association Paper, VII, London, Lund Humphries.

Tate, W. E. (1967) *The English village community and the enclosure movements,* London. A new standard work on this subject.

Thompson, F. M. L. (1963) *English landed society in the nineteenth century,* London.

Thorpe, H. (ed) (1966) *First Report of the Departmental Committee of Inquiry into Statutory Smallholdings,* HMSO Cmnd 2936. This includes an historical review of allotments and smallholdings.

Vince, S. W. E. (1953) 'Reflections on the structure and distribution of the rural population in England and Wales, 1921–31', *Trans. Inst. Brit. Geogrs.,* XVIII, 53–76.

Woodforde, J. (1969) *The truth about cottages,* London. One of the few accounts of the basic labourer's cottage from the fifteenth to the nineteenth centuries.

Wrigley, E. A. (ed) (1966) *An introduction to English historical demography,* London. Contains a useful bibliography of local studies, as well as articles on the methodology of the subject.

Notes on Contributors

Mr T. H. Bainbridge was headmaster of the Creighton School, Carlisle, having graduated B.Sc. in 1926 and M.Sc. in 1934 at Armstrong College, University of Durham, now the University of Newcastle. He wrote other articles on north-west England, including Carlisle, Alston and Wesley's ride around the Solway; and had made a previous contribution to *Economic Geography*. Mr Bainbridge died in 1949 at the early age of 43.

Professor M. B. Gleave is Professor of Geography, at Fourah Bay College at the University of Sierra Leone. The research upon which his study was based was carried out at the University of Hull and is embodied in his unpublished M.A. thesis, *The settlement pattern of the Yorkshire Wolds, 1770–1850,* 1960. Subsequently Professor Gleave has worked on social and economic change in West African rural communities.

Professor R. Lawton is Professor of Geography at the University of Liverpool. His main interests are in historical and social geography, with particular reference to nineteenth century Britain.

Mr I. Masser is lecturer in the Department of Civic Design at the University of Liverpool, where his main interests are in methodology and regional planning. In 1972 he published a book entitled *Analytical models for urban and regional planning.*

Dr D. R. Mills is staff tutor in Social Sciences at The Open University (East Midland Region). His main interests centre round the interdisciplinary study of rural life, economy and development, past and present.

Dr June A. Sheppard is a lecturer in Geography at Queen Mary College, University of London, where her principal interests are in rural settlement studies.

Mr D. C. Stroud is on the staff of the Department of the Environment, where he is concerned with aspects of urban economics, principally project appraisal and plan evaluation.

Professor J. N. Tarn is Head of the Department of Architecture at the University of Nottingham. His main interests are in urban housing problems and he has a special interest in Derbyshire.

Professor H. Thorpe is Head of the Department of Geography at the University of Birmingham. He has made a detailed study of rural settlement in Europe and is author of the standard chapter on rural settlement in the British Isles in J. W. Watson and J. B. Sissons (eds) (1964) *The British Isles: a systematic geography.*

Professor W. M. Williams is Head of the Department of Sociology and Anthropology, University College, Swansea. He is author of *The Country Craftsman,* 1958, and other books cited in the bibliography.

INDEX